CONFLICT
AND
COMPETITION

CONFLICT

AND

COMPETITION

The Latin American Church in a Changing Environment

edited by
Edward L. Cleary
Hannah Stewart-Gambino

Lynne Rienner Publishers • Boulder & London

Published in the United States of America in 1992 by
Lynne Rienner Publishers, Inc.
1800 30th Street, Boulder, Colorado 80301

and in the United Kingdom by
Lynne Rienner Publishers, Inc.
3 Henrietta Street, Covent Garden, London WC2E 8LU

Library of Congress Cataloging-in-Publication Data
Conflict and competition : the Latin American church in a changing
    environment / edited by Edward L. Cleary and Hannah Stewart-Gambino.
    Includes bibliographical references and index.
    ISBN 1-55587-251-4 (hc)
    ISBN 1-55587-332-4 (pb)
    1. Catholic Church—Latin America—History—20th century.
2. Latin America—Church history—20th century.   I. Cleary, Edward L.
II. Stewart-Gambino, Hannah W.
BX1426.2.C593   1992
282 '.8 ' 09049—dc20   91-44237
                                                                             CIP

British Cataloguing in Publication Data
A Cataloguing in Publication record for this book
is available from the British Library.

Printed and bound in the United States of America

The paper used in this publication meets the requirements
of the American National Standard for Permanence of
Paper for Printed Library Materials Z39.48-1984.

Contents

CHAPTER 1

Introduction:
New Game, New Rules

HANNAH STEWART-GAMBINO

The Catholic church in Latin America appears to be at a crossroads. After over two decades of dramatic theological and pastoral change, liberation theology, a theology born of the Latin American experience and grounded in the perspective of the poor, not only has survived attacks from opponents in and out of the church but also has influenced theological discourse among First World, minority, and feminist theologians. In many Latin American dioceses, the institutional church has flourished as a result of bishops' adoption of a preferential option for the poor. At the national level, the church in its role as "voice of the voiceless" has led hierarchies throughout the region to champion human rights and the struggles against oppressive regimes. Thus, on one hand, the terms of theological debate as well as the institutional pattern of the Latin American church appear to have been permanently, if not uniformly, altered. But more recently, observers have noted that the Latin American church faces new challenges that may limit its ability to continue to play such a prominent and progressive role. To different observers, the church appears to be embarking on a period of consolidation, maturation, reconciliation, or even retreat.

How the Latin American Catholic church will respond in the decades ahead to the challenges both within and outside the church is the subject of this book. The following chapters deal with the church in individual countries. The purpose of this chapter, however, is to introduce the reader to the general themes and challenges shaping the national contexts to which Latin American hierarchies must adapt in the coming years. The first section examines changing international conditions, specifically the pressure exerted by the Vatican on Latin American churches to rein in particularly their more progressive elements. A brief description of some of the early encounters between Pope John Paul II and Latin American progressives serves as a springboard for a more general discussion of various cleavages within the church today. The second section discusses

1

the impact of the political trend toward (re)democratization on churches that had found their prophetic voices during the harsh years of military repression and widespread misery of the 1960s through the 1980s. The third challenge to which Catholic churches throughout the region must respond is the explosion of Protestant and Pentecostal growth. The nature of this challenge and the varying ways in which it is interpreted within the Catholic church are reviewed in the final section.

Before discussion of these issues proceeds, it is important to place this book within the context of existing work on the church and politics in Latin America. Since the 1960s and Ivan Vallier's recognition that the Catholic church can play a central role in the process of modernization in Latin America,[1] the Catholic church as a political actor as well as a religious institution has become the focus of a steady stream of studies. Not surprisingly, the result of the proliferation of works on the church in Latin America has been a sharpening of debates concerning how observers should study the church. Scholarship has come a long way from its past formal-legal approach that suggested that church activity, either pastoral or social, could be directly deduced from encyclicals, pastoral letters, or pronouncements from national bishops' conferences. Collections of country studies such as those edited by Daniel Levine, Scott Mainwaring and Alexander Wilde, and Thomas Bruneau and his colleagues dispel the notion that a monolithic "Latin American Catholic church" does or ever did exist.[2] Rather, within the international church through which the orientations and priorities of Catholic social doctrine historically have been interpreted, national hierarchies always have made decisions regarding the application of social doctrine according to bishops' understandings of their own peculiar national contexts. These contexts include realities as diverse as the type of political system in a country; the nature of the social, economic, or political ills facing an individual country; and the availability of church resources, either tangible or symbolic. This book continues in the vein of works that deal with national churches as stages on which the ecclesiastical and theological concerns and priorities of the international Catholic church intersect with local hierarchies' struggles to make Christianity and the church meaningful in the concrete reality of believers' lives.[3]

Most of the contributions in this book adopt an institutional approach to the study of the church.[4] Most authors focus on bishops and their decisionmaking process to explain not only what "a church" perceives to be its challenges but also the interplay between the church as a religious institution with "nonrational" ends (i.e., faith and mission) and the church as a rational actor with institutional interests that it must preserve in order to pursue its religious ends.[5] This approach does not necessarily rule out competing definitions of the church. The church embodies both its institutional structures, which include patterns of authority and tradition, as well as the living, breathing community of faithful that make up the body of the church. Each of the following chapters provides a framework, within the context of a national hierarchy, for understanding the evolving relationship between the church as *institution* and the church as *community of faithful*. As several authors show, relations between groups that adhere to differing conceptions of the church can be quite strained under certain historical conditions, but the focus of this book is not a "battle for the church" waged by opposing sides.[6] Rather, the tensions described are framed within the historical continuity of the church's adaptation of its institutional integrity to changing temporal conditions.

The central theme presented here is that the ground beneath the Catholic church in Latin America appears to be shifting—calling into question the existing constellation of issues, debates, and influence within national hierarchies. Since the widespread acceptance of the notion that churches occupy an important "space" within national sociopolitical contexts that will not simply wither away with the advances of modernization, we have accumulated an impressive array of knowledge concerning the relationship between church and society in Latin America. We know a great deal more today about the church's vital role in (re)democratization, the championing of human rights, and the preservation (or at times creation) of a wide range of social organizations that have influenced the achievement of varying social goals such as social justice, economic equality, and the enjoyment of political rights. Unquestionably, the Latin American church is a stronger, more vibrant, and more progressive force for social change than it has ever before been in its history. Indeed, the progressive church has been the focus of the overwhelming majority of the social science literature on the Latin American church.[7] But the relationship between the church and its surroundings is neither unidimensional nor unidirectional; churches both influence and are influenced by their surroundings. Each of the contributing authors, although largely sanguine about churches' ability and willingness to build on the advances of the previous decades, examines the changing conditions that will place new constraints, new limits, and new challenges in the path of the Latin American church in its struggle to maintain its prophetic voice on the behalf of the poor. It is to these changing conditions that we next turn.

Changes Within the International Church

One of the most formidable constraints on the church's ability to strengthen its presence in the daily lives of many Catholic faithful in the future is John Paul II's intention to restore the authority pattern and traditional moral doctrines of the pre–Vatican II (1962–1965) era. Although not widely recognized at the time of the Second Vatican Council,

Archbishop of Krakow Karol Wojtyla (who took the name John Paul II when he ascended to the papacy) opposed the definition of the church as a "people of God." He argued then for a traditionally hierarchical defini-tion of an institution "in which laity worked under the direction of priests and bishops to achieve the 'truth' of a life lived in faith," and his policy has been consistent with this view since he became pope.[8] Penny Lernoux attributes John Paul's tremendous popularity to his energy and charisma, but argues that he is a "populistic intergralist." She states, "John Paul, who thinks in terms of peoples—not nation states—is deeply supportive of the populism that enables a people to express political, economic, or social aspirations through religious gestures and symbols." However, she warns that "John Paul's Catholicism has a clear set of rules and it is the respon-sibility of priests to make sure they are obeyed. . . . The civilization he envisions is essentially integralist—a throwback to a Christendom when the church was both the mediating force in secular society and the only source of spiritual salvation."[9]

Perhaps the best evidence of John Paul's "counterreformation" agen-da can be found in the tension between the Vatican and the more progres-sive sectors of Latin American hierarchies. Since John Paul's opening of the Latin American Bishops' Conference (CELAM) at Puebla, Mexico, in 1979, his two primary preoccupations with developments in the Latin American church have been increasingly clear: defense of theological orthodoxy against the taint of Marxism, and maintenance of traditional institutional authority patterns. John Paul's visit to Nicaragua in 1983 provided the stage for the pope's first highly publicized confrontation over these issues.

By the 1970s the Nicaraguan hierarchy had begun to distance itself from the Anastasio Somoza regime, which was notorious in the region for its repression and corruption. Although preferring to find a negotiated solution to the escalating civil war, the Nicaraguan bishops were pushed by Somoza's intransigence into finally endorsing the revolution as the last resort in the legitimate effort to topple the regime. Perhaps even more important was the participation of grassroots Catholic groups in the revolution that culminated in Somoza's overthrow in 1979. The consolida-tion of the new regime under Sandinista leadership, however, quickly ended the era of cooperation between the Nicaraguan bishops and the revolutionary forces, as the national bishops' conference under the leader-ship of Archbishop Miguel Obando y Bravo moved increasingly into opposition to the ruling junta. On the other hand, the grassroots coopera-tion between Sandinistas and Catholic progressives continued after the revolution, a bond symbolized by the inclusion of four priests in the new Sandinista government. The history of the worsening relationship be-tween the Nicaraguan bishops and the Sandinista government has been described at length elsewhere,10 but for our purposes it is important to note that the tension served to split the Nicaraguan church.

The divisions within the Nicaraguan church and John Paul's response to them in the early 1980s helped clarify the divisions within the Latin American church as a whole. These divisions can be roughly characterized as "vertical" (dividing hierarchies at every level) and "horizontal" (dividing lower echelons of the hierarchy, plus the laity, from those with higher positions of institutional authority).[11] The vertical cleavage is viewed as dividing radicals, progressives, and conservatives over the practical (and often political) implications of a preferential option for the poor. The horizontal cleavage, dividing progressives from traditionalists, results from the ongoing debate about the distribution of authority that stems from the basic disagreement over the definition of the church as either a people of God or a hierarchical institution.

Some early proponents of liberation theology seized upon the revolutionary potential of the church's preferential option for the poor and argued that the church cannot remain neutral in the historical struggles for liberation from manmade structures of oppression.[12] For "radicals," a preferential option for the poor must be understood in light of the Marxist notion that class conflict is the motor of history; thus, accommodationist or reformist political strategies that fail to bring fundamental change to existing power arrangements accomplish little more than to preserve the status quo. Christians not only may but must join with other forces, including Marxists, to fight for real political and economic transformation. As Mainwaring and Wilde point out, the radical position never crystallized into a broad or well-defined movement in the Latin American church, although brief organizational expressions of these ideas could be found especially in the late 1960s and early 1970s.[13]

Church progressives likewise condemn existing power arrangements; however, they stress reallocation of church resources to reach out to the poor or oppressed through the extension of grassroots organizations, the creation of base Christian communities (CEBs), and the initiation of parish-level study, self-help, and educational groups rather than an explicit focus on partisan activity. Nevertheless, progressives accept that these groups, which are first and foremost religious in nature, can result in a politicization among their participants that can lead to political, even partisan, activism.

Conservatives find the radicals' blurring of the line separating the church's religious mission and political agendas especially antithetical to the universal church's mandate to minister to the entire human family. Moreover, they argue that identification with particular political movements or positions ties the institutional authority of the church to the rise and fall of partisan fortunes. Conservatives also tend to find problematic the progressives' distinction between facilitating popular organizations and partisan activity.[14] "Conservative" in this sense does not necessarily

imply sympathy for the reactionary forces in Latin America, though the
political effect of such a position can be the appearance of tacit support
for the status quo that in most cases has been dominated by right-wing or
military forces. However, "conservative" can also imply a conscious right-
wing political preference, which appears to be the case for some Latin
American bishops.

The tensions between the grassroots church and bishops—tensions
that define the horizontal cleavage but overlap to a large degree the
vertical church cleavage—stem less from competing visions of society and
the church's role in it and more from debate concerning the appropriate
institutional strategy for implementing the church's commitment to the
poor or dispossessed. Progressives, already committed to a more activist
vision of the church's preferential option for the poor, find authority and
legitimation for their community involvement in their reading of the
gospel and the shared experiences of committed Christians in popular
organizations. Traditionalists regard authority and the determination of
the moral and social guidelines for the church as flowing primarily from
the top down from the Vatican through the international church. It is
possible, then, to be a church traditionalist without espousing conservative
political views, although these positions often accompany one another.

Philip Williams, in his chapter on the Nicaraguan church, shows that
in spite of the wide variation within the progressive sector of the church,
conservative Nicaraguan bishops since the early 1980s have accused laity
and clergy who continue to work with the Sandinista regime of political
"radicalism." They argue, with the support of John Paul II, that continued
Christian-Marxist cooperation reduces church activity to a merely political and fundamentally anti-Christian program. In addition to perceiving
vertical cleavage, the Nicaraguan bishops argue that the CEBs that were
founded on a participatory model of the church as "people of God" reject
the authority of the institutional church and establish, in effect, a "parallel
church" in which authority is derived from one's solidarity with the poor.
The Nicaraguan bishops characterize the so-called parallel church as a
direct challenge to the institutional pattern and, ultimately, to the
authority of the church itself. John Paul, in agreement with the Nicaraguan
bishops, repeatedly has rejected such a definition of the church, not only
in Nicaragua but also in other Latin American churches where he perceives the grassroots movement as affirming alternative sources of
spiritual or ecclesiastical authority.[15]

In many ways, confrontations such as the one between John Paul II
and the pro-Sandinista crowd at an open-air mass in Managua in 1983 have
exacerbated the divisions within the Latin American church as a whole.
Whereas in Poland his ecclesiastical traditionalism served as a symbol of
opposition to an oppressive Soviet system, these same traits in Nicaragua
served to reinforce not only Latin American church traditionalists but

political conservatives both in and out of the church. By reining in what he considers to be challenges or institutional threats presented by progressives, he gives the appearance of tying the church anew to its traditional allies, the military and economic/political elite. Such papal influence will not only constrain Nicaraguan progressives as the church adapts to the new right-wing government, but as the authors of this book argue, progressives in countries as diverse as Peru, Chile, Brazil, and Venezuela are finding that the terms of debate within their national hierarchies are increasingly influenced by Vatican traditionalism.

Also in the early 1980s, the Congregation for the Doctrine of the Faith, the Vatican office charged with maintaining orthodoxy, was gearing up for a protracted assault on liberation theology and its major proponents in Latin America. John Paul II named Cardinal Joseph Ratzinger, a Vatican hard-liner, to head the office; he pursued his work with fervor, beginning in 1983 with a list of criticisms of the work of Peruvian Gustavo Gutierrez, the recognized "father" of Latin American liberation theology. In 1984, the cardinal sent a letter to Leonardo Boff, a leading Brazilian theologian who most clearly has elucidated the Latin American church's commitment to grassroots CEBs, accusing him of serious "theological deviations," mainly infusing Christianity with Marxist symbols and meaning. In addition, he called Boff to Rome to defend his "challenge" to the institutional authority of the hierarchical church. Also in 1984, Ratzinger published a thirty-five page critique of liberation theology widely interpreted as particularly simplistic and reductionist in its condemnation of liberation theology as merely a Marxist, antiauthority ideology.

The confrontations between Vatican hard-liners and Latin American progressives are significant in two respects. On one hand, continued Vatican pressure has had a chilling effect on those Latin American progressives who want to renovate the church from within, not create a schism or break away from the institutional church. Thomas Bruneau and W. E. Hewitt in Chapter 3 and Jeffrey Klaiber in Chapter 5 explicitly examine this trend in Brazil and Peru, respectively, two of the primary stages for early conflicts between Cardinal Ratzinger and Latin American hierarchies. On the other hand, the flood of support for Gutierrez, Boff, and others under doctrinal scrutiny by the Vatican bureaucracy forced both John Paul and Cardinal Ratzinger to examine the claims and concerns of Latin American progressives with greater discernment and sophistication than they displayed originally. In fact, Ratzinger's final version of his "Instruction on Christian Freedom and Liberation," although retaining his virulent anticommunism and assertion of the traditional authority of the institutional church, did at least acknowledge the conditions of poverty and oppression in Latin America as well as tacitly recognize the religious validity of the notion of liberation. Ultimately, opponents in and out of the church failed to discredit liberation theology fully or successfully to equate Marxism with the commitment to social justice and the opposition to poverty and oppression that engenders liberation theology. Each contributor to this book concludes that although the "new church" of the 1960s and 1970s is increasingly circumscribed, the progressive sector has not disappeared partly because of the unchanging or worsening sociopolitical and socioeconomic conditions in much of Latin America.

In addition to continuing its doctrinal pressure on Latin American hierarchies, the Vatican has exerted its influence in other ways. John Paul has made some conciliatory gestures to progressives in Latin America, but he has filled the majority of vacancies in the Latin American hierarchies with conservatives and traditionalist Vatican supporters. Moreover, a number of outspoken progressive theologians both in Latin America and elsewhere have been relieved of their teaching duties in Catholic institutions or severely reprimanded by the Vatican. Changes in the complexion of national hierarchies, in turn, affect such vital decisions as resource allocations in local churches, curriculum content in Catholic seminaries where future generations of priests are trained, and local pastoral and social priorities. In many ways, these changes will have far more lasting effects on the opportunities available to progressives in the Latin American church than the more highly publicized, but more elite-oriented confrontations between church leaders.

Challenges at the National Level

In addition to the Vatican's efforts to rein in the Latin American churches' more political social commitments and to reassert traditional church authority structures, developments in Latin America also present new constraints to progressives. Whereas the wave of militarism and state-sponsored violence legitimated by the state's national security doctrine in the 1960s and 1970s helped consolidate the church's commitment to democracy and human rights in most countries, the recent trend toward (re)democratization has tended to undermine consensus and unity within the church. Democracy itself presents a challenge to the church. Historically the church, particularly in Latin America, was at best ambivalent toward democracy, often preferring an alliance with more authoritarian governments that were willing to provide a juridical basis for preserving the church's religious monopoly. Recent experiences with military dictatorships, however, clearly have strengthened Latin American bishops' commitment to democracy as the regime type that best allows for individuals to grow as human beings and as children of God. Yet democratic structures assume debate and dissent, the right for all to participate, and legitimation of authority from the bottom up. Although the international church now clearly commits itself to political democracy, the extent to which democracy extends to the church itself lies at the heart of the post–Vatican II struggle between progressives and traditionalists.

Church progressives claim the legacy of Vatican II, which they argue not only opened the church to the world but also opened the church's traditional authority pattern to greater collegiality and dialogue. The practical applications of these reforms, such as the worker-priest movement and greater autonomy of national bishops' conferences, initially resulted in a sense of tremendous optimism among progressive sectors who sought a fundamental reorientation of the church. The traditionalist challenge to Vatican II and the Latin American understanding of the council's reforms enunciated at Medellín, Colombia (1968), was mounted quickly, however, both in Rome and Latin America. Traditionalists have not scored a complete victory in rolling back Vatican II and its consequences, but most observers do agree that the progressives, who in the final analysis think of themselves as part of and loyal to the institutional church, do not want to be alienated from the church. Thus, in order to avoid schism and publicly damaging acrimony, progressives have resigned themselves to the reassertion of traditional authority patterns in the hopes of preserving a space for their work with the poor and popular sectors.[16]

(Re)democratization in Latin America not only highlights the tensions between traditionalists and progressives, but it also exacerbates conflicts between conservatives and progressives. With the reemergence of political parties, unions, and civil organizations, churches must now define their voices among a host of voices. The church can have a profound impact on the shaping of a nation's socioeconomic and political agenda, but the reverse is also true. Issues and debates within the church are shaped by the interplay between intrachurch theological and ecclesiastical concerns and national/international ideological and institutional patterns to which churches must adapt. Theoretically, the principles of tolerance and mutual respect required in democracy ought not conflict with the church's universal mission to all individuals regardless of class, gender, ethnic, or religious distinction. Yet as newly emerged democracies are consolidated, more fully articulated and competing political and economic programs will complicate the church's continued search for its prophetic voice: What will it mean to maintain a "preferential option for the poor" when countries' choices are shaped according to traditional political categories of left, center, and right? It is easier to build a consensus in opposition to a regime having an underlying ideology that not only assaults the humanity of its citizens but also attacks any individual or institution (including the church) that questions the legitimacy of the state's authority. In a democracy in which competition is phrased in terms of the best means to achieve such goals as economic growth or justice, clergy will find it more difficult to find their prophetic voice without at least appearing to endorse one political program over another.

Historically, national hierarchies have been overtly political in their support for or even participation in friendly governments. However, part of the process of renovation and renewal before and during Vatican II was the growing recognition within Latin American churches that in an increasingly politicized world, particularly in competitive democracies, the church should develop its own constituency by deepening its religious influence rather than by allying with political parties or interests. By the 1960s, most Latin American churches had broken their formal ties to conservative parties or regimes and asserted their mediating role "above politics." With the reemergence of democratic politics, many within the church want to return to this position and allow parties, unions, and voluntary associations to serve their legitimate political functions.

On one hand, the desire to return to a space above politics reflects a consolidation of trust in democracy and democratic institutions. On the other hand, many progressives, whose work and suffering were sustained during the harsh years of dictatorship by a concept of Christian faith that propelled them into political opposition and activism, will find the notion that there exists a space "above politics" difficult to accept, much less that the church should retreat to this space. Progressives argue that faith orients their vision of what it means to be not only human and a Christian but also a citizen of the national and international community. One's faith cannot be divorced from one's participation in the community and, thus, must imply concern with temporal matters. To retreat from "this world" (including its political realm) would imply an abandonment of Christian faith. Likewise, a church that retreats to a position above politics abandons its faithful in their struggle to witness their faith in their daily lives. In light of the worsening socioeconomic conditions throughout Latin America, progressives argue that the need for the church's prophetic voice on behalf of the poor is as urgent as ever.

Adding to the confusion is the apparent realignment of the international left and its consequences in Latin America. Progressives typically (although not necessarily) have been sympathetic to leftist ideologies and programs. For countries where church progressives developed ties with leftist parties, the scramble to redefine party ideologies and platforms in the wake of the East European crises further limits the clarity of progressives' prophetic voice in the political sphere. This is particularly true in Chile, where the Marxist left has the longest and strongest tradition in Latin America. The reunified Socialist Party has joined the governing coalition that essentially champions the export-oriented development policy of the Augusto Pinochet regime, and the Communist Party has been decimated (at least temporarily) by internal infighting. At present, no significant political actor is articulating a coherent alternative to the neoclassical development model offered by the government coalition.

Many Chilean church progressives, with ties to a sizable number of grassroots organizations with more traditionally leftist views, no longer have a clear political ally or expression. To articulate such an alternative from within the church not only would exacerbate the tensions between progressives and conservatives/traditionalists but might also present a challenge to the stability of the newly founded democracy, a result that progressives want to avoid as it would most likely benefit the non-democratic right.

Even in the case of Brazil, where the democratic party system does offer alternatives that are compatible with the views of the progressives, Thomas Bruneau and W. E. Hewitt argue that the progressives are increasingly isolated in the national hierarchy. In the decade before the 1964 coup, the church distanced itself from its previous neo-Christendom, elite-oriented strategy for building national influence, thus providing a foundation for the church's postcoup ability to eschew relations with military and right-wing elites. However, after adopting a preferential option for the poor and the people-centered strategy that it implies during the repressive years of military control, the national church appears to be returning to an elite-centered strategy of influence building. With the encouragement of the Vatican, progressive clergy and organizations are increasingly marginalized in the church's public statements. Bruneau and Hewitt maintain that in addition to a reassertion of a traditionalist non-political or pastoral role of the church, a clear trend toward politically moderate or even conservative sympathies appears to be emerging. As in Chile, the Brazilian bishops initially were careful to confine their participation in early elections to political education, avoiding the appearance of endorsing particular candidates. However, Bruneau and Hewitt offer evidence of an increased willingness among the clergy to embrace publicly candidates and platforms that are antithetical to the progressives' understanding of the church's preferential option for the poor.

Carol Drogus's chapter on base Christian communities (CEBs) in Brazil suggests that in addition to the church's apparent retreat from its more progressive commitments, the progressive sector appears to have overestimated its ability to influence mass political (or at least electoral) behavior significantly. Drogus points out that although active participants in CEBs often undergo a dramatic personal liberation from their sense of alienation from the religious hierarchy or even the political hierarchy, this phenomenon does not necessarily translate into active political participation, nor does it necessarily lead to mass political organization or mobilization. Drogus's research, which focuses primarily on women participants (who compromise on average 90 percent of the active participants in CEBs), confirms the conclusions reached by others that both male and female participants appropriate changes in church teachings in a far more complex way than is normally assumed.[17] The realization that progressive

trends within the church hierarchy are not directly or immediately repli-
cated in general belief patterns has helped to erode the original optimism
concerning the impact of the changes in the church over the past several
decades. For many progressives throughout Latin America, this more
sober view has resulted in a reevaluation of the importance of remaining
in the institutional church and working to transform it from within, in spite
of continued tensions with traditionalists and the conservative Roman
curia. Drogus's chapter also makes a major contribution to our understanding specifically of women's participation in CEBs. Her typology of
ways in which women approach their understandings of religious participation adds new prisms for analyzing the ways in which changes in
church doctrine are refracted through the community of faithful.[18] This,
in turn, contributes not just to the discussion of the Latin American church
but also to an increasingly sophisticated international feminist interchange
of ideas.

Brian Froehle's chapter on the Venezuelan church adds an additional
dimension to the discussion of the limits of the influence of the church,
both in its progressive and traditionally pastoral ambitions. Froehle argues
that the Venezuelan case can serve as a model for other churches in Latin
America in two senses. Unlike most other churches, the Venezuelan
church has enjoyed several decades of uninterrupted democratic rule in
which to find its voice amid the plenitude of other voices. Historically, the
Venezuelan church also has suffered from an acute shortage of resources,
both tangible (for example, financial and personnel resources) and symbolic (such as close relations with friendly regimes or a clear religious
monopoly). Under such conditions, the same tensions exist between
progressives and traditionalists, but Froehle argues that the church's
struggle even to maintain (much less strengthen) its presence in
Venezuelan society has resulted in a pragmatic coexistence between these
groups. None of the intrachurch groups can begin to meet the range of
religious needs of the country; thus, a rough "division of labor" has
emerged along with a realistic tolerance of differences.

Interestingly, the one case portrayed in this book as offering new
promise to progressives is the Cuban church. John Kirk argues that the
Cuban church, after years of denying the Cuban revolution, has begun
to reconcile itself to the Fidel Castro regime in a way that portends well
for the possibility of renewal and expansion of the church's presence
in Cuban society. The author writes, however, in anticipation of John
Paul II's visit to Cuba, that the reasons already mentioned may complicate the Cuban hierarchy's attempt to become a "Cuban church"
rather than a "church in Cuba." Castro's intransigence in the face of
the changes throughout communist Europe and communist parties
worldwide also may retard the process of reconciliation between the
Cuban government and the church. Finally, it is particularly difficult to

predict with any certainty the path of the Cuban church when the identity of Castro's successor is unclear.

Challenges to the Church's Religious "Monopoly"

In addition to the dramatic political changes of the past decade, many Latin American societies also have been experiencing an equally dramatic socioreligious transformation. Statistics have only recently appeared in the North American mainstream press, but Protestant growth has exploded in the past twenty-five years in what was once considered a "Catholic continent." Characterized as forming a "revolution" by sociologist David Martin, Protestants now comprise as much as 10 percent of the overall population (and more in certain areas). Given that active participants in the Catholic church may number no more than 15 percent of the general population, the rapidly expanding Protestant presence can be considered a major challenge to the Catholic church.[19] According to David Stoll, Brazil, Guatemala, El Salvador, and Honduras could be predominantly Protestant by the year 2000, followed by 40 percent in Chile and 35 percent in Costa Rica and Bolivia. Thirty-five percent of the Mexican population is already Protestant, and an estimated 30 million Brazilians identify themselves with non-Catholic or Protestant sects.[20] The phenomenal growth in non-Catholic religious identification has yet to be fully quantified, but most observers agree that the preponderance of the growth has occurred among Pentecostal and neo-Pentecostal groups rather than within traditional, mainstream Protestant churches.

Protestantism—and especially Pentecostalism—with its emphasis on one's personal relationship to Jesus Christ—offers individuals a psychological sanctuary in an otherwise chaotic and hostile world. The typical focus on personal salvation, securing one's place in the afterlife, provides new value to the sufferings of this life. As well, great stress is placed on living one's life as a witness to Christ. Converts must give up their "old sinful ways" (drinking, extramarital relations, gambling, and the like), a change that not only confers a new sense of control over one's life but also may increase a family's standard of living as money previously spent on such activities is brought back to the family budget. These characteristics tend to be especially attractive to the lowest socioeconomic groups that are most marginalized. Moreover, because authority is conferred not by education or training but by (the often highly emotionalistic) evidence of the blessing of the Holy Spirit, Pentecostalism is far more accessible to the poor and uneducated than is the Catholic church. In turn, Pentecostal preachers of humble origin have more in common with, and hence can reach more effectively, potential converts in the popular sector, although as Edward Cleary indicates in Chapter 9, conversion to Pentecostalism increasingly crosses class lines in places like Guatemala. Finally, because religious authority is primarily charismatic, Pentecostal churches have proved to be quite prone to schism, resulting in a tremendous proliferation of worship sites. In this sense, Pentecostal churches do not suffer from the same resource constraints as the Catholic church. Few "wealthy" Pentecostal churches exist, but there are far more Pentecostal storefront churches in many (particularly urban) areas than the Catholic church, with its chronic shortage of priests, can staff.

Some observers have attributed Protestant growth to North American–sponsored and –funded political organizations that seek to strengthen right-wing regimes and undermine the progressive Catholic potential to mobilize popular dissent. Although evidence exists that confirms such a strategy among a number of North American religious, political, and quasi-governmental institutions, the rapidity and degree of Protestant growth cannot be explained solely as a North American conspiracy. More responsible studies, including Cleary's chapter on Protestant growth and Catholic revitalization in Guatemala, identify a myriad of factors that account for the rapid increase in rival religious organizations in Latin American societies. According to Cleary, the stresses associated with dependent development, coupled with an ongoing climate of political violence in a society with a historically high degree of popular religiosity create a heightened need for religious institutions that provide order and security in the midst of chaos.

Both Catholic traditionalists and progressives consider the tide of Protestant growth a threat. Progressives have tended to view Protestantism, which stresses one's personal relationship with God, as contrasting sharply with liberation theology's communitarian emphasis that often fosters sociopolitical commitment and community activism. Certainly, it is easy to find examples of Protestant groups that encourage political quietism or even explicit support for right-wing governments, such as Pentecostal support for Guatemalan dictator Efraín Ríos Montt or Chilean dictator Augusto Pinochet. Thus, Catholic progressives most criticize many of the Protestant groups for espousing a religious worldview that can be used to legitimate political regimes and social orders that are contrary particularly to progressive interpretations of Catholic social doctrine. Traditionalists, on the other hand, see Protestant growth as an assault on Latin American culture that they assume is inextricably linked historically to the Catholic church. The belief that to be Latin American is to be Catholic has long served as a source of influence and power for the church. Traditionalists view Protestantism as not only a cultural invasion but also an attack on the integrity of the church. Both groups recognize the threat to the historical influence of the Latin American Catholic church posed by the multiplication of rival religious institutions.

Although church traditionalists and progressives share a common sense of threat from Protestant growth, their prescriptions can be quite different. To date, the trend has appeared to be that Pentecostal churches tend to win converts among the popular sector, the very sector most targeted by Catholic progressives.[21] Indeed, as some of the contributors to this book point out, many urban areas where the Catholic church has most developed its presence through active CEBs are precisely where one can find a proliferation of Pentecostal worship sites. Progressives see the CEBs as well as other forms of Catholic community organization as critical to strengthening the church's presence in these areas. The church must continue to build on its new network of community groups in order to dispel the historical perception of the church as an ally of the rich, indifferent to the daily concerns of the popular sector. Such community presence would not only result in a renewed relevance for the church in the lives of individuals, but it also would serve an educative function that could undermine the natural appeal of Pentecostalism. In contrast, traditionalists want to reallocate resources toward a more pastoral orientation of church and a renewed focus on expanding the church's traditional sacramental function. Traditionalists argue that Pentecostal attendance has increased as a natural response to the shortage of Catholic parishes and personnel in a population known historically for a high degree of popular religiosity; the proliferation of Pentecostal worship sites fills a void left by the Catholic church for sacramental services.

The Vatican has tended to agree with the traditionalists' interpretation of both the scope of the Protestant threat as well as their prescription for how to meet it. Thus, not only are CEBs and other neighborhood or grassroots groups being tied much more closely to the institutional church and its hierarchical authority structure, but the renewed emphasis on pastoral rather than political work has resulted in a distancing of the church from some of the organizations that it protected or fostered under previous military regimes.[22] This distancing, in turn, further reinforces the church's attempts to pull back to the realm "above politics."

Jeffrey Klaiber's chapter on the Peruvian church, in which he shows that Protestant groups in Peru do not necessarily eschew political or communitarian goals and strategies, adds an interesting new dimension to the discussion of the relationship between Catholicism and Protestantism in Latin America. The presidential election of Alberto Fujimori, himself a Catholic but the candidate endorsed by many of the Peruvian Protestant churches, indicates that Protestants, particularly the newer Pentecostal and neo-Pentecostal groups, may begin entering the political realm in unexpected ways in the next decades. Should this occur, Protestants likely will not enter politics in any uniform pattern because groups differ widely in religious principles (and hence, potentially, in political views). Especially among Pentecostals, political principles can vary according to the beliefs of the individual leaders of the churches. Moreover, religious differences may be mitigated by other shared concerns in countries facing desperate socioeconomic and political conditions. For example, Cleary points out that in Guatemala, the desire for a solution to the economic crisis and widespread violence cuts across classes as well as religious affiliation, resulting in similar voting patterns among Pentecostals and Catholics. Jorge Serrano, widely recognized as former dictator Rios Montt's surrogate, won the 1990 presidential election with votes from rich and poor, Catholic and non-Catholic alike. Because no uniform Protestant "movement" or sociopolitical doctrine exists, it is impossible to predict how widespread Protestant political activity would affect the Catholic church; however, it is clear that it would add another layer to the competition between Catholic and non-Catholic churches and, in turn, further complicate relations between Catholic traditionalists, conservatives, and progressives.

Conclusion

Changing intrachurch, national, and interreligious conditions undergird the following examinations of the new challenges to and complexities of maintaining the church's prophetic voice and preferential option for the poor in the coming years. Yet no author here argues that the church can or will return to its pre-1960 status in Latin America. The space available to the progressive sector is in many ways more constrained and its boundaries less clear; however, conditions in Latin America ensure that this progressive sector will not disappear. The democratic trend is good news in Latin America, but very real threats to the political gains of the past decade still lurk behind the nearest corner. Militaries that have stepped out of the front halls of power often still exert enormous influence on civilian leaders and fragile democratic institutions from behind the scene. The United States, through its militarized "drug war" as well as a continued reliance on arms as a primary tool of diplomacy, ensures the institutional strength of militaries while often undermining civilian governments' capacity to rule. Moreover, the economic forecast for the foreseeable future is bleak. The relentlessness of the debt crisis and its "solutions" result in ever more dramatic indicators of worsening conditions for the majority of Latin Americans. To be "voiceless" is still a reality for many, not only in nondemocratic countries. Many in the church will continue to speak on behalf of the voiceless throughout Latin America—in the countryside in Guatemala, in the Brazilian hinterland, in the violence-torn regions of Peru—albeit within a shifting context of intrachurch and church-politics relations.

Notes

1. Ivan Vallier, *Catholicism, Social Control, and Modernization in Latin America* (Englewood Cliffs, N.J.: Prentice-Hall, 1970).

2. Daniel H. Levine, ed., *Church and Politics in Latin America* (Beverly Hills, Calif.: Sage Publications, 1980); Levine, ed., *Religion and Political Conflict in Latin America* (Chapel Hill: University of North Carolina Press, 1986); Scott Mainwaring and Alexander Wilde, eds., *The Progressive Church in Latin America* (Notre Dame, Ind.: University of Notre Dame Press, 1989); and T. Bruneau, M. Mooney and C. Gabriel, eds., *The Catholic Church and Religions in Latin America* (Montreal: Center for Developing-Area Studies, McGill University, 1984).

3. The list of country-specific studies that examine these issues is too long to list fully. Among the best-known books in this tradition are: Thomas Bruneau, *The Political Transformation of the Brazilian Catholic Church* (Cambridge: Cambridge University Press, 1974); Bruneau, *The Church in Brazil: The Politics of Religion* (Austin: University of Texas Press, 1982); Margaret E. Crahan, *The Church and Revolution in Cuba and Nicaragua* (Bandoora, Australia: La Trobe University Institute of Latin American Studies, 1988); Daniel H. Levine, *Religion and Politics in Latin America: The Catholic Church in Venezuela and Colombia* (Princeton, N.J.: Princeton University Press, 1981); Scott Mainwaring, *The Catholic Church and Politics in Brazil, 1916–1985* (Stanford, Calif.: Stanford University Press, 1986); Brian Smith, *The Church and Politics in Chile* (Princeton, N.J.: Princeton University Press, 1982); Hannah W. Stewart-Gambino, *The Catholic Church and Politics in the Chilean Countryside* (Boulder, Colo.: Westview Press, 1992); Philip J. Williams, *The Catholic Church and Politics in Nicaragua and Costa Rica* (Pittsburgh: University of Pittsburgh Press, 1989).

4. The exception is Carol Drogus's chapter on women and base Christian communities in Brazil. Drogus examines the way in which changes in church orientation are refracted in the belief patterns of CEB participants rather than the struggles between elites regarding the proper role or orientation of the church.

5. Among others, Scott Mainwaring explicitly criticizes an excessively institutional approach that envisions the church as simply a rational actor that seeks to preserve its interests: Mainwaring, *The Catholic Church and Politics in Brazil*, pp. 7–11. A similar critique is made by Daniel H. Levine, *Religion and Politics in Latin America*, pp. 6–14. Other recent works that adopt an institutional approach that at once recognizes the unique religious ends of the church while examining its pursuit of its "interests" are Williams, *The Catholic Church and Politics in Nicaragua and Costa Rica*; Stewart-Gambino, *The Catholic Church and Politics in the Chilean Countryside*.

6. A good example of a study that views the two conceptions of the church as necessarily opposed is Luis H. Serra, "Religious Institutions and Bourgeois Ideology in the Nicaraguan Revolution," in Laura Nuzzi O'Shaughnessy and Luis H. Serra, *The Church and Revolution in Nicaragua* (Athens, Ohio: Monographs in International Studies, Latin America Series No. 11, Ohio University, 1986).

7. The most recent major work on the progressive church is Mainwaring and Wilde, eds., *The Progressive Church in Latin America*. This book seeks not so much to offer an alternative viewpoint to their work as to continue the story of a changing environment in which the progressive church is increasingly constrained within both national churches and the international church.

8. Penny Lernoux, *People of God: The Struggle for World Catholicism* (New York: Penguin Books, 1989), p. 29.

9. Lernoux, *People of God*, pp. 35–36.

10. In addition to those sources already cited, see Philip Williams, "The Catholic Hierarchy in the Nicaraguan Revolution," *Journal of Latin American Studies*, vol. 17, pt. 2 (November 1985), pp. 241–269; Michael Dodson and Tommie Sue Montgomery, "The Churches in the Nicaraguan Revolution," in Thomas Walker, ed., *Nicaragua in Revolution* (New York: Praeger, 1982); Margaret E. Crahan, "Varieties of Faith: Religion in Contemporary Nicaragua," Kellogg Institute Working Paper, no. 5; Phillip Berryman, *The Religious Roots of Rebellion: Christians in Central American Revolutions* (London: SCM, 1984).

11. The following several pages are borrowed heavily from Hannah W. Stewart-Gambino, "The Evolving Role of the Latin American Church," in Abraham Lowenthal, ed., *Latin American and Caribbean Contemporary Record* (New York: Holmes and Meier, 1989), pp. A100–A117.

12. Michael Dodson, "The Christian Left in Latin American Politics," *Journal of Interamerican Studies and World Affairs* 21 (February 1979), pp. 45–68; Michael Dodson, "Liberation Theology and Christian Radicalism in Contemporary Latin America," *Journal of Latin American Studies* 11 (May 1979), pp. 203–222.

13. Scott Mainwaring and Alexander Wilde, "The Progressive Church in Latin America: An Interpretation," in Mainwaring and Wilde, eds., *The Progressive Church in Latin America*, pp. 15–28.

14. Levine characterizes the line dividing popular organizations and partisan activity as the difference between the church serving as an "activator" versus "activist." Levine, *Religion and Politics in Latin America*.

15. The most recent expression of this concern for maintaining traditional authority patterns is John Paul II's warning made on January 10, 1991, to Latin American religious to "obey their local bishops, especially regarding pastoral programs for the 500th anniversary in 1992 of the arrival of Christianity in the Americas." The pope expressed "profound worry" about alternative plans for the official celebration of the anniversary (i.e., the Word-Life catechetical program designed by the Confederation of Latin American Religious to offer the native American view of the colonial experience). The Word-Life program already has been banned by the Vatican as too critical of colonial evangelization. "Pope Warns Latin American Religious to Obey Local Bishops," *National Catholic Reporter*, January 25, 1991, p. 13.

16. A number of authors have noted this phenomenon recently. See, for example, the chapters by Williams, Mainwaring, Doimo, Ireland, and Romero in Mainwaring and Wilde, *The Progressive Church in Latin America*.

17. W. E. Hewitt, "Myths and Realities of Liberation Theology: The Case of the Basic Christian Communities in Brazil," in Richard Rubenstein and John Roth, eds., *The Political Significance of Liberation Theology* (Washington, D.C.: Washington Institute Press, 1988), pp. 135–155; Hewitt, "The Influence of Social Class on Activity Preferences of Comunidades de Base (CEBs) in the Archdiocese of Sao Paulo," *Journal of Latin American Studies*, vol. 19 (1987), pp. 141–156; Thomas Bruneau and W. E. Hewitt, "Patterns of Church Influence in Brazil's Political Transition," *Comparative Politics*, October 1989, pp. 39–61.

18. See also Lisette van den Hoogen, "The Romanization of the Brazilian Church: Women's Participation in a Religious Association in Prados, Minas Gerais," *Sociological Analysis*, vol. 50, no. 2 (1990), pp. 171–188.

19. Tim Stafford, "The Hidden Fire," *Christianity Today*, May 14, 1990, p. 23; David Stoll, *Is Latin America Turning Protestant? The Politics of Evangelical Growth* (Berkeley: University of California Press, 1990); and David Martin, *Tongues of Fire: The Explosion of Protestantism in Latin America* (Oxford:

Blackwell Press, 1990).

20. "A Quiet Revolution in Latin America: Is the Roman Catholic Bulwark Turning Protestant?" *World Press Review*, March 1991, p. 30.

21. As recent research indicates, this trend may be changing in areas where the Pentecostal churches have a strong foothold. Two recent publications on Protestantism are Stoll, *Is Latin America?* and Martin, *Tongues of Fire.*

22. John Paul II's eighth encyclical, released January 22, 1991, and entitled *Redemptoris Missio*, is an indication of this Vatican trend. This encyclical reminds the church that Christ's work is not yet completed and the church must continue and reinvigorate its missionary activity. The encyclical's call on Islamic countries to concede religious liberty received the most attention in the press because the encyclical was published in the early stages of the Gulf war. But the real thrust of the encyclical is the reassertion of the Catholic church as the "ordinary means of salvation and that she alone possesses the fullness of the means of salvation." Not only does this deal a blow to interreligious dialogue, but it places renewed emphasis on the pastoral function of the church. Latin American CEBs are cited as an antidote to the "sects which are sowing confusion by their activity" in Latin America, but within the context of their specifically pastoral and religious function as a means of outreach for the institutional church. Peter Hebblethwaite, "Mission Encyclical's Many Caveats Lean Most Heavily on Theologians," *National Catholic Reporter*, February 1, 1991.

CHAPTER 2

Redefining the Changes and Politics in Chile

HANNAH STEWART-GAMBINO

Because of its history of progressive leadership, both in Chile and Latin America, the Chilean Catholic church has been the object of intense scrutiny in recent years. Ivan Vallier, the first North American social scientist to see the church's potential contribution to Latin American modernization, pointed out the relatively early emergence in the 1930s and 1940s of a progressive faction of Chilean priests and bishops committed to expanding the church's ties to the working class.[1] The steady radicalization of the progressive wing of the church in the 1960s and early 1970s, evidenced by the splintering of the church between reformist and radical factions, has been examined at length by such authors as Brian Smith, Thomas Sanders, and others.[2] Further, the crucial role of the Catholic church in preserving a space for democratic opposition to the Pinochet regime and in providing individuals protection from the human rights violations of the military government has been the focus of much scholarly as well as journalistic analysis.[3]

Virtually all of the literature on the Chilean Catholic church suggests that the hierarchy's progressivism, especially the majority's courageous role under the Pinochet regime, strengthened the Chilean church's national influence, broadened its scope of authority, and allowed the church to develop a truly national, multiclass, and ideologically inclusive community of faithful. Indeed, not only did the Chilean church serve as a symbol of opposition to the military regime, but it also lent its substantial institutional resources to the struggle for democracy, resulting in the creation of a broad array of ecclesial and quasi-ecclesial organizations from the grassroots to the national level. But with the election of President Patricio Aylwin and the return to democratic rule and party politics, the challenges facing the church changed significantly. What role will the church play in democratic Chile in the 1990s? Can the church maintain the same level of national (particularly political) influence and the same scope of authority? What will the emergence of a cacophony of "new voices" mean for the

21

institution that so successfully served as "the voice of the voiceless" for the past decade and a half?

This chapter is divided into four sections. Because some call for the church to return to its historical position "above politics," the first section briefly reviews the unique features of the pre-1973 relationship between the church and Chilean politics and society. The second section describes the role adopted by the church during the dictatorship, and the third focuses on the way in which the church contributed to the transition to democracy. The final section analyzes the present and future role of the Catholic church in the context of the challenges facing Chilean politics and society. Can the church return to a space above politics, and will this space have the same parameters as in the precoup period?

The Church and Pre-1973 Chilean Society

Chile's pre-1973 political history contrasts sharply with that of most other Latin American countries. Not only did Chile enjoy one of the longest and strongest democratic traditions in the region, but its political party system was perhaps the most highly developed. From the 1930s, democratic competition in Chile depended largely on the parties' ability consistently to recruit new members and establish ties with new social groups. Thus, unlike in many countries that have yet to experience the "deepening of democracy," the evolution of the Chilean party system in which party elites spent a preponderance of their time maintaining and expanding clientelistic ties to their constituencies resulted in an extraordinarily high degree of party penetration into all areas of social life. Political parties served as the fulcrum of virtually all sociopolitical activity, reinforcing and being reinforced by stable, multiclass political subcultures. According to Manuel Antonio Garreton, nonparty organizations "managed to become actors of national significance precisely to the extent that they were related to the party political structure."[4]

Another distinctive characteristic of the Chilean political system was the early emergence of primarily class-based political parties. By the end of the 1930s, the political arena was divided into rough thirds: a strong right, a viable center, and a well-institutionalized Marxist left. The relatively even distribution of the vote created incentives for party elites to engage in politics of accommodation and compromise instead of extralegal or extraconstitutional political strategies.

Because of the distinctive features of Chilean political development, the twentieth-century Chilean Catholic church had to devise a strategy for maintaining its influence in national society far earlier than other national churches that continued to rely on their relationships to dominant conservative parties or authoritarian regimes. Many Chilean church leaders, who initially felt threatened by the development of a democratic, class-based party system that included both traditionally anticlerical and Marxist parties, clung to the church's traditional alliance with the Conservative Party. However, a significant minority argued that severing the church's historical identification with the Conservative Party and withdrawing from the partisan political arena could strengthen the moral authority of the church. Maintaining an alliance with the Conservatives would only identify the church with the economic interests of traditional elites, and the church would risk losing the allegiance of the increasingly mobilized Chilean working and middle classes.[5] By the 1940s, under the progressive leadership of Cardinal José María Caro, the majority of the hierarchy came to agree that the church should remain above politics—a position from which church leaders could address national issues without taint of partisan identification. Of course, in keeping with Vatican policy, the Chilean church uniformly opposed the parties of the Marxist left. Many within the church continued to sympathize openly with the Conservative Party, and a few, like Bishop Larraín of Talca, championed the so-called Social Christians (who later merged with several smaller parties to become the Christian Democratic Party).[6] However, the church as *institution* remained neutral.

The significance of the Chilean church's official withdrawal from partisan politics is threefold. The presence of new political and social associations competing for the allegiance of urban working and middle classes forced significant factions within the church into increasingly progressive theological and policy stances. In turn the church created its own organizations targeted at the working and middle classes and thus legitimated their interests and participation in national debates. Finally, unlike in a number of other Latin American countries where battles over religious issues continued to place the church at the center of national politics, social and class issues came to define the political agenda in Chile. National economic and political debates were framed largely by the political parties through which workers' and employers' associations articulated their demands. The church contributed to these national debates through a variety of public and private means, and its views influenced the Conservative and Christian Democratic parties' positions. But although the "above politics" stance increased the church's moral authority and influence, the post-1930s Chilean church did not wield the same degree of political power as did some other Latin American churches. The pattern of economic and political modernization in Chile resulted in a process of secularization and rationalization more common to Europe than to other Latin American countries.

Nevertheless, the church did play an important mediating role within the Chilean sociopolitical arena. On a number of significant occasions, political battles tempted church officials to equate Catholicism with par-

ticular partisan positions. Indeed, one of the hallmarks of the Chilean
political system until the late 1960s was an intense competition between
the Conservatives and Social Christians/Christian Democrats for the
church's endorsement, and many within the church were happy to use
their positions to bless publicly one or the other. However, both because
of papal instructions to remain neutral[7] and precisely because the church
itself was divided internally, the leadership preferred to avoid the potential dangers of partisan identification and to develop the church's own
agenda separate from any party platform. Over time, the church's official
neutrality came to be synonomous with not only an acceptance of but also
a support for democracy. As others have described in detail, both in the
1970 election and especially in the latter half of Salvador Allende's tenure,
the national church leadership hosted meetings between opposing
politicians in an attempt to avoid the collapse of Chilean democracy.[8] The
pre-1973 church's refusal to descend into the partisan fray from its official
above-politics position[9]—a move that could have eroded the delicate
compromise between left and right and led to an earlier breakdown of
democracy—is arguably the most important contribution the church made
in the fifty years before the coup.

The Church and Dictatorship: 1973–1983

To the surprise of many Chileans who had assumed that military personnel
would simply "restore order" and return to their barracks, the military's
postcoup behavior quickly demonstrated its more radical intent to restructure Chilean society and politics. Consistent with Cardoso's characterization of bureaucratic-authoritarian regimes, the military struck hard
at eliminating the left and severely curtailed the scope of activities open
to the center.[10] It was not until 1975, however, when the military adopted
the neoliberal "Chicago-boys" economic model, that the ramifications of
the goal to restructure society became evident. From the team of free-
market technocrats, the military adopted a set of policies consistent with
both its desire to lead the country to rapid economic development and its
aim to depoliticize Chilean society.

The economic logic behind these policies was to concentrate capital
in the hands of "efficient" sectors (for example, private export enterprises
where Chile is considered to have a comparative advantage) and to attract
foreign investment. More important, the military hoped that simultaneous
economic growth and the availability of cheap, imported consumer goods
resulting from a reduction of trade barriers would eliminate political party
allegiance. With economic prosperity and the satisfaction of consumer
demands, the military planned to transform permanently the democratic
tradition of channeling demands through political parties to the state to a

more "stable" state structure that satisfied the majority's demands from above.[11] In some ways, it can be argued that the military initially succeeded. The rightist parties simply disbanded in favor of the new regime, and the combination of sophisticated repression and the economic boom of the late 1970s enabled the state effectively to shut down the center and left and fragment the opposition.

This strategy was common to Latin American militaries' self-appointed mission as defined by the national security state ideology, but it had a special significance in Chile. As Manuel Garreton argues:

> The elimination of the party political arena and of the political system was not simply the elimination of a channel for demands, as in other Latin American societies. In the Chilean case, it meant the destruction of the principal mode by which social actors and subjects were constituted. Thus in breaking up the political system the military took a step which was both reactive and transformative.[12]

Because Chilean democracy had been built around the political party structure, the military's success in driving the parties underground allowed the government to disarticulate the various sectors of society (for example, *campesinos*, students, *pobladores*, and others) in a successful divide-and-conquer strategy.

Into the political void created by the military policies stepped the Catholic church. Until 1983, the church served as virtually the only channel through which opposition to the Pinochet regime could be voiced. By the late 1970s, church leaders began issuing stronger and more pointed public criticisms of the regime's human rights violations as well as its social and economic policies. Scores of new church or church-affiliated neighborhood, academic, and workers' organizations were created to facilitate especially working-class Chileans' social, political and economic struggles against the regime. To the extent that a democratic space remained open between 1973 and 1983 in which the opposition could survive, it was provided largely by the church.

The church's willingness to provide a "protective umbrella" had important consequences for the Chilean opposition. First, until 1983 the traditional parties, particularly on the left, managed to preserve their basic structures and contacts with their bases primarily because of the (albeit limited) space provided by the church. More importantly, a slow mobilization of a network of grassroots social organizations began under the protection of the church that was new to the traditionally party-dominated Chilean sociopolitical arena. Much of the initial organization was defensive in nature: A host of such resources as *ollas comunes* (community kitchens) and community self-help groups were born to fulfill needs created by the military's economic and political policies.[13] By the 1980s an additional network of nongovernmental organizations (NGOs) emerged to provide new avenues for organization of specific interests. Many NGOs were founded by the church itself or by groups with close links to the church. Although these new NGOs differed substantially in the specificity of their constituencies and level of local, regional, and national organization, they represented a partial transformation of the historical political arena in Chile.

The church's leadership role under the military dictatorship strengthened dramatically the relationship between church and some sectors of society. Certainly, if "influence" is measured by the degree of salience the church has in individuals' lives, then the willingness of the church to serve as a surrogate for the suppressed parties and unions greatly expanded church influence in Chile. Relations between the church and the left were never better. In working-class neighborhoods where survival often depended on church or church-sponsored self-help, community organizing, or human rights groups, the church became far more visible than it was in the years preceding the coup. Many involved in church work or base Christian communities experienced a revitalization of their religious faith that continues to strengthen the ties that bind together the church-as-institution and the church-as-community of faithful. In many ways, by the early 1980s the church had become a far stronger institution than it had been before the coup.[14] One indicator of this increased influence is the dramatic rise in numbers of seminarians in Chile, from 111 in 1972 to 946 in 1987, or a 752 percent increase.[15]

On the other hand, the church's willingness to assume vital political functions placed the church at the center of the political arena for perhaps the first time since its disestablishment in 1925. For many including Pinochet, the church *itself* became a critical political issue. In the absence of political parties or other properly "political" actors to define national issues, Pinochet successfully reduced the political agenda to a single issue: support or opposition to the military regime. Clearly defined institutional mechanisms were not necessary for channeling support for the regime. And given that virtually every institution that could channel opposition had been outlawed but the church, Pinochet could accuse the church's Vicaría de Solidaridad and its leadership of being "more communist than the communists themselves."

The price of leadership, then, was a perceived politicization. The church gained a new relationship with the poor and working class, but it lost authority among the wealthy and the rightwing. It was not uncommon to hear regime supporters say that they were Catholic but owed no obedience to Chilean prelates, especially to such outspoken opponents of the regime as Cardinal Raúl Silva Henríquez or Bishops Carlos Camus or Tomás Gonzalez. The church's reduction to a "mere political actor" in the eyes of the right also resulted in frequent attacks, both verbal and physical. Other less obvious costs were exacted as well. Pinochet, in an effort to undermine the church's authority throughout Chilean society, courted leaders of Pentecostal churches. Non-Catholic and particularly Pentecostal churches have grown at a phenomenal rate in the past twenty-five years, and estimates are that as many as 20 percent of the Chilean population are practicing non-Catholics, 90 percent of whom are Pentecostal.[16] This is a religious challenge to the Catholic church of the first magnitude. Pinochet for the first time opened the ranks of the military to non-Catholic evangelization and extended social benefits to Protestant ministers and their families that had been reserved to Catholic personnel in the past. In return, top military brass were celebrated at an annual *Acción de gracias* hosted by the Methodist Pentecostal Church, the largest non-Catholic church in Chile. This annual event alone lent a legitimacy to non-Catholic churches that they had never enjoyed historically in Chilean society.

Even the most progressive and activist members of the hierarchy recognized the institutional costs of having the church involved in leading the struggle for democracy in Chile. But until other actors emerged to fulfill the functions of an opposition, most felt that the church could not morally retreat or return to its previous role above politics. In turn, without the church to preserve a space for democratic opposition, it seemed unlikely that other actors could emerge to take on the church's more political functions. Underlying the broad consensus regarding the church's role in supporting democracy and protecting human rights, however, lay a fundamental tension between those who yearned to reestablish a more pastoral line within the church and those who supported the church's new activist role in Chilean society. This tension flared after the emergence of the Chilean protest movement in 1983.

The Reemergence of the Party System and Transition to Democracy: 1983–1989

On May 11, 1983, Chileans responded to a call to protest issued by the leadership of the national copper-workers' union in numbers that astounded even the organizers of the event. This national protest, the first in ten years of military rule in Chile, marked the formal beginning of the process that led to the democratic transition in late 1989. In the wake of its overwhelming success, the opposition parties vowed to call monthly demonstrations for airing the Chilean people's demand for a return to democratic rule and an end of the Pinochet regime. Political elites from the center and left rapidly reconsolidated their party structures and solidified their political positions in order to take advantage of the reawakened mobilization potential. Clearly, the military had grossly underestimated the depth and endurance of the societal cleavages underlying party allegiance in Chile. The parties had not withered away, but had maintained their links to civil society through a host of informal associations—for example, professional organizations, student associations, even sports clubs—many of which had been provided or protected by the church after the coup. Although there has been some change in the lineup of political parties since 1973, it is remarkable the degree to which virtually the identical political parties and leadership cadres that existed before the coup reemerged after a decade of repression.[17]

The revitalization of party politics in 1983 signaled a new hope for democracy in Chile, but the immediate result was an intensification of party competition and ideological rigidification that initially hindered progress toward the ouster of the military. Because of the success of the first protests, the major opposition parties and alliances fell prey to an "election mentality"—their immediate goal became the demonstration of party strength rather than subordination of party interests to the goal of unifying a cohesive opposition movement. Moreover, both the extreme left and right erected obstacles to broad cooperation across the political spectrum. The democratic right refused to participate in any coalition that included the Communist Party (PC), especially after the attempt on Pinochet's life in 1986 and the discovery of caches of arms allegedly linked to the communists in 1987. The PC, on the other hand, refused to abandon its legitimation of violence as a potential strategy for struggle or its ties to the extremist Manuel Rodríguez Patriotic Front (FPMR). All of these factors reduced the possibility of constructing a coalition capable of either ousting the military or offering a political alternative attractive enough to induce the officers to step down.

At the same time that the protest movement erupted, the Catholic church experienced several significant internal changes that would affect the prospects for democracy. The most important of these changes was the retirement of Cardinal Raúl Silva Henríquez and his replacement with Juan Francisco Fresno. Fresno was widely considered to be sympathetic to the military regime before he became head of the Santiago diocese.[18] A traditional man of the church, Fresno maintained a sharp distinction between the public and the private, the pastoral and the political. In his view, the church's authority should be consigned to the religious realm of person's life; public life should be left to the authority of the state and political actors. Thus for Fresno, the legitimate role of the church excluded any activities that could compromise the integrity of its pastoral mission by placing it on either side of temporal, political issues. He argued that the hierarchy's apparent endorsement of the opposition and its political goals in the late 1970s and early 1980s reinforced the divisions in Chilean society, alienated many believers from the saving grace of the church, and contributed to the loss of the church's moral authority. For Fresno, the church should not become the ally of any one group or organization, nor should the heirarchy perform the functions of a political party, trade union, or state apparatus.

Because Fresno's vision of the proper role of the church in Chilean society appeared to differ markedly from that of Cardinal Silva Henríquez, many in the opposition, and especially the left, feared that the struggle to oust the military government would be weakened. Privately, many argued that a nonpolitical Church would simply legitimize the status quo. For their part, the military and the right anticipated that the church would, if not legitimate the military regime, put an end to its role in maintaining international attention on the regime's human rights abuses and in sheltering domestic pressure to restore democracy.

Fresno's appointment also highlighted the tension within the church between more activist progressives and traditionalists who emphasize the church's pastoral versus social mission. The Chilean church has never suffered the kind of horizontal cleavage that has divided contemporary Nicaraguan church elites from the so-called popular, or parallel, church. However, tensions have existed for decades between bishops and between bishops and clergy over the line distinguishing between pastoral care and partisan activity—between mediation and political meddling. In the several years following the coup, the extreme nature of the military's socioeconomic and security policies muted previous debates over such issues as liberation theology and the meaning of the church's preferential option for the poor. But as the church moved into ever-wider areas of social responsibility and its protective umbrella extended further and further, the old debate over the legitimate role of the church re-emerged.

Moreover, church elites like Fresno pointed to surveys indicating that the Pentecostal sects predominate in a number of Santiago *poblaciones* where the Catholic church has difficulty providing basic pastoral services because of a chronic shortage of priests. Losses among the lower classes, coupled with substantial alienation of much of the upper classes over the church's apparent endorsement of the opposition, strengthened the argument of the traditionalists who hearkened back to the church's more pastoral, less activist pre-1973 position. Others, notably Bishops Camus of Linares and González of Talca repeatedly spoke out against the military regime and publicly endorsed the opposition. In an interview with *El Mercurio*, Bishop Camus stated that given the depths of immorality of the military regime, virtually any form of opposition would be warranted and legitimate, calling the authors of the assassination attempt on Pinochet "heroes."[19] Bernardino Piñera, in his capacity as president of the Episcopal Conference, described the nature of the divisions within the church in a statement made to John Paul II during the papal visit in 1987:

When we (the Episcopal Conference) meet twice a year, some difficulties arise. Those of the strictly pastoral order are not the most grave, but they exist. The diverse currents of thought in the universal church . . . also divide us. More difficult to reconcile are the differences in judging the reality of the country—social and cultural, but also economic and political—and the attitude that our episcopacy should adopt toward it.[20]

In spite of the concern produced by Fresno's promotion, both within the opposition as well as the church, his insistence on the reassertion of the church's pastoral and mediational roles allowed the church to play a decisive role in the exceedingly difficult process leading to Pinochet's defeat in the 1989 plebiscite. Fresno's first attempt to alter the church's role was an offer in 1983 to host meetings between the Democratic Alliance (AD) and the government.[21] After several meetings, the dialogue fell apart because the representatives of the government did not appear to have the power to commit the government to concrete steps toward redemocratization. More importantly, the talks excluded the Popular Democratic Movement (MDP), the Marxist opposition alliance having as its largest member the Communist Party. In order to stall negotiations, the government insisted that the AD publicly deny the Communist Party any role in the future of the country. While the AD wavered on this issue, the MDP launched a series of its own protests to demonstrate that any transition excluding the left would be doomed. The net result of the failed talks were (1) greater polarization and distrust between opposition alliances, (2) greater unease on the right and hence a greater tendency to continue support for Pinochet, and (3) embarrassment on the part of the church. In the end, Fresno, who had committed the moral force of the church behind sponsoring dialogue, was forced to issue a statement defending the leaders of the AD for their decision to abandon the talks; in effect, he placed the blame for the breakdown on the government for refusing to offer any timetable for the transition on the basis of which the talks could continue.

The failed attempt at dialogue was a turning point for Fresno. Because both the right and the military had misread Fresno's call for a nonpolitical church as a call for an antipolitical church, his role in the attempts at negotiation were seen as a betrayal. By virtue of hosting a dialogue, Fresno in effect endorsed democracy and legitimated the centrist opposition (if not the opposition in the MDP). By blaming the government for the breakdown in talks, Fresno refused to lend the church's unconditional support for the military. As a result, the number of physical and verbal attacks on churches and church personnel increased dramatically after an initial lull following Fresno's appointment.

Attacks on the church were significant beyond the physical violence to either church property or personnel. Government attacks were a direct assault on the integrity and the authority of the church. Even for church leaders such as Cardinal Fresno who sincerely desired to pull the church within the boundaries of legitimate pastoral activity, such attacks could not be tolerated. Regardless of the inevitable politicized interpretation, the hierarchy had to lodge official protest to direct assaults, a response that in turn further strained church-state relations and complicated Fresno's ability to play the mediational role he desired.

Cardinal Fresno was more successful in providing a forum for dialogue between moderate opposition parties seeking bases for mutual cooperation. After a series of negotiations hosted by the cardinal, the National Accord for the Transition to Full Democracy was born on August 15, 1985. This alliance, which included a broad spectrum from the democratic right to sectors of the left, raised anew Chileans' hopes for a broad front capable of pushing the military from power. Once again, however, the accord proved to be weaker than the traditional cleavages between the left and the right. Fear of the left led the right to lend only lukewarm support to the mobilization efforts of the alliance. The moderate Socialists faced a loss of potential support to a seemingly more militant Communist Party and socialist faction still within the MDP. And the Christian Democrats in the center remained pulled between left- and right-leaning factions either supporting or eschewing cooperation with the Marxist left.

Pope John Paul II's visit to Chile in April 1987 gave the national leadership a renewed impetus for unification. The slogan for the pope's six-day visit was "Messenger for Life." The pope repeatedly stressed dialogue, reconciliation, nonviolence, and forgiveness—studiously non-political words designed to deny any group the opportunity of using the pope's visit for partisan purposes. In both words and actions, John Paul II fully supported Fresno's vision of the church as a mediator. Consistent with the Chilean church's traditional support for democracy, the pope endorsed the government's official commitment to a transition beginning in 1989: "Man is naturally inclined to organize political and legal structures. All citizens, without exception, should have the chance to freely and actively participate in the establishment of the legal foundations of the political community, and in the administration of public affairs, in the determination of areas of action and boundaries of the different institutions, and in the election of public officials."[22] The pope also made clear that the church would exert not only a mediating but also a moderating influence and that the goals he identified must be achieved through negotiation and dialogue: "Violence is not Christian. Violence is not evangelical. Violence is not a path to solving the real difficulties of individuals or the people."[23]

The pope's full endorsement of democracy had an enormous symbolic impact on the Chilean political scene at a time when the improving economy and opposition fragmentation had strengthened Pinochet's position. But more importantly, the pope helped rekindle hopes of opposition unity by meeting with representatives from an extraordinarily broad array of opposition actors, from human rights and neighborhood groups to officials of all the opposition parties, including the Communist Party. In order to demonstrate his understanding of Chilean politics, public appearances were staged at such places as the National Stadium, the scene of such brutality in the months following the coup. Yet while confronting squarely the most vivid symbols of repression and state-led violence, the pope repeatedly emphasized the need for dialogue, reconciliation, and compromise. His message was clear: Chile's hope lay in a peaceful transition in which nonextremist forces, both civilian and military, mutually agreed in advance to specific steps and shared rules of the political game. The role of the church should not be so much to participate in the negotiations over specific steps or political procedures, as to facilitate the discussion and to provide a forum for its pursuit.

Perhaps the most important immediate consequence of the pope's visit was the recapturing of some of the influence the church had lost among the right and Pinochet's supporters. One representative of the rightist National Party (PN) said before the plebiscite:

> There is no doubt that the church has enormous influence in spite of the fact that we live in an increasingly secularized world. On one hand, it has great temporal power and on the other hand, it has an enormous moral reserve. The best expression of the latter is the pope's recent visit. Perhaps there has never been such a powerful call to come together in this country.[24]

That the pope was careful to commit the church to respect for human rights and democracy and not to specific proposals that could be viewed as partisan was well noted by the (at least democratic) right.

Nevertheless, the right continued to insist that although it might be the church's legitimate function to facilitate political dialogue, the church should only exercise this function under extraordinary circumstances. "Today in Chilean politics, there are two actors facing one another that paradoxically should not be political actors: the armed forces and the church. . . . This is one of the central distortions of Chilean politics, this dislocation of the natural institutional role."[25] John Paul II's firm rejection of the church's political role helped facilitate the right's legitimation of its mediational role; however, the question of the boundary between pastoral and political remained crucial to the right. As one leader of the National Party asked: "How far can the church go? How far can the church push [into politics]?"[26] Another National Party militant answered:

> I would say that the church has a great mission to accomplish. . . . [T]he church should disseminate the fundamental Christian message . . . which naturally inspires people—civilian leaders, the laity—to realize this message through unified actions of reconciliation, legality, respect for human

rights, opposition to dictatorship. [But] the practical application of this message must be brought about by the Catholic lay leaders. I must do it, as a politician, not Bishop Camus. Bishop Camus can talk with me and I talk with the press, but he should not talk to the press.[27]

What Now?

General Pinochet's defeat in the plebiscite on October 5, 1988, is one of the more dramatic events in recent Latin American politics. Supporters of the regime were convinced that given a yes-no choice for Pinochet, the majority of voters would choose to continue being ruled by the military, which was portrayed as the guarantor of economic growth, stability, and anti-Marxist law and order. The victory of the "no" forces, which grouped together seventeen parties ranging from a newly moderate leftist faction of the Socialist Party to the center right, is a remarkable story of political cooperation and restraint. In spite of improved economic conditions and state manipulation of such resources as the national media, the "no" faction won 55 percent of the vote with 90 percent voter turnout. The next step in the transition was a three-way presidential race scheduled for December 1989 between Christian Democrat Patricio Aylwin, who headed the coalition of seventeen parties that formed the Concertation for Democracy (CPD), and two conservative candidates: Hernán Buchi and Francisco Javier Errázuriz. The military, not surprisingly, manipulated the electoral rules of the game to ensure a rightist victory in the presidential as well as congressional elections—for example, by gerrymandering congressional districts and manipulating the political party laws. Not only did the CPD parties successfully unite behind Aylwin's candidacy, but they managed to put together a single list of national congressional candidates. Aylwin's election and the CPD victory in both congressional houses can be seen as a testimony not only to the ultimate failure of the Pinochet regime to depoliticize Chilean society but also to the strength of Chileans' political will to overcome the obstacles to democratic transition erected either by the military or traditionally narrow partisan self-interests.

The party leadership's ability to overcome previous animosities as well as the logic of electoral competition confirmed observers' belief that the historical strength of the Chilean party system provided the best hope for democracy. Certainly, the most distinctive feature of the Chilean transition to democracy is the degree of resilience not only of the particular parties but also of the party leaderships. A remarkably high percentage of the top officeholders today were political leaders in 1973.

However, this party and leadership resilience may present the most profound political challenge for the immediate future of Chilean democracy. The transition was possible to the extent that (in many cases) the same politicians who could not resolve their differences before the 1973 coup successfully negotiated both the CPD's national program as well as the often more thorny, practical questions of how to allocate political resources and authority to seventeen parties ranging a broad political spectrum. Yet in order to achieve this degree of political cohesion, the party leaderships have exercised firm control over their constituencies, resulting in a degree of disaffection with the political leadership, especially among the youth and the *pobladores*. These two groups particularly served as the vanguard of mobilization after 1983 and claim responsibility for opening the space within which the party elites could operate for the first time since the coup. Grassroots leaders' perception that the transition was negotiated (albeit successfully) over their heads at the potential expense of legitimate demands and interests contributes to this sense of alienation.

As the difficult problems inherited by the Aylwin government go unresolved, these tensions could flare. Finance Minister Alejandro Foxley has made it clear that the government plans to maintain the military's basic export-oriented, free-market development strategy with modifications only to provide for increased social spending.[28] A study published by the National Institute of Statistics shows that whereas consumption for the average family remained stable between 1978 and 1988, consumption for the poorest 20 percent of the population dropped 15.4 percent. At the same time, intake of the wealthiest 20 percent rose 7.6 percent.[29] In spite of the government's initial prediction of an increase of 20 percent in expenditures in health, housing, and education between 1989 and 1991, the 1991 budget resolution introduced in Congress in September 1990 revealed that public spending remained virtually the same in 1989 and 1990 with only a 7 percent increase in 1991.[30] The government's position, in apparent agreement with the leadership of all the CPD parties, is that this economic model maximizes Chile's potential for economic growth, yet increasing criticism can be expected from the poorest sectors whose lifestyles were further squeezed by a 36 percent increase in the consumer price index in 1990.[31]

These statistics, coupled with the 17 percent of government spending allocated to the military in 1990, could prove to be powerful political symbols in the future. Moreover, although the government has passed legislation increasing the power of negotiation for workers and legally recognizing the United Alliance for Workers (CUT), CUT President Manuel Bustos asserts that these reforms are "insufficient and it will be necessary to continue fighting for a radical reform of the Work Code imposed by the dictatorship."[32] In addition to issues of economic justice and distribution, items remaining high on the Aylwin government agenda will be reform of the penal code, effective civilian control over the security forces (particularly the former Central Nacional de Informaciones [CNI] officials), and a resolution of human rights violations of the past regime. All of these issues are politically explosive, and none will be easily resolved. Not only do governmental policy initiatives have to be negotiated with the seventeen CPD parties, but the 1980 constitution allowed Pinochet to designate nine of the forty-seven senators and all of the mayors as well as to control the courts and the army, giving the promilitary opposition an effective veto over government policy. In late 1991, resolution of these matters remained under intense negotiation.

A crisis of expectations is probably inevitable among sectors that expected to see immediate and structural solutions to their demands from the new regime. Such a crisis would present a fundamental political challenge to the party leadership (and hence the government). It should be noted here that the Communist Party (PC), which historically would have served as a natural channel for this discontent, has been decimated by the transition process. The voters' rejection of the PC and its post-1980 abandonment of the electoral process have left the party plagued by internal bickering, public and massive resignations of longtime and prominent Communist leaders, and acrimonious expulsions of dissenters. On the other hand, a network of organizations that could serve as an alternative to the traditional parties for grassroots mobilization exists that did not exist before 1973. Significant mobilization through nonparty structures could undermine the very strength of the party system that supports the current democratic compromise of the CPD parties. Moreover, if nonparty organizations successfully mobilize public opinion in an attempt to affect the terms of national debate (for example, over economic policy), the cohesion of the political consensus in the CPD could fray. Speaking as a representative of the CPD, Enrique Krauss referred explicitly to the danger of competition between the traditional parties and grassroots organizations at a conference of ninety-seven NGOs in September 1989:

> I am one of those who is conscious of the fact that the way of doing politics in Chile has changed. . . . [In] these 16 years our people . . . learned to construct their own solutions. . . . What Aylwin and the Concertation hope is that the solutions to the extremely grave problems that to some degree will be exacerbated after March 11 [the inaugural date for the new president] will come from the social base.[33]

A crisis of expectations would present a new challenge to the church as well. Because much of the organizational work has occurred through church-affiliated base Christian communities and NGOs or groups protected by the church, tension between party and nonparty leaders could create a dilemma for bishops who want to support the new regime but also maintain the influence that the church has gained through its new institutional ties with the popular sectors. It is not clear what it would mean to remain "above politics" in this case. In the traditionally party-dominated political system, remaining above politics meant refusing to endorse any partisan agenda or equating Catholicism with participation in a particular party. Historically, a consensus about the distinction between pastoral and political was difficult enough to attain in a system defined by electoral competition between national parties. But today, the church cannot return to a pre-1973 position merely above parties in order to be above politics. Much of what is "political" is now expressed through the church's own roots that extend throughout Chilean society.

As in 1983 when changes within the political scene coincided with the appointment of a new archbishop of Santiago, the retirement of Cardinal Juan Fresno in 1989 left the Vatican with the opportunity to choose new leadership for the challenges brought with redemocratization. Many within the church and the political left initially hoped for the naming of a more progressive archbishop than they perceived Fresno to be, but realistically it appeared unlikely that a candidate from the more progressive sector of the church (for example, Bishops Camus or Gonzalez) would be chosen given that the Vatican had filled virtually every new position in the 1980s with a "conservative." For example, Archbishop of Concepción Antonio Moreno, the Vatican's most recent appointment before Fresno's resignation, is widely considered to be an active supporter of the military. Bishop Jorge Medina was the candidate most often mentioned as a possible choice for the next appointment and the one most opposed by the progressives. Progressives recognized the necessity of mobilizing pressure in Rome for a sympathetic appointment, but it was the elevation of Adolfo Rodríguez (the head of the rightist clerical group Opus Dei) to episcopal status that precipitated what was known as "the red alert."

The first step was taken by a group of women who wrote to nuncio Giulio Einaudi saying:

> Have pity on the thousands of disappeared, tortured, exiled, unemployed [whose] voices are raised demanding justice and social revindication. For us, it would be a great affliction and a scandal for our people if the naming [of the new Archbishop] fell on someone who . . . had remained silent or, worse, had worked in complicity with the military government that has assaulted the dignity of mankind and the values of the Gospel.[34]

Another group of laity issued a statement accusing Medina of "sympathy and identification with the dictatorship that has oppressed the Chilean people for sixteen years."[35] The national effort to prevent the naming of Medina included extensive use of public graffiti, distribution of petitions through parishes and church organizations, and a letter-writing campaign to the forty-two cardinals in the Bishops Congregation and the other Episcopal Conferences.[36] Under these conditions, the naming of Bishop of Antofagasta Carlos Oviedo, in spite of his self-identification as a conservative, was considered a victory for the progressives.

> [H]e is a man of recognized obedience to the Pope and Vatican policy, who in the vulgar classification between progressives and conservatives classifies himself as the latter, [but also] he is a priest with great pastoral endowment, preparation, open to dialogue, very receptive to the problems of the popular sectors and not indifferent to the problems of human rights.[37]

Oviedo's history of work on behalf of prisoners (both common and political) and public commitment to human rights, democracy, and the needs of the poor have been highlighted by the progressive sectors of the church.

Archbishop Oviedo also is welcomed by the right. He has used every public opportunity to reaffirm the church's "commitment to be a sign, instrument and endorsement of unity . . . serving everyone with full political independence in such a way that we can shelter everyone . . . so that no one feels rejected, excluded or scorned."[38] In his first major interview after his appointment, the new archbishop described himself as "friend of the poor and the rich, pastor of all and for all."[39] Added to the fact that Oviedo thinks of himself as a "priest's priest"[40] and refuses to be placed on a political spectrum, he follows the pope's lead carefully on intrachurch issues. On liberation theology he states: "When liberation theology substitutes the poor or the people for Jesus Christ, clearly that is not theology. . . . [T]hose who follow it [liberation theology] without knowing theology have been quite confused."[41] About the so-called popular church he states: "In general, I can say that a church that calls itself popular means that it is not in communion with its bishop, that it is marginalized from him. That is not the Catholic church because the Catholic church is a church-communion guided by its pastor through the will of Jesus Christ."[42] Oviedo, in some ways like Fresno, articulates a traditional view of the church more than a conservative political agenda.[43]

Oviedo's task as the leader of the Santiago diocese (which houses much of the bureaucracy of the church's new commitments) as well as that of the rest of the hierarchy is to define the location of the church's space in the new democratic order. Consistent with its pre-1973 position, the church's most recent pastoral agenda for 1991–1994 is a full endorsement of democracy. The bishops say: "It is necessary to create an authentically pluralistic and respectful society, without ignoring the moral principles that rest in the nature and dignity of man, and that are a reflection for believers of God's wisdom. Democracy offers a framework for these aspirations."[44] This pastoral plan, however, also can be viewed as an attempt among men of differing persuasions to carve out those areas of legitimate church support for the project of building a democracy. The bishops' collective statement is an attempt to return to a space above politics without giving up the new spaces conquered during a punishing sixteen years of dictatorship.

Archbishop Oviedo and the Episcopal Conference have consistently stated that although the church is nonpartisan, it has a central role to play in the ongoing process of national reconciliation. Reconciliation includes "closing wounds in the climate of truth, justice and pardon. It does not mean leaving wounds without healing, but neither does it mean wanting revenge. God's justice is expressed, before all, in mercy."[45] The bishops identify the church's mission, in part, as forming individuals' consciousness of the Christian values that must underlie true reconciliation.

At the same time, reconciliation cannot be achieved wholly in the hearts of individuals. The church's position is that reconciliation requires disclosure of the truth about the abuses, especially the human rights violations, of the past regime. Thus, the church, particularly through the legal department of the Vicaría de Solidaridad, continued its crucial work in gathering human rights information in cooperation with the government's Commission on Truth and Reconciliation (the Rettig Commission), which gave its final report in May 1991.[46] The Aylwin government charged the commission with collecting testimonies concerning human rights violations (although limited to those resulting in death) during the military regime in order to obtain an officially recognized accounting of abuses. Under pressure to address the demands for justice from the families of victims of repression, the government has embraced the call for national reconciliation based on truth. On the one hand, the government acknowledges the necessity of publicly recognizing previous abuses; on the other, it has argued that "revenge" will only further divide Chileans and has called on victims' families to contribute to reconciliation through forgiveness.

Oviedo has tried to steer clear of the explosive political question of whether reconciliation requires justice, meaning the trying of human rights abusers in the civilian courts. But there has been an inevitable outcry for criminal proceedings from sectors of the left and victims' families, many of whom have organized through church or church-affiliated organizations like the Vicaría de Solidaridad.[47] Part of the complaint is that names of those responsible for violations should have been published and that the information should not merely have been passed on to the courts to pursue. The courts proved quite ineffectual in protecting human rights under the military government, and until the judicial system is restructured to provide more autonomy from the legacy of the Pinochet years, few anticipate that the courts can adequately pursue the issue of criminal responsibility. The courts are further hampered by an amnesty law passed by the military as well as constitutional fetters tying the hands of the judges. Thus, many within the human rights organizations feel less than sanguine about the achievement of real justice for past abuses. Finally, leaders of the organizations of the victims' families reject the proposal to set up a system of monetary reparations if it is unaccompanied by tangible steps to bring known perpetrators of violence to justice. Because of the church's central position in the human rights movement in Chile, the tensions between the government's attempt to heal past wounds and the cry for greater justice from many who depended on the church for sustenance will place the church in a very difficult position.

It is likely, however, that the church's commitment to the theme of reconciliation will distance the institutional church from the sectors demanding justice. President Aylwin, invoking Pope John Paul II's words during his visit, stated during his address to the nation concerning the commission's report: "Chile has a vocation for understanding and not for confrontation. We cannot progress by digging deeper into division. It is time for pardon and reconciliation."[48] The wave of terrorism (from both the extreme right and left), particularly the assassinations of Jaime Guzmán (leader of the rightist Independent Democratic Union [UDI], the party most closely aligned to the military) as well as others known to be human rights violators, strengthens the view that reconciliation and pardon are necessary for the consolidation of the new political order. Unfortunately for the victims' families, the pervading view that terrorism is on the rise and constitutes the greatest challenge to the Chilean system helps marginalize the legitimate claim for a more energetic pursuit of those responsible for violations who are still housed within the military and *carabineros*.[49] It is especially regrettable given that the military's response to the commission's report was a complete rejection of responsibility for any abuses; the military insisted instead that "the report overlooks . . . the subversive war situation existing during the period. . . . To any serious armed institution faced with a war situation, the only objective to be pursued should be total victory."[50] General Manuel Contreras Sepulveda, former director of Dirección de Intelligencia (DINA), said of the Rettig report: "They [the Rettig Commission] only listed the false declarations of the same Marxists defeated yesterday and today supported by the Vicaría de Solidaridad, where infiltrated Marxists exist, with and without priests' robes."[51]

The concept of reconciliation does stretch to include the hierarchy's continued preferential option for the poor. Although the bishops state that the export-led strategy of the military has "with great sacrifices modernized and perfected . . . the country's economic structure and productive system," they also say that reconciliation is jeopardized by the "unjust distance" this policy has created between social classes.[52] Not only does the church call the privileged to charity but also to "distributive justice" because "Chile should not be a country of great economic and social differences."[53] As of late 1991, the left is fragmented between a Communist Party in disarray and a newly moderate tendency within the majority of socialist factions. As a consequence, no political party or movement currently is articulating an alternative economic model to the modified export-led strategy proposed by the Aylwin government. In contrast, the rightist opposition can be divided on issues such as the degree of civilian control over the military, but these opposition parties have demonstrated a remarkable unity on their long-term economic interests. That the church continues to assert an economic vision of a preferential option for the poor (and that it fits this vision within the concept of reconciliation) leaves a space open for those who would like to assert alternatives to export-oriented growth. This issue, perhaps more than any other, will go to the heart of Chilean politics in the next decade.

It is clear, then, that Oviedo, like Fresno before him, intends to pull the church back to a position above politics and restore to the church a pastoral orientation that is inclusive and nonpartisan. This is a goal that is fully supported by the Vatican as well as others within the Chilean hierarchy. However, the exact parameters and the location of this position above politics are not clear. Beneath a general democratic consensus, the hierarchy remains divided—between political liberals and conservatives and between theological progressives and traditionalists. But the choice is no longer merely between partisan agendas or between pastoral versus political activity. The choice is between claiming the legitimate right to continue to champion the interests of the popular and grassroots groups now found within the church or supporting democratic stability achieved through the firm control of national party leaders. The church risks loss of hard-won national influence if it cedes setting the national agenda to properly "political" organizations. For grassroots leaders for whom the church offered not only solace but also organizational structure for the mobilization of their demands during the dictatorship, a perception that bishops are retreating to a position above politics could lead to an atrophying of the church's new roots in Chilean society. Yet the church risks loss of moral authority if it continues to provide nonparty channels for the expression of many Chileans' demands of the new democratic government. Given that the church now must "compete" with a variety of aggressively evangelizing non-Catholic churches and sects, many within the hierarchy argue that the church must reassert the universality of its message and concentrate its efforts on responding to the often unmet pastoral needs of the Chilean population. According to this view, not only should the church avoid alienating the conservative wealthy, but it must strengthen its pastoral presence among the poor in order to prevent their defection to rival religious institutions.

The prospects for the Catholic church in the next years are not clear. On one hand, the fears of many progressives that the church will simply retreat to its pre-1973 space are probably unfounded. The pattern of institutionalization of Chilean civil society has been transformed to some extent, primarily through church or church-related organizations. The same space above politics simply does not exist to retreat to, nor will many within the church be willing to forfeit the influence that the church has gained by trying to recreate exactly the same space. On the other hand, the Chilean church has a historical commitment to democracy; moreover, the hierarchy understands that the church has much greater flexibility to develop its own sphere of moral influence separate from national or partisan actors in a democracy. To the extent that the full transition to democracy in the next few years probably will require a degree of control exercised by party elites over their grassroots constituencies, the bishops will not stress the mobilization potential of church organizations as they did during the dictatorship. Some sectors within the church may well argue that in spite of redemocratization, the reemergence of party-dominated politics leaves them without a voice. To the extent that these are the same sectors that came to depend on the church to serve as the voice of the voiceless, the bishops' position will be perceived as a fundamental retreat.

Notes

1. See, for example, Ivan Vallier, "Church 'Development' in Latin America: A Five Country Comparison," in Karl M. Schmitt, ed., *The Roman Catholic Church in Modern Latin America* (New York: Alfred A. Knopf, 1972), pp. 167–193.

2. Thomas G. Sanders, "The Chilean Episcopate: An Institution in Transition," in Schmitt, *The Roman Catholic Church*, pp. 105–138; Brian Smith, *The Church and Politics in Chile* (Princeton, N.J.: Princeton University Press, 1982). For a differing view, see David Mutchler, *The Church as Political Factor* (New York: Praeger, 1971).

3. See, for example, Thomas G. Sanders, "Catholicism and Authoritarianism in Chile," *Thought: A Review of Culture and Ideas* 59 (June 1984), pp. 229–243; Brian Smith, "Chile: Deepening the Allegiance of the Working-Class Sector to the Church in the 1970s," in Daniel H. Levine, ed., *Religion and Political Conflict in Latin America* (Chapel Hill: University of North Carolina Press, 1986), pp. 156–186. See also Sanders, "The Chilean Episcopate"; Smith, *The Church*; and Mutchler, *The Church*.

4. Manuel Antonio Garretón, "The Political Evolution of the Chilean Military Regime and the Problems in the Transition to Democracy," in Guillermo O'Donnell, Philipe C. Schmitter, and Laurence Whitehead, eds., *Transitions from Authoritarian Rule* (Baltimore: The Johns Hopkins University Press, 1986), p. 96.

5. By the end of the 1930s, the transformation of the Chilean political system into one defined by class-based parties led the Conservative and Liberal parties, traditional enemies, to ally in a right-wing electoral coalition based on shared economic interests. Thus, the Conservative Party continued to proclaim its proclerical roots, but its primary function had become representation of economic interests. The Conservative-Liberal alliance in turn made the argument for a church-Conservative alliance based on proclericalism difficult to sustain for Conservative sympathizers within the church.

6. That many within the church advocated maintaining political alliance with the Conservative Party is not surprising given that the rapid influx into the political arena of new urban sectors resulted in substantial gains by the Marxist and radical parties that produced a fair degree of concern within the church about potential anticlerical persecution.

7. The first such Vatican instructions came in the form of a letter from Cardinal Eugenio Pacelli (later Pope Pius XII) in 1933. For an explanation of events leading to Pacelli's letter, see Hannah W. Stewart-Gambino, *The Catholic Church and Politics in the Chilean Countryside, 1925–1964* (Boulder, Colo.: Westview, 1992).

8. By the final days of the Allende period, significant numbers of church elites, like the majority of Chilean citizens, welcomed the coup as a necessary corrective measure to deal with a chaotic political situation.

9. It is important to note that days before the coup, Cardinal Silva Henriquez called on the military to step in to restore order, a request indicating the degree to which the hierarchy thought things had gotten out of control.

10. Fernando H. Cardoso, "On the Characterization of Authoritarian Regimes in Latin America," in David Collier, ed., *The New Authoritarianism in Latin America* (Princeton, N.J.: Princeton University Press, 1979), pp. 45–49.

11. Jaime Guzmán best articulated this argument before the military coup in an article in *El Mercurio*, December 26, 1981. He argued that underdevelopment engenders irresponsible parties that artificially create political divisions by seeking votes on the basis of ideological promises to the politically naive and economically disenfranchised. The solution to this problem is economic growth "from above" that would undermine the artificial bases of Marxist electoral support, create political "stability," and lead to "responsible" political elites. Cited in Arturo Valenzuela and J. Samuel Valenzuela, "Partidos de oposición bajo el régimen autoritario chileno," *Revista Mexicana de Sociología* XLIV, no. 2 (Abril–Junio 1982), pp. 606–607.

12. Garretón, "The Political Evolution of the Chilean Military Regime," p. 118.

13. In 1989 in the Santiago metropolitan region alone, over 2,000 popular economic organizations of various types were operating. For a breakdown of their numbers, see Roberto Urmeneta, "Los pequeños (y grandes) esfuerzos de las organizaciones económicas populares," *Mensaje* 383 (Octubre 1989), p. 442.

14. In addition to the increase in symbolic influence acquired as a result of the church's commitment to prevent the military from completely controlling the public discourse, the church has acquired important new sources of financial resources. First, it has successfully raised international aid through Catholic and non-Catholic sources for its expanded commitments. As well, for reasons of security, the church served as a conduit for funds for a variety of non-Catholic organizations until the late 1980s.

15. *Statistical Yearbook of the Church 1987* (Vatican City: Typis Polyglottis Vaticanis, 1989), p. 241; and Felician Foy, ed., *Catholic Almanac 1975* (Huntington, Ind.: Our Sunday Visitor, 1974), p. 409.

16. For example, *Der Spiegel* projects that if Protestant membership continues to grow at the same rate, 40 percent of the Chilean population will identify themselves as Protestant by the year 2000. The assumptions behind this projection can be questioned, but this kind of statement presents a fundamental challenge to the Catholic church. "A Quiet Revolution in Latin America: Is the Roman Catholic Bulwark Turning Protestant?" *World Press Review*, March 1991, p. 30.

17. By late 1991, the dominant strains of the Socialist Party, excluding the Partido Socialista-Almeyda, had reunited after shattering into a variety of schisms after the coup. Perhaps the most significant new party is the Party for Democracy (PPD) under

the leadership of Ricardo Lagos, though its future as of late 1991 is uncertain.

18. Mrs. Pinochet was widely quoted in the press for exclaiming when she learned of Fresno's appointment that "God had finally answered her prayers."

19. For an excellent discussion of the role of Bishop Camus in the process of redemocratization and the differing views of his contribution across party lines see Patricio Dooner, *Iglesia, Reconciliación y Democracia* (Santiago: Editorial Andante, 1989).

20. José Antonio Viera-Gallo, "La iglesia chilena en su actuar público," *Mensaje*, Enero–Febrero 1989, p. 12.

21. The Democratic Alliance included parties ranging from the center-right to portions of the fragmented socialists.

22. Jaime Ruiz-Tagle, "La visita del Papa: Perspectivas sociopolíticas," *Mensaje* 358 (Mayo 1987), p. 134.

23. Ronaldo Muñoz y Manuel de Ferari, "Juan Pablo II en Chile," *Mensaje* 358 (Mayo 1987), p. 142.

24. Dooner, *Iglesia*, p. 101.

25. Ibid., pp. 113–114.

26. Ibid.

27. Ibid., p. 114.

28. The government passed a tax reform that raised corporate and value-added taxes in June 1990 in order to fund increased social spending. Arturo Valenzuela and Pamela Constable, "Democracy in Chile," *Current History*, February 1991, p. 54.

29. *Chile Report* (Santiago, Chile: Justice and Peace Commission of Maryknoll Missioners, July–August 1990), p. 9.

30. *Chile Report* (Santiago, Chile: Justice and Peace Commission of the Maryknoll Missioners in Chile, September–December, 1990), p. 11.

31. Ibid., p. 13.

32. Ibid., p. 2.

33. Ivan Radovic, "ONG en democracia," *Mensaje* 385 (Diciembre 1989), p. 535.

34. Jaunita Rojas, "Nuevo arzobispo de Santiago: Los entretelones de la designación," *Análisis*, 16–22 de Abril de 1990, p. 18.

35. Ibid.

36. Ibid., p. 19.

37. Ibid., p. 18.

38. "Arzobispo de Santiago hizo llamado a la unidad y al imperio de la razón en Chile," *La Epoca*, Miércoles 19 de Septiembre de 1990, p. 13.

39. "Amigo de pobres y ricos," *El Mercurio*, 1 de Abril de 1990, p. D3.

40. Raquel Correa, "El arzobispo, a lo humano y a lo divino," *El Mercurio*, 8 de Abril de 1990; p. D1.

41. Ibid., p. D4.

42. Ibid.

43. The best evidence of Fresno's traditionalism is the trend toward more conservative training of diocesan priests during his leadership of the Santiago diocese. Among other indicators, teaching or discussing liberation theology or even specifically Latin American theology is now prohibited. Interview conducted by Pascale Bonnefoy with Luis Maldonado, professor of theology, September 10, 1990.

44. See Conferencia Episcopal de Chile, "Nueva evangelización para Chile: Orientaciones pastorales 1991/1994," Santiago, Area de Comunicaciones de la Conferencia Episcopal de Chile, 1990, p. 19.

45. Conferencia Episcopal de Chile, "Nueva evangelización," p. 23.

46. According to Eduardo Rojas, head of the Department of Solidarity Action and Education of the Vicaría (DAES), the Vicaría is quite satisfied with Oviedo's commitment to the Vicaría and to human rights and will abide by the archbishop's decisions regarding the Vicaría's future with "satisfaction." Interview with Pascale Bonnefoy, September 14, 1990.

47. The Supreme Court upheld a law passed by the military granting a blanket pardon for any abuses committed before 1976; however, the issue is far from resolved.

48. "Aylwin Addresses Nation on Human Rights Report," *Foreign Broadcast Information Service (FBIS)*, March 5, 1991, p. 30.

49. A study conducted by *La Nación* reveals that although terrorism may be up (for example, murders and bank robberies), the public's fear that crime in general is on the rapid upswing is unfounded. "Statistics Reveal Number of Crimes Committed," *FBIS*, May 7, 1991, pp. 30–31. The church, of course, is not immune from these attacks. In addition to a sustained assault on progressive priests and parishes throughout the past decades, the government recently reported that a bodyguard and police protection have been extended to Father Raúl Hasbún, the most public of Catholic supporters of the military government, because of terrorist threats.

50. "Government, Armed Forces Respond to Rettig Report," FBIS, March 29, 1991, p. 18.

51. "Former DINA Director Contreras Denies Torture, Disappeared," *Chile Information Project (CHIP)*, March 26, 1991.

52. Conferencia Episcopal de Chile, "Nueva evangelización," p. 22.

53. Ibid., p. 79.

CHAPTER 3

Catholicism and Political Action in Brazil: Limitations and Prospects

THOMAS C. BRUNEAU & W. E. HEWITT

A large number of scholarly and popular works have recently examined the changing politico-religious role of the Latin American Catholic church during the second half of this century. Students of the church have indeed been very much captivated by the way in which, in a number of key countries, national churches formerly supportive of the status quo have, within a relatively short time, increasingly appeared to cast their lot with the social justice cause of the poor and oppressed.

As most church observers are aware, the developments they examine in this respect are very much conditioned by a complex set of relationships linking culture, society, and religion.[1] Yet rather interestingly, many authors have concerned themselves only with the *positive* effect of the wider social milieu on church-based political activation in recent years. By contrast, much less emphasis has been given to the study of *constraints* imposed upon politico-religious innovation by the broader sociocultural context.

In the case of Brazil, the nature and effect of positive cultural inducements to church involvement in politics have been much discussed to this point. After 1950, the Brazilian Catholic church moved to reorient its institutional goals away from support for conservative elites and toward the promotion of social justice. This change in church orientation occurred, and in fact was encouraged, within the context of a variety of sociopolitical factors, including modernizing tendencies within international Catholicism (especially in the post–Vatican II period) and increasing competition from secular and religious value movements, such as communism and Protestantism, respectively. Still another important factor was the assumption of power by the Brazilian military in 1964. In the decade that followed, Brazil approximated the model of a bureaucratic-authoritarian state, characterized by a strong push toward economic and political modernization within a context of severe repression. Most avenues of formal protest for labor, students, minorities, and other interest

45

groups were either prohibited or tightly controlled by government legislation. It was within this repressive political milieu that the Brazilian church initially assumed its now-famous "preferential option for the poor," acting essentially as a surrogate for prohibited social movements. In the late 1970s and early 1980s, this stance was then consolidated, largely during a time when the military began to relax its grip on Brazilian politics and to broaden its base of popular support through a reintroduction of basic rights and liberties. The church, in fact, helped to play a role in this liberalization process, which eventually culminated in the official transfer of power to civilian hands in January 1985.

Throughout the military period, the role of the church as defender of the poor and oppressed was relatively clear. More recently, however, the church's continued involvement in this area has been threatened by certain politico-religious constraints. Since 1985, for example, political life in Brazil has opened up considerably, and parties and value movements of all stripes have begun to flourish. Elections for legislators at all administrative levels have also been held on several occasions, a new democratic constitution was promulgated in 1988, and Brazil's first democratically elected president since 1961—Fernando Collor de Mello—was inaugurated in 1990. Complementing these changes on the political front, the Vatican has given clear signals of its distaste for overt political action, while competing value movements, especially Protestantism, are once again reported to be expanding at the expense of Catholic religious hegemony.

Such developments within the spheres of domestic and international politics and religion have most assuredly caused complications for the church. During the past two decades, its actions have been largely in favor of the lower classes and the church's allies, the left or progressives. Now, with the emergence of parties and groups of various ideological stripes in ascension and the changes in the national and international religious milieu, the church has had little choice but to adapt and rechart its course through relatively unknown and potentially dangerous waters.

Certainly, there are already strong hints as to what the church's new course will likely be. In response to the new climate in Brazil, the church appears to be reconsidering seriously the desirability—in fact, the necessity—of maintaining an overtly political role in favor of social change. Indeed, although the "option for the poor" is far from dead, the church has already moved to replace this strategy with one designed to serve better the more devotional needs of the faithful.

In this chapter, we examine the historical context of these developments and investigate the factors—emanating from domestic and international secular and religious sources—that have worked for and, more recently, against the continued politicization of the institution. We conclude with an assessment of where, in light of its current situation, the

Catholic church in Brazil is likely to move in the near future.

The Historical Context of Church Activism in Brazil

Within the literature, there has without question been more attention given to the Brazilian church than to any other in Latin America. This is due not so much to the large size and population of the country or to the energy of Brazilian and foreign researchers as to the existence of a wide and varied richness of events and processes occuring within the church that have demanded attention in recent years.

Most students of the Brazilian church clearly recognize that the institution, as part of the worldwide Catholic community, has as its primary role the religious function: administering the sacraments and providing other services to the faithful. Nevertheless, the attention of the vast majority of researchers has been directed toward the more explicitly this-worldly activities of the church in Brazil—in particular those relating to the church's growing concern for social justice.

The specific sociopolitical and religious context of the emergence of the church's preferential option for the poor, the origins of which can be traced as far back as the mid-1950s, has been examined from several perspectives. One view, which might be termed the "institutional opportunism" approach, focuses mainly on the institution itself (the episcopacy, in particular); its primary goal is seen as the retention and augmentation of organizational power within Brazilian society. If the aims of the church have changed in recent years, this approach suggests, it is because the institution, in the face of threats from competing value movements, has made a conscious decision to approximate itself to the concerns of its historical constituency—the lower classes—in order to preserve its hegemonic position.[2]

At the opposite end of the scale is another approach that might be termed the "people ascendent" view. This perspective is basically an exercise in class analysis, insofar as it gives primary attention to the involvement and demands of the lower classes in reorienting the church.[3] Proponents of this approach suggest that the poor, who in recent years have suffered under a government strategy for economic development that favors economic expansion over social welfare, have essentially pushed the institutional church to act in their class-based political interests.

Although attractive to many, in their extremes, both of these approaches are somewhat flawed. Certainly, they do reflect on some rather salient societal influences on church change. Nevertheless, they neglect too many central dimensions of the church, and tend to totalize certain features of the church that are best viewed in relative terms. The institutional-opportunism approach, to begin with, ignores the role of theology in legitimating church initiatives and pays little attention to the momentum furnished by the response and support of the lower classes to the institutionalization of the social justice cause. The people-ascendant view, on the other hand, fails to explain how and why a whole complex institution could be usurped by the poor and also tends to neglect the international dimensions of the church. Indicative of a strong totalizing tendency, moreover, is how this approach adheres to the closely interrelated phenomena of liberation theology and the *comunidades eclesiais de base*, or CEBs. For its proponents, the theology of liberation becomes the only way to understand the church and its mission. Once this interpretation, which locates the church in a historical and concrete context, is accepted, certain roles in society follow. In a situation of underdevelopment, the church must be involved, it must opt for the poor, and it must use its resources to assist the poor in their liberation. The CEBs, for their part, become the privileged vehicle to work with the poor and promote their awareness, mobilization, and organization. In the opinion of some proponents, the CEB becomes literally a new way of being the church with the structure of authority inverted; the base is now the real source of legitimacy in the institution.[4]

There can be little question, however, that the Brazilian church itself and the relationship it maintains with the predominant sociocultural milieu, are far more complex than these incomplete, totalized visions would offer. To begin with, it must be recalled that the church is first and foremost an institution which is international in scope and behavior—and one that finds its justification, and even justification for change, in centralized theology sanctioned by the Vatican. The church is also a community unto its own right, with power exercised at different levels by the various sectors operating within it. Although the episcopacy is clearly the most important level in the national context for understanding change, there is at least some scope for other clerical and lay actors to affect policy. The response of the population, affected as it is by the prevailing social and political environment, does matter in determining the extent and durability of innovations.

Using this broader understanding of the church as institution and its role in society, a number of authors have attempted more accurately to place the church's preferential option within the broader socioreligious and political contexts.[5] In his attempt to understand church change, Mainwaring, for example, has focused upon the interaction between the institutional church, middle-class activists, and the popular classes in urban areas. Some researchers have looked at the development and impact of church-sponsored programs of national or regional scope favoring human rights or natives and other oppressed groups. There is also much attention paid to Brazilian contributions to the development of the theology of liberation and its resultant effects upon church activation.

Our own work in this area has also been guided by a basic belief that the church is a complex international institution that seeks to influence individuals and society within the context of specific sociohistorical factors. As we have argued elsewhere, the religious influence of the church in Brazil has traditionally been problematic, with various forms of popular religiosity and spiritism much in evidence. Because of historical factors making for weak influence and also perpetuating that status, the church has tended to view politics as a valid means to gain influence. The term *politics* as used here is not restricted to party politics but rather includes any form of link with the state or elites holding power. Traditionally, the use of politics by the church resulted in its playing a conservative role in state and society.

In the context of Brazil in the 1950s and early 1960s, we have suggested, the church's political base of support was challenged by encroaching religious and secular value movements, and the church responded in part by redefining its base to be the lower classes. This was encouraged by theological trends in the universal church that culminated in the Second Vatican Council (1962–1965) and in the regional church at the CELAM meeting in Medellín (1968). By late 1968 and the consolidation of the military regime in Brazil, the church had assumed sufficient commitment to promote change in favor of the lower classes; subsequent repression orchestrated by the military against dissidents did not discourage but rather solidified the commitment among dominant sectors of the institutional church. Later, such moves toward an institutional commitment to the poor and oppressed were reinforced by the response of the lower classes themselves to the organizational adoption of a preferential option.

Implementation of an Option for the Poor Within the Church

On the issue of the quality and extent of the commitment to social justice undertaken by the institutional church since the 1950s, most students of the Brazilian church are in agreement. In contrast to its historical (and largely unconscious) involvement in support of the *status quo*, church involvement during the 1970s and 1980s is seen, in essence, as having been conscious and intentional, with the church seeking to promote change in specific ways and in accordance with the clearly defined preferential-option program. There is also consensus about the ways in which the strategy came to be implemented at various levels within the church.

The most important vehicle for the direct stimulation of the church's program, most observers agree, has been the CNBB (Conferência Nacional dos Bispos do Brasil). Formed in 1952 by progressives within the upper hierarchy of the church, this body has spoken regularly and forcefully for nearly two decades on many important and polemic sociopolitical issues. The CNBB has also maintained extensive contacts with other hierarchies and foreign sources of funding that have allowed it to fill a broad sphere of activities within the social justice area. In addition, it has provided the umbrella organization for a number of programs—operating within specific societal milieus—that hold obvious political implications, such as the Indian Missionary Council (CIMI), the Pastoral Workers' Commission (CPO), and the Pastoral Land Commission (CPT).[6]

The CNBB is also seen as instrumental for its role in promoting the basic Christian communities, or CEBs.[7] These small cell-like organizations, of which there are reported to be 60,000–100,000 in operation, may well be the most widely recognized innovation in the Brazilian church and have received considerable popular and scholarly attention. Even if the CEBs have not, as some have suggested, turned out to be the "new way of being Church" and have definitely not inverted authority within the institution, they are important as a means of relating to society, particularly for the lower classes. Closely linked to the institution, they have constituted a network whereby the institution can promote a variety of sociopolitical issues such as agrarian reform and popular participation in politics. They have also led to the formation of other movements such as cooperatives, unions, and similar associations for promoting the interests of their lower-class membership.

The degree of success the CNBB has had in converting the entire church to the preferential-option approach has, of course, been questioned. It is well known that the actual implementation of most programs, including the CEBs, has varied from diocese to diocese. Some dioceses are known as progressive—São Paulo, Fortaleza, and Vítoria, for example—others as conservative—Rio de Janeiro, Porto Alegre, and Aracaju. These designations normally refer to the orientation of the local bishop. When the bishop is changed for one with a different orientation, it is not long before the overall orientation of the diocese changes, as is the case of Recife on the one hand, and Manaus on the other.

Generally, though, most authors would agree that support for the preferential-option strategy has been remarkably strong from the CNBB right down through the entire institution. Within the CNBB itself, a majority of the almost 400 members of the hierarchy have supported the church's role in promoting change. Since 1970, moreover, the CNBB has been led by progressive and active bishops. This holds with regard not only to the presidency (including a president, vice-president, and general secretary) but also the majority of commissions and other organizations within and affiliated to the CNBB. Outside of the hierarchy, probably a majority of the 13,000 clergy also have supported this role, as have a lesser percentage of the 40,000 nuns—although numerical strength likely has varied a great deal among Brazil's nearly 225 dioceses. Brazil is exceptional, as well, in having available a well-prepared and committed laity. Emerging from sectors of the Catholic Action organization in the 1950s and early 1960s, a relatively large number of lay people have continued to be involved with church organizations and programs with important sociopolitical content. Their involvement within the institutional church has tended to be somewhat ad hoc, but they have certainly kept pressure on clergy and bishops to ensure a continuing commitment to the poor.

Recent Changes in Society, Religion, and Politics in Brazil

The Brazilian church's preferential-option program, thus shaped, has provided direction to church activation for the better part of two decades. Nevertheless, the religious and sociopolitical context that provided fertile soil for its sustenance and growth is now unquestionably changing. Such changes are both national and international in scope, and religious and secular in nature.

At the national level and within the secular realm, the changing political agenda in Brazil has without question imposed certain constraints on space for the continued implementation of the church's program. First of all, with the primary source of societal evil-doing (i.e., the military) in retreat, church leaders have been left without a solitary target to focus upon. Second, the new civilian regime has been securely bent on a liberalizing path, removing restrictions on pornography, divorce, birth control, and other matters of historical concern to the church. Government initiatives in these and other areas have thus effectively forced church leaders to attend to matters they had not been forced to deal with for at least twenty years. The military may have been the physical embodiment of evil in the sphere of economy and politics, but its leaders at least claimed to be moral purists. And third, with the political market open, there are increasing numbers of political parties, popular associations, and labor union organizations now flourishing in Brazil. In effect, these groups have not only siphoned off leading church activists, but have also essentially reduced the need for the church to remain actively involved with the cause of social change.

On the national religious front, an opening up of a different kind has also been occurring. Indeed, the religious monopoly of the Catholic church has been seriously threatened in recent years—and at an accelerated pace—by a number of newcomers to the Brazilian religious marketplace. Of particular significance in this regard has been the advance of Protestantism. Although US-style evangelical preachers have traditionally drawn large numbers to regional soccer fields (as many as 150,000 in fact), the percentage of the population claiming Protestant affiliation has historically been rather low. In 1950, Protestants accounted for less than

2 percent of the population, and most of these were concentrated in German-speaking (Lutheran) areas of the south. By 1980, however, the figure had risen to nearly 7 percent, and 1991 estimates are that as many as 10 percent of Brazilians may now call themselves Protestant.[8]

To a considerable extent, the monopoly of the Catholic church in Brazil remains secure, insofar as well over 80 percent of the population still claims Catholicism. Nevertheless, with a growth rate nearly double that of Catholicism (currently at about 2.5 percent per year), the various Protestant denominations serve as a stark reminder to church leaders that Catholicism's numerical supremacy is threatened.

Within the institutional church, a number of developments have contributed as well to a more restricted platform for further sociopolitical activation. To begin with, there has emerged a crisis of leadership within the institutional elite. Although clearly an advocate of the option for the poor, current president Luciano Mendes de Almeida of the CNBB is a true moderate who disdains confrontation. His leadership style is markedly more subdued than that of his predecessors during the middle to later years of military rule.

It has also recently become apparent that the church has been operating with far less popular support for its initiatives than many institutional leaders had supposed. The Catholic church in Brazil remains one of the country's most trusted institutions, but research based on national surveys of public opinion undertaken during the height of the church's engagement with the option for the poor in the early 1980s has revealed that only between one-third and one-half of practicing Catholics in Brazil supported specific individual church initiatives in the political sphere at any one time, with popular support for all church initiatives combined far lower still. This was true, moreover, for all social classes and age groups.[9]

Making matters worse, the Brazilian print media—and São Paulo's influential *O Estado de São Paulo* in particular—have subjected the church lately to considerable criticism for certain of its activities in the social justice sphere. Most of the accusations stemmed from actions reportedly undertaken by the church's more vociferous agencies and commissions. In 1987, one of these, the Indian Missionary Council (CIMI), publicly suggested that Brazil, and in particular the Amazon region, be subjected to more intense international scrutiny in order to protect the local Indians and their forest reserves. In the press, this was generally interpreted as a call to "internationalization" and thus served to fuel intense criticism from a historically nationalistic Brazilian government and public. The fact that the suggestion came from a commission as part of one of the world's largest international religious conglomerates only added insult to injury. In a similar manner, the Pastoral Land Commission (CPT) was accused of using money donated by European churches to purchase arms for land-hungry peasants engaged in skirmishes with large landholders. Though the church vehemently denied the charges, the reputation of the CPT remained effectively stained.[10]

The church has also come under direct criticism from the Brazilian government for charges it had leveled concerning the pervasiveness of high-level corruption. Condemnation in 1988 of financial illegalities orchestrated by top government officials, for example, made by CNBB president Luciano Mendes de Almeida, was in fact met with howls of derision in Brasília. Seizing the moment, President José Sarney, in a much publicized response, sarcastically reminded Dom Luciano of the Vatican's own troubles with Roberto Calvi and the Banco Abrosiano.[11]

Although such domestic religious and secular changes have certainly given the church pause to consider its present political strategy, perhaps the most potent force weighing on the institution originates from a source outside the country—the Vatican. As is well known, the Vatican has generally moved to adopt a more conservative position with respect to the political defense of the poor and oppressed within national churches.[12] In the papacy of John Paul II, the Vatican has certainly supported political change in certain circumstances, including the Marxist regime of Poland and the authoritarian regimes of Haiti, Paraguay, and the Philippines. The support is less clear in Chile, but there it may not have been so necessary. However, the Vatican clearly opposes political involvement, broadly understood, in democracies and where transitions are under way. Brazil fits into the latter category, along with Portugal and Spain. In the Brazilian case, the pope has made this very clear in his speeches in Brazil in 1980 and in discussions with the Brazilian bishops. For example, in a February 1990 speech to bishops from Brazil's southern states, the pope warned that it is necessary for the church "to make a clear distinction between the action that the faithful do, individually or in groups, guided by their Christian conscience, and the actions they undertake in communion with their pastors, in the name of the Church." He continued: "The specific mission that Christ confided to his Church, is certainly not of a political, economic, or social order."[13] The Vatican has also actively discouraged the theology of liberation, which provides much of the justification for political involvement at the grassroots level. Cardinal Ratzinger, prefect for the Congregation for the Doctrine of the Faith, has attacked the credibility of well-known liberationists, such as Leonardo Boff, while at the same time minimizing the legitimacy and jurisdiction of episcopal conferences that sympathize with this theological tendency, such as the CNBB.[14]

Perhaps even more signficantly, the Vatican has moved to replace or to marginalize predominant progressives within the Brazilian hierarchy. Virtually all new appointments for archbishops and most for bishops are conservatives. The change is clearest in Recife, where the outspoken Dom Helder Cãmara was replaced by Dom José Sobrinho. In Salvador, a moderate archbishop was replaced by the somewhat more conservative Dom Lucas Moreira Neves. And in the elevation to the cardinalate in mid-1988, the two Brazilians were Moreira Neves and the conservative archbishop of Brasília, Dom José Freire Falcão. These two archbishops were in fact the only two Brazilians raised to the cardinalate during the first ten years of John Paul II's papacy.

In São Paulo, the most important center of the progressive church since the early 1970s, other changes have been evident. In an attempt to undermine the power of well-known activist Cardinal Archbishop Paulo Evaristo Arns, the archdiocese was split in 1989 into five dioceses. Even though the bishops for the four new units are not considered to be conservatives, the division indicates a setback for the cardinal and will probably slow the momentum in sociopolitical programs.[15] Momentum was also lost because of the transfer from São Paulo of the president of the CNBB, Dom Luciano Mendes de Almeida, to the isolated rural archdiocese of Mariana.

Alterations in Church Strategy

Given the changes in Rome and the very fluid (and often confused) domestic political and religious context, the church in Brazil consequently finds itself in a new situation. Indeed, it is clear that for a growing number of the hierarchy, both the desirability and the necessity of upholding the preferential-option strategy may be questioned. To an increasing extent, far more appealing—and indeed safer—to growing numbers within the church leadership, is a return to more devotional concerns and more traditional forms of maintaining influence in Brazilian society.

This is not of course to say that the option for the poor is dead. Recent events demonstrate that in some respects at least, the approach has continued to instruct church thinking and action in some fundamental respects.

Without question, the five years of the civilian-led Sarney administration—the first civilian regime since the transfer of power from the military in 1985—gave the church much to react against, insofar as the government has been characterized by economic crisis, social instability, corruption, politicization of every imaginable issue, and the continuing fragility of political institutions, including parties.

A good synthesis of the Church's sociopolitical involvement during the Sarney administration was its role in the elaboration of the new constitution.[16] As early as 1977, the CNBB advocated a new institutional framework in its *Exigências Cristãs de uma Nova Ordem Política*, and throughout the late 1970s and early 1980s, remained at the forefront in demanding not only the return of civilian rule but a new constitution for the country as well. Many in the church calculated that mobilization in favor of a new basic charter would result in the rupture with Brazil's history of mass apathy and populist politics. As part of this thrust, elements within the church were, for example, key players in the Plenário Pro-Participação Popular na Constituinte, the umbrella organization seeking to guarantee lower-class interests. Broad sectors of the church also remained active in the general process associated with framing the new constitution, from as early as mid-1985 through the promulgation in October 1988. Overall, such lobbying efforts were successful, and many of the Church's goals—with the notable exception of agrarian reform—were achieved in the constitution.

The high level of church involvement in the elaboration of the constitution led right into the campaign for the presidential elections in late 1989. In August 1989, for example, the CNBB issued a document entitled *Participar com Esperança*, which requested the Congress to pass laws implementing the constitution, encouraged popular participation in the elections, and defined the criteria for evaluating a candidate for the president.[17] During the actual campaign, the church was also involved, although it did not officially support a candidate. In the first round of voting and more obviously in the second, the CEBs, many clergy, and a number of bishops demonstrated support for Luis Inácio da Silva (Lula).[18] Lula and the Workers' Party (PT) had a long relationship with the archdiocese of São Paulo and the CEB movement. In addition, Lula had a program in accord with the CNBB's criteria; he was in line with the constitution of 1988, and he belonged to a real political party. Thus, Lula was a much closer approximation in the political sphere to the church's preferential-option program, than was conservative rival Fernando Collor de Mello.

Such recent church involvement in Brazilian politics is noteworthy. Yet in some ways, it obscures another reality because the signs of a new, more conservative agenda within the church have slowly been appearing for at least a half dozen years.

To begin with, there have occurred subtle changes in the way the church comports itself politically. As part of its commitment to the poor and its people-centered strategy for effecting change, the church largely eschewed high-level interaction with bureaucratic and political elites in favor of a strategy of popular mobilization. More recently, however, there appears to be a return on the part of the church leadership to the elite-level political maneuvering characteristic of the period before the poor-oriented strategy.[19]

Since José Sarney's assumption of the presidency in 1985, the church has in fact been a constant fixture in the halls of power. Dom Luciano Mendes, for example, as secretary-general of the CNBB, had been a frequent visitor to the presidential palace and at one time was thought to be one of Sarney's closest advisers. Moreover, in his capacity as president of the bishops' council, he has certainly been less than shy about calling on influential power brokers to resolve church problems. In late August 1987, he met with several congressmen to demand a government inquiry into "fraudulent" press criticism of the CNBB's Indian Missionary Council (CIMI). Again, in 1989, he requested that the president personally intervene on behalf of agricultural workers engaged in disputes with landowners in Rio Grande do Sul and Bahia states.

There has also been strong evidence of increased church involvement in electoral politics and political decisionmaking—involvement highly reminiscent of church action during the 1930s, when church leaders attempted to influence public policymaking through such means as voting leagues and high-level influence peddling. Before the 1986 general elections, some of the bishops, including outspoken progressives such as São Paulo's Cardinal Arns and Bauru's Cândido Padim, released lists of candidates deemed worthy of church support. Such activity was not generally undertaken during elections some four years earlier, when church leaders took great pains to educate voters politically without appearing to favor any one particular party. As mentioned earlier, during the debate surrounding the formulation of the country's new constitution, the church played an active and direct lobbying role; it did so once again during the 1989 presidential elections, when many of the bishops and clergy also publicly announced their electoral preferences.

In addition to reviving old forms of political lobbying, church leaders have increasingly demonstrated a growing conservatism and return to dogmatism that in some cases has ironically been prejudicial to the needs of the socially disadvantaged the preferential option traditionally defended. A few of the more salient examples of this latter tendency may be presented chronologically.[20]

In 1986, to begin with, Cardinal Arns of São Paulo reportedly requested and was granted a government-imposed ban of Jean Luc Godard's controversial film on the life of Mary, *Je Vous Salue, Marie.* At one point, Arns even requested that the São Paulo state governor call in the military police (a body he had fought tooth and nail with during the years of the military regime) to prevent a screening of the film at the Pontifícia Universidade Católica—of which he is chancellor.

In 1987, the bishops of Brazil's impoverished northeast region undertook to purge the area's long-standing basic education movement (based in large measure on radical pedagogy developed by educator Paulo Freire) of progressives linked to the Communist Party and various working-class movements. That same year, soon after assuming the presidency of the CNBB, Luciano Mendes de Almeida publicly scolded liberation theologian Leonardo Boff for suggesting that the communist states of Eastern Europe and the Soviet Union were examples of the values of the kingdom of Heaven in practice. Again in 1987, Bishop Serafim Araújo criticized the state government of Minas Gerais for promoting the use of condoms to prevent AIDS, while a colleague, Bishop Benedito Vieira (formerly vice-president of the CNBB) cautioned federal politicians against establishing a national family-planning program. In the year following, documents released by the CNBB, including *Diretrizes Gerais da Ação Pastoral da Igreja no Brasil* and *Igreja: Comunhão e Missão na Evangelização dos Povos*, were among the most moderate in tone—in terms of criticism of the status quo—in nearly twenty years.

In 1989, Archbishop of Recife José Cardoso Sobrinho (who replaced Dom Helder Câmara), following a repressive strategy employed by Cardinal Arns in São Paulo some three years earlier, called upon the local military police to disperse a group of peasants who had arrived unannounced to request an immediate audience with the archbishop. When the Recife chapter of the CNBB's Justice and Peace Commission protested the move, moreover, Cardoso henceforth forbade the agency from speaking officially on behalf of the archdiocese. In other moves, Cardoso purged four coordinators of the local Pastoral Land Commission for their involvement in working-class political movements and forbade priests sympathetic to the theology of liberation from celebrating mass on local television.

Again in 1989, some church leaders openly advocated an enhanced role for the conservative Catholic charismatic movement as a way to combat the growth of Protestant evangelical groups. By early 1991, the concerns about the Protestant threat were so generalized that the CNBB went so far as to convene the first National Seminar on Religious Pluralism in Brazil in Caieiras, São Paulo, to stimulate discussion about the necessity of creating pastoral methods capable of resisting the Protestant groups' advance.

Also in 1991, the CNBB's Comissão Episcopal de Doutrina began a review of the new Bíblia Pastoral, first released for use by Catholics in Brazil in 1990. In the view of a sufficient number of the bishops, the new bible was tied too closely with the theology of liberation. The CNBB also vowed that year to work diligently to fight government plans to reopen the country's gambling casinos; renewed gambling, according to secretary-general Dom Celso Queiroz, would lead to "moral decomposition" on a national scale.

Perhaps the most significant development of all over the years, however, has been the way in which concrete support for the all-important basic Christian community phenomenon has suffered.[21] References to the CEBs in official church documents, for example, have been relatively rare since 1988. Occasionally, reference is made to *comunidades eclesiais*, but this is used in the generic sense and refers not only to CEBs but also to dioceses, parishes, or Catholic associations. There also appears to have been a significant alteration in the way the church conceives of the role of CEBs. Whereas once seen as the "new way to be Church" or the seeds of the new society, the mission of the CEBs is increasingly tied to leadership building. In essence, the CEBs and other similar types of lay groups or associations are seen no longer as agents acting autonomously in the name of the church. Rather, they serve to provide militants on an individual basis a way to operate within secular bodies such as labor unions and popular movements. In any case, by all accounts, the CEBs appear increasingly to be in a period of stagnation. After twenty years, these groups still vary tremendously in size, composition, and role. Certainly, they have received a good deal of attention, not a little of which is more an indication of commitment and hope than a description of reality. Much was expected of the CEBs, and indeed their importance in the late 1970s and early 1980s in providing alternate forms of organization and mobilization cannot be denied. Nevertheless, they have not matched expectations, despite inflated figures on their numbers. An independent lay leadership has not emerged from the CEBs, and they still rely very much on clergy and bishops. They have not been unified on sociopolitical matters, and their general impact is weak. It seems likely that the CEBs will turn out to be one more organization or movement in the long line of church-generated entities aimed at relating to sectors of society at different periods.[22]

Overall, then, whether in terms of support for the CEBs or changes in statements and undertakings of the upper hierarchy directly, the ability and the willingness of the church to intervene in Brazilian society and politics appear to be increasingly constrained. Without question, through relationships at the elite level, specific target groups and programs, and mobilization of the lower classes through the CEBs, the church up until recently has had a highly publicized impact. Increasingly, however, predominant sectors within the church appear engaged in an attempt to restore its traditional religious role in the face of some very salient social, political, and religious pressures.

Future Trends in the Church's Political Role

In January 1990, Fernando Collor de Mello assumed the presidency of Brazil. A member of the Brazilian elite, Collor won the election on a populist platform, vowing to take Brazil into the twenty-first century by wrestling inflation to the ground and modernizing the economy. In practice, he has attempted to do this through a combination of innovative policy measures, including stringent monetary controls and a progressive opening up of Brazil's highly protected domestic economy to foreign competition.

Such initiatives have certainly brought the inflation rate down, and more and more foreign goods are available for consumption in Brazil, but in the short run these measures have also had a seriously dampening effect on the national economy. Production of goods and services has fallen dramatically, and this in turn has resulted in ever-rising levels of unemployment.

During the first days of the Collor administration, the Brazilian church indicated, through CNBB secretary-general Dom Celso Queiroz, that it would cooperate with the president for the good of Brazil, as it had with previous presidents. And to a considerable extent it has. Indeed, a year and a half into Collor's term, CNBB president Dom Luciano Mendes de Almeida offered his tacit support to the Brazilian president's latest proposed agenda for economic restructuring, known as the Projeto de Reconstrução Nacional (or simply Projetão), in the interest of national harmony and development.

Nevertheless, the Collor government has given large sectors within the church much to complain about, especially those members of the hierarchy most closely tied to the preferential-option strategy. The CNBB and affiliated organizations (the CPT and CIMI, for example), several dioceses (such as São Paulo and Vitória), and the popular movement based in the CEBs have to this point continued to use the option, along with the 1988 constitution, to judge the performance of the government. There has been at least some criticism of Collor's lack of support for agrarian reform and of his perceived tendency to work around the constitution. In early May 1990, for example, eight organizations linked to the CNBB, including the Workers Pastoral Commission (CPO), the National Commission of the Laity (CNO), and the Pastoral Land Commission (CPT), issued a document critical of the Collor administration. They criticized his style, and in their view, the technocratic and authoritarian approach to administration compromised even promising economic measures.

Even in the face of continued poor economic and political performance, there is little question, though, that the cracks and fissures in the Church's option for the poor will likely widen. Throughout the 1970s and early 1980s, as was shown, the Brazilian church was very active in the social justice field, primarily because of the leadership of progressives in key dioceses and the CNBB. Because of the changes that have occurred in the domestic and international context of church operation, however, and the evidence of problems with the preferential-option already apparent (as described in the previous section), it is logical to anticipate still less commitment and action in the future.

To begin with, given the Vatican's relentless moves to pacify the Brazilian church through the appointment of more moderate bishops, the press attacks on the institution, and the ever-present Protestant threat, consensus within the ranks of the upper hierarchy on social justice issues will be difficult, if not impossible, to reach. Moreover, the ongoing confusion and fragmentation inherent within Brazil's presently open political system will likely ensure that any political position the church does assume will alienate at least some large sectors of the population. The logical response, then, will be to hesitate or equivocate in assuming positions—or at the very least to issue only generic statements.

Within the CNBB, a lack of consensus is already much in evidence. During the twenty-eighth general assembly of the CNBB at Itaici, São Paulo, in May 1990, divisions were in evidence regarding the chances for success of the Collor government. In addition, the CNBB did not adopt an official position on the government's tough economic program, despite its apparent social costs (especially unemployment). As for the potential for alienation, this in fact has also already been realized in the attacks in early 1989 of Leonel Brizola, candidate of the Democratic Labor Party (PDT), on the church and its putative support for the PT. Finally, the tendency of the church to define its position more generically has been made clear in the document prepared by the CNBB at its March 1989 assembly, entitled *Exigências Eticas de uma Nova Ordem Institucional*, in which specific suggestions for changes in political direction are all but absent.

The Church may be becoming more fractious and cautious with respect to overt political action, but it is showing increasing signs of unity where the promotion of the devotional is concerned. Perhaps more than any other single factor, the principal catalyst for the growing consensus is the perceived Protestant threat.

Some within the church, in fact, now see nominal affiliation with Catholicism falling to as low as 75 percent of the population during the 1990s. This has so alarmed the bishops that during their April 1991 meeting in Itaici, São Paulo, there emerged strong support for a realignment of the church's this-worldly role with the more conservative directives on church action outlined by Pope John Paul II. In the months ahead, this will unquestionably contribute to still less emphasis on the direct forms of social action that the preferential option for the poor mandates and more on the spiritual role of the church.[23]

Conclusion

In the early 1950s, the Brazilian church became extremely active and innovative within certain spheres of Brazilian society—especially politics. Within a context of competing value movements, progressive tendencies in international Catholicism, and political repression orchestrated by the ruling military, the church effectively redefined its base in part to be the lower classes and eventually adopted the preferential option for the poor as its principal operating strategy.

The context in which such activism grew, however, has changed in recent years. Not only has the Vatican become less supportive of church activities in the sociopolitical sphere, but Brazil has been engaged in a long and arduous transition from authoritarian state structure to civilian democracy. Moreover, the threat of competing value movements has proved to be a long-term problem the church has been increasingly unable to ignore. Such factors, as we have argued, have been conducive to a diminution of church activation in the sphere of politics.

Because the process involved in developing and implementing the preferential option was long and complicated, it must be stated that there is no reason to anticipate a rapid and obvious retreat from that commitment. Indeed, in the days ahead, large sectors of the church will likely continue to promote and implement the preferential option. Nevertheless, these will operate in ever-greater isolation, and certainly implementation of the strategy will not proceed with the intensity of the late 1970s and early 1980s.

Whether there will be a return sometime in the future to the preferential option as the church's primary operative strategy is open to considerable doubt. Clearly, despite the severe political and economic stress, Brazil is modernizing, and traditional religion per se may become less relevant, much as it has in the industrialized countries. As it does, the available sacral and religious space for the church to continue to exercise influence of any kind will likely be restricted still further.

Notes

1. On this point, see Donald Smith, "The Limits of Religious Resurgence," in Emile Sahliyeh, ed., *Religious Resurgence and Politics in the Contemporary World* (Albany: State University of New York Press, 1990), p. 33.

2. See especially Roberto Romano, *Igreja contra estado* (São Paulo: Kairos, 1979).

3. The more theoretical statements on this position are given in Luiz Alberto G. de Souza, "Igreja e sociedade: Elementos para um marco teórico," *Síntese* 13 (April–June 1978), pp. 1–25; and Luiz Gonzaga de Souza Lima, *Evolução Política dos Católicos e da igreja no Brasil* (Petrópolis: Vozes, 1979).

4. A forceful statement on both of these elements is Leonardo Boff's *Igreja: Carisma e poder* (Petrópolis: Vozes, 1981).

5. See, for example, Paulo Krischke and Scott Mainwaring, eds., *A igreja nas bases em tempo de transição, 1974–1985* (São Paulo: L&PM, 1986); Scott Mainwaring, *The Catholic Church and Politics in Brazil, 1916–1985* (Stanford, Calif.: Stanford University Press, 1986); Vanilda Paiva, ed., *Igreja e questão agrária* (São Paulo: Loyola, 1985); and Heléna Salem, ed., *A igreja dos oprimidos* (São Paulo: Brasil Debates, 1981).

6. On the nature and extent of these programs, see Thomas Bruneau, *The Church in Brazil: The Politics of Religion* (Austin: University of Texas Press, 1982);

and Mainwaring, *The Catholic Church and Politics.*

7. On the CEBs, see Marcello de Azevedo, *Basic Ecclesial Communities in Brazil: The Challenge of a New Way of Being Church,* trans. John Drury (Washington: Georgetown University Press, 1987); and especially W. E. Hewitt, *Base Christian Communities and Social Change in Brazil* (Lincoln: University of Nebraska Press, 1991).

8. On the extent of Protestant evangelical growth in Brazil, see David Barrett, ed., *World Christian Encyclopedia* (Oxford: Oxford University Press, 1982), p. 186; and Instituto Brasileiro de Geografia e Estatística, *Anuário estatístico do Brasil* (Rio de Janeiro: Fundação IBGE, 1982), p. 74.

9. Thomas C. Bruneau and W. E. Hewitt, "Patterns of Church Influence in Brazil's Political Transition," *Comparative Politics,* October 1989, pp. 39–61.

10. For reports of the controversy surrounding these agencies, see, for example, *O Globo,* September 5, 1987, p. 8; and *Jornal do Brasil,* February 22, 1989, p. 7.

11. See *O Globo,* February 5, 1988, p. 5.

12. This factor is also discussed by Ralph Della Cava, "The 'People's Church,' the Vatican, and Abertura," in Alfred Stepan, ed., *Democratizing Brazil* (New York: Oxford University Press, 1989), pp. 143–167.

13. Taken from *Catholic New Times* (Toronto), March 4, 1991, p. 2.

14. The pope's position is clearly stated in his letter to the Brazilian bishops of April 1986. He reiterated support for the instruction of August 1984 on the theology of liberation and emphasized the church as mystery. On Ratzinger, see *The Ratzinger Report: An Exclusive Interview on the State of the Church* (San Francisco: Ignatius Press, 1985).

15. This issue was covered extensively in the Brazilian media. See, for example, *Folha de São Paulo,* March 15, 1989; and *Veja,* March 22, 1989.

16. Bruneau has discussed the general process of elaborating the constitution in "Constitutions and Democratic Consolidation: Brazil in Comparative Perspective," *NPS Technical Report* (NPS-56-89-009), March 1989, pp. 1–30. For a discussion of the CNBB's role, see José Ernanne Pinheiro, "A Ação da CNBB na constituinte," *Revista da Cultura Vozes* 82, July–December 1988.

17. Among the eight criteria were the following: Does the candidate favor agrarian reform; promote the just distribution of urban land; assist in the struggle of workers for social justice and workers' rights; and intend to review carefully the country's foreign debt? See *Folha de São Paulo,* August 26, 1989.

18. See *Veja,* November 15, 1989, and December 6, 1989, for examples of church involvment in the campaign.

19. For a more thorough account of the developments cited in the rest of this section, see W. E. Hewitt, "Origins and Prospects of the Option for the Poor in Brazilian Catholicism," *Journal for the Scientific Study of Religion* 28 (1989), pp. 120–135.

20. Ibid.

21. See W. E. Hewitt, "Religion and the Consolidation of Democracy in Brazil," *Sociological Analysis* 59 (Summer 1990), pp. 139–152.

22. On these points, see Hewitt, *Base Christian Communities and Social Change.*

23. Such tendencies have now been widely reported in Brazil's print media. See, for example, *O Globo,* April 10, 1991, p. 9; and April 17, 1991, p. 5.

CHAPTER 4

Popular Movements and the Limits of Political Mobilization at the Grassroots in Brazil

CAROL ANN DROGUS

In the Brazilian autumn of 1981, expectations surrounding the return to electoral politics were building. The Party Reform Law of 1979 had legalized a range of political parties, and Brazilians eagerly anticipated direct elections in November 1982. In this heightened political atmosphere, the Catholic *comunidades eclesiais de base* (CEBs) held their fourth National Encounter at Itaici, São Paulo.[1] Journalists speculated about the role Catholics organized in the CEBs would play in the new electoral system. Most predicted a party endorsement—probably of the leftist Partido dos Trabalhadores (PT)—from Itaici.[2]

The creation of a unified leftist voting bloc was widely seen as a natural outcome of the CEBs' activities. Because of their association with liberation theology and religious and political *conscientização* (conscientization), CEBs were perceived "as seedbeds of a new, democratic culture and social order, providing norms that legitimate equality and the promotion of social justice."[3] Their democratic practices posed a potential challenge to traditional Brazilian electoral populism.[4] Moreover, thousands of working-class CEB members took to the streets of São Paulo and other cities in movements that challenged the state and speeded the democratic opening, providing plausible evidence of emerging new political attitudes.

In the end, however, no political endorsement ensued. Subsequent events showed the electoral weight of the CEBs and the progressive church more generally to be slight. They have had limited success in cultivating class-based party identification.[5] Overall the record is clear: Despite success in mobilizing popular political movements, the CEBs will not influence national politics through the ballot box.

Although their political limitations are now obvious, the groups have achieved important, sometimes overlooked, successes as well. They have roused many individuals on the margins of Brazilian political life to activism, including protest on behalf of the needs of their families and communities. Specifically, they have brought many women—poor, rural-born, and uneducated—into the political arena. It is true that partisan affiliation remains weak and the numbers reached through the communities are, in any case, too few to translate into electoral clout. The importance of the personal transformation experienced by CEB members in general, and women in particular, however, is profound.[6]

Understanding the strengths and weaknesses of the CEBs' political accomplishments requires analysis at two levels. First, we must examine the constraints that limit the political influence of the progressive wing of the church as a whole.[7] Of particular interest here is the progressives' limited ability to reach a wide public.

Second, a full explanation requires that we also understand patterns of response to *conscientização* by CEB members. Low interest in partisan politics has been documented, but too often it is merely described or attributed to a "failure" of conscientization. Members' preferences for some modes of political activism rather than others must be explained. This is best done by working outward from the religious ideas of the participants to their political behavior.[8] Thus, after I briefly discuss some limits on the church's larger role, I focus in this chapter on individual responses, attitudes, and behavior. In particular, I discuss the often-neglected majority of urban CEB members: women.[9] The responses of this group are important not only to the success of the CEBs' political project but also to the continued vitality of the communities and the church itself.

Limits on the Progressive Church's Political Role: The Institutional and Social Level

That the progressive church's political potential was exaggerated in the waning years of the military government is now clear. Many factors, however, contributed to overestimating the numerical strength and political cohesiveness of the CEBs. Several of these are illustrated by the archdiocese of São Paulo, where my research was carried out and which, under the leadership of Dom Paulo Evaristo Cardinal Arns from the mid-1970s to the late 1980s, was considered one of the most progressive in Latin America. In fact, São Paulo's importance and Cardinal Arns's prominence probably contributed to misperceptions of the strength of the progressive movement within the Brazilian church as a whole.[10]

The archdiocese strongly encouraged the formation of CEBs, a pastoral priority from 1976 to 1980.[11] One source of the very high political expectations was the CEBs' activism and visibility. São Paulo's CEBs generated numerous social movements. As the *abertura* (opening) permitted more activism, poor people—especially from the CEBs—took to the streets to voice a growing variety of demands. Although the fact was little noted at the time, women, and especially those from the CEBs' *clubes de maes* (mothers' clubs), spearheaded these movements.[12] The Church provided crucial material and logistical support for many movements, unifying the atomistic peripheral neighborhoods and motivating participation in the first place. In São Paulo, high participation rates in popular movements were correlated with the fact that invitations to join were issued by the local church.[13]

The São Paulo church's visible role in the two-party elections before 1982 also enhanced the image of CEB political strength. Cardinal Arns's public moral stand for social justice and the political *abertura* helped shape the political debate and lent legitimacy to the opposition. The church's endorsement may have helped candidates more than political endorsement as *autênticos*, or historical members of the opposition. For example, Dom Paulo's endorsement and CEB votes were probably crucial to Fernando Henrique Cardoso's victory in 1978, especially in working-class areas with many CEBs, including the one in which this research was conducted.[14] In the two-party context, then, church mobilization affected opposition voting.

The accomplishments were real, but expectations for the progressive church as an electoral force faltered for several reasons. Most obvious were the strictures that multiparty democracy and the growing concern of the Vatican placed on the hierarchy (see Chapter 3). In contrast to their willingness to back a united opposition to the authoritarian regime, the bishops were reluctant to risk a party endorsement that would alienate some Catholics, and the Vatican discouraged this as well.[15]

The CEBs themselves might have remained more active than the hierarchy after 1982 because as lay groups they could claim a right to make a party option. In fact, as the journalists at Itaici predicted, many individual CEBs directly or indirectly endorsed the PT.[16] But the presence and impact of the progressive church in the urban periphery had been tremendously overestimated. The most fundamental impediment to the church's political role was the fact that its ability to reach significant segments of the population with *conscientização* and a clear liberationist message was always limited for a variety of reasons. The number of core participants in each CEB is small. The groups have not been successful in recruiting nonpracticing Catholics. There is considerable variability in CEB members' participation and in different CEBs' commitment to progressive practices. Finally, disagreements among progressives on political issues are a further obstacle restricting the Church's influence.

We know that São Paulo's 756 CEBs are nearly all located in the urban periphery.[17] There are no membership records, however, that may have contributed to the equation of the popular church with popular religiosity. Nothing could be farther from the truth.[18] Brazilians are a religious people, but most practice a folk Catholicism that is essentially private and unconnected to the institutional church. Moreover, the CEBs were formed by already practicing Catholics, not from among folk Catholics as many thought.[19] The CEBs I studied, for example, were formed largely by women with lifelong ties to the church who had been recruited via the CEBs' parent parish.[20]

In any case, numbers in the CEBs were never large. Each community has about fifteen core activists who run both religious and political affairs. A similar number regularly assist when called upon. As many as one hundred people may attend mass if a priest is officiating. Even if we estimate one hundred members per CEB, however, the CEBs' weight in São Paulo's electorate would be limited.[21]

But such an estimate itself overlooks the heterogeneity of experience in the CEBs. Occasional participants, especially, are unlikely to engage in regular Bible study or political conscientization groups. Only about 65 percent of working-class CEB members participate in religious reflection, which might expose them to the ideas of the progressive church. A mere 35 percent engage in specifically political consciousness-raising.[22]

Moreover, the CEBs themselves are quite diverse.[23] The character of a CEB depends greatly upon its clerical and lay leadership. Although São Paulo's clergy overwhelmingly agree that part of their mission is the formation of Catholic political consciousness, they are not all equally accepting of liberation theology or certain political ideas.[24] Thus, although all CEBs fulfill basic religious functions, they vary in the degree and form of their political involvement. The hegemony of progressives within the local and national church concealed a range of political and religious opinion among clergy implementing the "option for the poor."[25]

Overall, then, the progressive church's presence among the poor is weaker than the ferment of CEB-backed popular movements suggested. This alone restricts their potential political weight, but another institutional factor also necessarily limited the transformation of political movement activism into electoral organization. The progressive bloc itself is divided over the issue of the relationship between the CEBs and political parties. Many priests are skeptical of political parties and fear that they will manipulate the CEBs.[26] A few take an anarchist position; most believe that popular social movements are more valuable than political parties.[27]

Three basic models of CEB-party relations exist: neo-Christendom, in which CEBs are the basis of a party of the church; complementarity, in which CEBs eschew political functions in favor of a purely religious role; and dialectic, in which the CEBs discuss the political dimensions of faith but the party develops the concrete program that expresses religious and ethical beliefs.[28] The debate over the CEB-party proper relationship has raged since the late 1970s. At the 1989 National Encounter of CEBs, opinion ranged from the view that the CEBs were no longer playing a political role, to Clodovis Boff's call for a "party-political pastoral" enabling Christians to "create a party that is popular, transforming and democratic."[29] The practice in individual CEBs is thus bound to vary widely. Many—including those in my research area—identified with the PT and come closer to the third model, a tendency Bruneau and Hewitt in Chapter 3 suggest continued to the 1989 elections. In others, the desire to avoid partisanism and favor a more ethical approach to politics led groups to limit their involvement in politics. Membership in a CEB thus does not guarantee exposure to partisan political debate.

The party debate suggests an important point: the difficulty of transforming an ethical critique of society into a practical political strategy. It is clearly a fundamental obstacle to the CEBs' exercising a major role in electoral politics. Given the dilemmas theologians and other church leaders experience in connecting the ethical and religious teachings of liberation theology to a practical political strategy, it is not surprising that CEB members find this a perplexing task at best; many choose not to address it at all.

Despite their clear political limitations, however, the CEBs did manage to turn out thousands of working-class men and, especially, women in a variety of social movements. Their political impact was real, although limited, and may have involved important transformations for those individuals who were reached with a message of liberation and *conscientização*. What did this activity mean? How much did it reflect changing religious and political values? To raise these questions is to inquire into individuals' experience within the CEBs.

Responses to Conscientization in the CEBs:
The Individual Level

A profile of the average CEB member in São Paulo is virtually a portrait of political marginality. The vast majority are poor, were born in rural areas, work in low-skill jobs, and have little education.[30] At least two-thirds of all and perhaps as many as 90 percent of the most active members are women.[31] Poor, rural-born, religious, uneducated women—according to most studies of political behavior, this is a recipe for political conservatism, if not apathy and alienation.[32]

Before their involvement in the CEBs, the women in the Itaim Paulista region of São Paulo conformed to that stereotype. They unanimously affirmed that they had never participated in any social movement or organization. Most had no interest in politics and simply voted the way their husbands told them to. Like most poor Brazilian housewives, they were on the margin of politics.

For many the CEB was a revelatory experience, giving them practical skills and opening up a realm of unimagined possibilities for participation in the public arena.[33] As one woman said:

Being in the struggle, with the participation we have, is a beautiful thing. Even if we haven't had a chance to study, like me, myself, I don't know much. A person without schooling doesn't know much, not even how to get around, eh? And that was a very important thing. While we were that way, I, like I said, was a housewife. And look, nowadays we go to every blessed place trying, looking for things.[34]

The CEBs' importance in providing these opportunities for poor women cannot be overemphasized.

Individual women's political participation, however, replicates the pattern of political mobilization at the municipal level. They confronted bureaucratic hostility, police, and fire hoses in a variety of social movements, but their activism was largely confined to those movements. The ability of conscientization to raise specifically class-based consciousness appears to have been slight. They were more likely than their non-CEB female neighbors to support the PT, but that support was soft. Even women with a more politicized commitment restrict party activism to voting and minor campaign activities.

Why do women who have taken the difficult, dangerous step of confronting the state in authoritarian Brazil often fail to move into the easy activities of voting and campaigning for a party that is seen as the natural ally of their social movements? To answer this question is to inquire into the women's motivations and their own perceptions of their activism. Two themes emerge as important. First, we must understand the way in which the women's religious practices and beliefs sustain and shape their political involvement. They have not been passive recipients of the ideas of the progressive church. Understanding their interaction with these ideas—what they accept, reject, and reinterpret—will help us to understand the form and future of their political activism.[35] Second, we must ask to what extent and in what ways the gender identity of the overwhelmingly female CEB members plays a role in their political activism. For women in the CEBs, this question is linked to their religious self-image as well, through their understanding of the traditional Catholic model of womanhood described by *marianismo*, the cult of Mary, the mother of Jesus.

Religious Orientation and Conscientization

The parish of Santo Antônio provides favorable conditions for *conscientização* along classic liberationist lines. At least until late 1986, the progressive line was dominant in the parish.[36] The pastoral agents laid the groundwork for the CEBs by inviting catechists, about fifty women, to weekly Bible groups. These moved from liberationist-inspired reflection on the Bible to a discussion of the area's concrete problems.

The catechists in Santo Antônio took up the challenge to find a "new way to be Church," in Leonardo Boff's phrase. Six groups of catechists went on to form CEBs, which spread until by 1986 there were nearly thirty.[37] But the results have not been precisely those that a knowledge of liberation theology and the ideas of the progressive church would lead us to predict. Even in a propitious environment like Santo Antônio, the path to *conscientização* is neither easy nor direct.

The new religious practices and liberation theology were jarring for the parishoners in Santo Antônio. Some simply rejected the CEBs, convinced that the new priests were either communists or evangelicals.[38] For those who continued, the transition was difficult. As one woman commented: "We received a big shock. We were going to church just to pray, and now we go to church to participate, and to help. To participate!"[39] Nearly all of the women who became extremely active in the CEBs expressed a lifelong attachment to the church, which probably both motivated and facilitated their assimilation into the CEBs.[40] But even among those who remained active, not all responded to conscientization in the same way.

Three Broad Religious Orientations

There is growing evidence that individual religious experience varies greatly, even within a single denomination.[41] Thus, we might expect to find different patterns of adaptation to the progressive church among base community members. Because CEBs are integral parts of the institutional church in Brazil, not sects, we can anticipate nearly as great a range of personal religious orientations within the CEBs as within the practicing Catholic population as a whole.

In Santo Antônio's CEBs, three general tendencies in religious orientation can be discerned. Using the terminology of Peter Benson and Dorothy Williams, we can describe the women roughly as people-concerned, self-concerned, or integrated religionists.[42] Each orientation is reflected in a different response to the ideas of liberation theology and the challenge of *conscientização*.

People-concerned religionists. People-concerned religionists emphasize the importance of community, connectedness, and responsibility to others. But they extend this sense of connectedness beyond face-to-face relations. Iracema described her participation this way: "[It is] not just for our own children—we are doing this for *all* of our children, for all the poor children of Brazil."[43] People-concerned religionists are unusual in the degree to which religion motivates them to seek fairness, justice, and well-being for all—even people outside their family and immediate community.

More than any other group, people-concerned women also perceive religion as a challenge: It motivates them to act on their faith in the world. These women expressed the challenge dimension of their faith in describing their response to the CEBs. Some felt they were signing on for an "apprenticeship."[44] Others described the call to participate as a physical force: Iracema felt "a weight fall on [her] shoulders" when the priest said people needed to participate more. She promptly went out and joined the CEB's women's group.[45]

The value orientation of people-concerned religionists is characterized by an emphasis on social justice. Although we cannot establish the extent to which the interviewees held those values before becoming involved in the CEBs, this group more than the others embraces the theology of liberation. Asked about the meaning of symbols such as the kingdom of God and Christ as liberator, they replied in classic liberationist terms. They were quite clear that God wills the material liberation of the poor and the oppressed. Although often unsure about the exact form it would take, they believed that some kind of socialism would move Brazil closer to God's plan. They thought it would do so because it would end injustice, create equality, and give people their rights, including the right to participate.

Zélia's comments provide a succinct example of this religious type. While her seven sons were growing up, she was waiting for an opportunity to get out and do something in the world. "Captivated," she said, by the idea of the CEBs, she fought and argued with her husband and even went on the sly to participate.

Zélia spontaneously offered an interpretation of Christ's message. Describing conditions against which some workers were striking at the time of the interview, she said:

> I perceive very clearly that when we go and look at Christ, that isn't what he wanted. Christ, he died, he came to fight against all that. And now we have to ask ourselves what we will do. I think we have to fight, too. That's my thinking. That alienated religion that just sits there, that isn't being the church of Jesus Christ.[46]

Later she offered this description of the kingdom of God, the objective toward which the CEBs are struggling: "To really have equality, that would be a type of socialism. . . . We who study the Bible, we see that the kind of society Christ wanted was that kind. [Was] socialist.[47]

Such internalization of the message of liberation theology is what pastoral agents hope to achieve through *conscientização*. In fact, however, it sets the people-concerned religionists apart within the CEB. Other religious types coexist with the people-concerned religionists in the CEBs, but reject their understanding of liberation theology.

Self-concerned or traditional religionists. The second group is distinguished by a strong emphasis on morality. These respondents expressed concern over the breakdown of the family, loose morals among youth, and crime.[48] They are absorbed with their personal relationship with God, with individual salvation. For them, finding God is a personal experience, not something that occurs through relationships with others. But this is not so marked for the women as the ideal type of self-concerned religiosity would have it. For these women, individualism is mitigated by their traditional value-emphasis on the role of women as caregivers. Given this tendency to muted individualism, these women might be described more aptly as "traditional religionists."

This group views religion as a source of comfort in a harsh world, in contrast to the people-concerned religionists' perception of religion as challenge. Margarita says:

> You go to church with a thirst, a thirst for God. . . . Ah, it seems you've forgotten all the problems you left behind! . . . Then, a person who left the house desperate, slapped, pushed, her kids in the brush where she took them so her husband wouldn't kill them, she arrives in church and you begin to speak of God, she begins to see him. Here, I've found a peace, a relief. . . .[49]

Traditional women also place much more value on the institution of the church, with its sacraments and so on, than the others.

Unlike people-concerned religionists, traditional women have accepted few of the new ideas put forward by the progressive church. They have, however, fused their traditional beliefs with the new language of liberation theology. As a result, they often sound like people-concerned women in group meetings and church services. But deeper questioning reveals that the key concepts of liberation theology have very traditional meaning for them.

Traditional women believe strongly in the separation of faith and politics. Unlike the first group, they expressed the view that poverty is natural and inescapable.[50] As a result, they rejected the concept of Christ as a liberator of the materially poor and oppressed. Margarita distinguished political liberation from "liberation with Christ": "Let's not mix politics with the church. . . . 'Ah, Jesus worked that way, it's in the Bible . . .' No! That's not written there, church and politics, no. 'Ah, but Jesus died for . . .' No! Jesus died for the salvation of sinners!"[51] She added that "conversion in Jesus's name" means "liberation of faith, of morals."

Traditional women share the people-concerned religionists' belief that it is incumbent upon us to "struggle" in this world. Given their rejection of liberationist Christology, however, they did not conclude that struggle includes fighting for a change to a socialist—or indeed any other—political order. Rather, they perceived the fight in religious and individual terms. One common theme is the idea that Christians must struggle for a conversion of hearts: their own above all but also those of other people. In another vein, the women often describe as God's will their personal struggles to improve the lot of their families, especially their children. Margarita, for example, equates the need to "struggle" with her sacrifice, working in menial employment so that her children could finish school.[52]

The traditional women realize that their views are at odds with the values often preached in the CEBs. They can reconcile themselves with the CEBs, however, in part because those groups still represent the Catholic church. Many are able to separate the actions and words of lay CEB members from the institution of the church/CEB itself. Cristina, for example, claimed that laypeople using liberationist concepts were "confused" and misunderstood what the church stands for.

Moreover, the CEBs offer many opportunities for direct participation in church life. Whatever their disagreements with lay leaders (and even pastoral workers), many traditional women are thrilled by the chance to participate in liturgy groups and as lay ministers. Thus, they are able to separate out and reinterpret the liberationist concepts they do not share and the CEB, which continues to represent the church they love.[53]

Integrated religionists. In many respects, integrated religionists fall between the two extremes of people-concerned and traditional women: "Integrated religionists present a portrait that shows them balancing between the extremes . . . able much of the time to be 'both-and' rather than 'either-or.'"[54] Thus, for example, the integrated religionists share the traditional women's concern with individual salvation, but also have a much higher emphasis on community, love, and charity that places them close to the people-concerned religionists' orientation. What sets them apart from the social justice orientation of the first group, however, is the greater degree to which they stress face-to-face acts of charity, rather than seeking justice for individuals in the abstract as the first group does.

Integrated religionists presented mixed interpretations of religious symbols. They are likely to agree that Christ desires the liberation of the materially poor and oppressed. They have more sympathy for poverty and those affected by it than the traditional women, who often describe the poor (other than themselves) as "lazy." Traditional women view crime as a result of moral degeneracy. Integrated religionists take a "love" position: Criminals are often driven to their acts by great necessity and should be helped rather than condemned. As Maria Angela says, "badness is born from misery," and God will not punish the thief.[55] Chica blames social neglect of children for criminality: "It's very sad, isn't it? That shouldn't happen. Because God put us all in the world, all pure. But society is what spoiled all that."[56]

Unlike the people-concerned women with whom they share this interpretation and who endorse socialism, integrated religionists do not perceive a clear connection between the socioeconomic and political situation and its results in terms of poverty and crime. They see the Kingdom above all in terms of small, individual, face-to-face acts of love and kindness:

> We go to help our brother in his needs, his problems. . . . And if we act that way, we are going more into the kingdom of God here on earth. . . . I should listen to you, because you have problems and I do, and listening is what is lacking. That for many is missing among us, the Kingdom. For us to listen to people, also to give when necessary, that also is part of the kingdom of God.[57]

Whereas most of these respondents began their descriptions of the Kingdom by discussing face-to-face charity and concrete examples of love, they do not reject the connection of religion and politics as the traditional women do. Though less essential for them than for the people-concerned religionists, politics is still viewed as a legitimate religious concern by this group. They simply do not endorse the position that a change in socioeconomic system alone is the single or even primary way to move society closer to the Kingdom.

Marcela began by saying that conversion of one's own heart is the first step toward the Kingdom—a very traditional-sounding view. But she added that the next step is to conscientize people and organize them to demand their rights.[58] For the most part, integrated religionists speak of reforms that would ease the lives of the poor, especially poor children. Or they wish to gain greater equality of treatment before the law and government officials.[59] Through a combination of personal change by the poor and the rich and of political reform, they believe that capitalism can be transformed into a humane, salvageable socioeconomic system.

In sum, there are three broad patterns of response to the liberationist ideas of the CEBs. Similarities as well as differences emerged from the interviews, however. The women vary in their religious attitudes, but all share the view that women have a special role to play in society—a role the unique character of which comes from their experience as mothers.[60]

Gender Attitudes and Conscientization

Simone, a people-concerned religionist, eloquently expresses the belief in women's "special" role:

> At the bottom, the very bottom, it's for the children that we do everything. There are people who see all this [misery] and don't really see,

don't understand. But we understand, we see with the hearts of mothers. That's why women are in every fight. Not for ourselves, but for all the people.[61]

This is an echo of Iracema's view that women were fighting for the well-being of all the children of Brazil.

People-concerned religionists are not alone in this perspective, however. Margarita, a traditional religionist, described her belief that women have a special gift of love that they should use to help others.[62] Integrated religionists also described the love and compassion they feel for the abandoned street children and their wish to do something to help them.[63]

Concern for children and families may result from women's concrete tasks in the gender-based division of labor in urban Brazil: Women must occupy themselves with the health, education, and care of their children, for whom they are primarily responsible. But the most active women in the CEBs have no children at home. Their activities are not a product of personal interest. They stem from deeply held beliefs about the role of women. These may be traceable in part to the powerful cultural influence of *marianismo*.

Some differences emerged in the women's interpretations of the Virgin Mary. Traditional women, for example, strongly emphasized Mary's moral example of virginity. In contrast, a people-concerned woman recalled a book that "took off some of those clothes" and uncovered Mary as a woman like herself.[64] Another said Mary pushed Christ to begin his ministry with the miracle at Cana and thus was a "participant" in his ministry.[65] These interpretations may reflect the CEBs' attempt to reconceptualize Mary as an active, courageous participant in history, like the women themselves.[66]

All of the women, however, held Mary's traditional image in high esteem. Traditional and people-concerned religionists alike stressed her model of motherhood, love, and compassion. They shared the notion that Christian women have particular responsibilities toward others in the community, especially children. Indeed, the CEBs' appeal to women to become politically active is sometimes couched in terms of their responsibilities as wives and mothers, modifying but reinforcing, rather than challenging, traditional gender roles and stereotypes.[67] Most of the time, however, the women said the CEBs had not encouraged reflection on Mary as it had on religious symbols. Thus, traditional interpretations were left unchanged and unchallenged for many. They provide a common language and set of issues that bind the women together.

Because past research has shown that religious orientation is correlated with political attitudes and behavior, we can expect to see divergent patterns of political activism among CEB members.[68] Integrated and people-concerned women are likely to be more liberal or radical in their political views and perhaps more activist as well. Traditional women should be more conservative. We can also expect areas of shared concern, however, especially regarding children. As Iracema pointed out, even the most conservative women want the CEB to support activities that help children, though most women vote against activities like discussion groups on "faith and politics."[69] It is from this mixture of divergence and shared concerns that the pattern of women's political activism has evolved.

Religious Orientation, Gender, and Political Activism

The CEBs in Santo Antônio have promoted two types of political mobilization. They initiated or supported a variety of social movements: for daycare, sanitation, water, street paving, street lights, land title. At the same time, the local church has encouraged electoral participation generally and especially on behalf of the Partido dos Trabalhadores (PT). As already mentioned, CEBs in this part of São Paulo have come closer to the neo-Christendom model of CEB-party relations.

Participation in Social Movements

How have the women responded to the two types of mobilization promoted by the CEB? Looking first at social movements, we see that nearly all of the women have participated in at least some of the social movements in some way. Many have participated in several. But there are differences in the degree and form of women's participation according to their religious orientation.

People-concerned religionists emerge as the leaders of both the CEBs and the social movements. Iracema, Zélia, and women like them organize the movements and recruit others to join them. These women moved from one issue to another as each movement's goals were achieved. Most of the CEBs in Santo Antônio began with a sanitation movement, and once the garbage dumps were cleaned up, the women leading the mothers' clubs quickly found other neighborhood concerns around which to organize.

Integrated religionists present a more mixed profile of participation. Some, especially those with young children, expressed support for the movements, but claimed that they simply could not be away from home enough to participate fully.[70] A few, like Marli and Chica, have worked hand in hand with the people-concerned religionists as organizers, though they are not generally the recognized leaders. For the most part, however, integrated religionists are the faithful rank and file of the movements. They "make up the number" when people are needed to protest at a government office, to do the door-to-door canvassing, and so on. Like the first group, many move from issue to issue, participating in a wide range of movements.

Traditional women followed a similar pattern. Again, younger mothers rarely or never participated in social movements.[71] Most traditional women, however, participated in at least one of the movements. A few, like Neide, were active in nearly all.[72]

Several characteristics of this group's participation are distinctive, however. First, some traditional women consider charitable work as a form of participation, but had little interest in or knowledge of more political activities. One older woman described her activities visiting the sick as part of the community's "health pastoral," although the CEB has also promoted a movement to demand a health post as part of its pastoral activities.[73]

Second, they select movements in which to participate and are more critical of them. Cristina participated in a sanitation movement, but does not participate in the daycare movement. Her reasons for refusing reflect her traditional value emphasis:

> I don't agree much with the ideas of this daycare movement. Just for this reason, that daycare takes children out of the home.... They won't have that idea of family.... Daycare, movements like that, I think the church is being too unilateral in these, you know?[74]

Similarly, Margarita participates in the land movement, but in keeping with her traditional values, she does not support the movement's use of illegal invasion as a tactic. Although she acknowledged the movement's claim that God gave the land to all in common, she said that the "laws of man" that divided it up must be respected.[75]

Traditional women may also confine their participation to certain activities. Only Neide mentioned participating in demonstrations, for example. Margarita could not recall participating in any protests. She attends meetings, and she provides follow-up and support work, however. She and Neide are both on the advisory board of the health post. They represent the CEB at meetings, make lists of needed equipment and medicine, and inform the mothers' club of the problems.

Although religious orientation seems correlated with differences in participation, nearly all of the women have found at least one movement they were willing to support actively. The women's descriptions of their own activism suggest a reason for the acceptance of social movements even by those rejecting liberation theology's political analysis. Most construed the movements in terms of common gender values.

We have already seen expressions of maternal concern by people-concerned activists. Integrated religionists also often expressed a personal desire to help children, and their movements for daycare centers and an after-school care program are expressions of this compassion. Similarly, both Simone, a people-concerned religionist, and Fátima, an integrated religionist, described their efforts to form a sewing cooperative in the same terms. They do not need the work or income, but they hope the cooperative will help young girls from a nearby *favela* (shantytown) to learn a marketable skill and avoid prostitution or other sad fates.[76]

Traditional women also spontaneously linked the movements with a concern for the children. Neide's participation in the sanitation movement was motivated primarily by the health hazards that the open garbage dumps posed "to poor people and to children."[77] Cristina explained her participation in the sanitation movement as follows:

> I like a movement that brings something good to the people. It was with Darcy, Father Darcy that got married, that we started that movement, and we even got rid of the garbage. I mean, that was a productive thing, it was good. In addition, it was a shame to see the children that lived there.[78]

Margarita's greatest efforts at the health center focused on trying to guarantee distribution of free milk for infants.[79]

Despite the radical character imputed to the social movements by many observers in the early 1980s, understanding the motivations of CEB members who participated in these movements puts them in a rather different light. Even women who reject the political options made by pastoral agents and social justice activists in the CEBs felt at home in the social movements. The less-conscientized women saw the movements as a way to "care" for children and community in a larger arena. Traditional women were also able to perceive participation as an extension of charitable activities in a new direction. They recognized that they were acting politically, but in effect, political implications were for them merely incidental. The government needed to be challenged to do something good for people. This was much more a moral than a political position.

Church sponsorship reinforced the moral validity of the movements. For Cristina, the sanitation movement is inextricably linked with the presence of Father Darcy, who encouraged the parish to organize it. Neide was afraid to participate at first, but said the fact that "the priests were together with us" in the movements made it easier.[80] In another community, a lay activist complained that the women would "follow behind Sister Gabriela, crying, into every movement." As a layperson and one who understood the women's conflicts and difficulties, she could not make them feel "guilty" enough to leave their domestic duties and participate.[81]

None of the women, including the traditional women, regarded the movements as wholly nonpolitical. But the "helping" aspects of the movements, their construction as an extension of women's traditional religious and familial roles, and their locus in the church made it easier for women with no particular political or ideological convictions to view the movements as a positive contribution to the community. In essence, they became a moral or charitable act rather than a statement of political belief.

Electoral Participation

As noted earlier, translating moral beliefs into effective political action is much more difficult than making them the basis of a social movement or a generalized critique of the regime. This difficulty is reflected in the degree to which consensus among the women in the social movements breaks down when electoral issues are at stake. In this second mode of participation, the people-concerned religionists are exceptional in both party identification and degree of political involvement.

Pastoral agents in the parish and the diocese claim that the PT in Itaim Paulista is a direct result of *conscientização* in the CEBs.[82] Among the regular CEB participants—women in the mothers' club, the liturgy groups, *conselhos* (councils), and so on—there is a general, expressed consensus in favor of the PT. CEB activists often use ostensibly religious services and meetings to do a little propagandizing for the party as well.

The agreement at the meetings, however, hides a wide degree of variation in political attitudes. Traditional women, especially, may feel compelled to voice the same "line" as the others at meetings. Neide said she did not support any particular party, but she mistrusts the PT leadership and is strongly anti-Communist. Shortly after privately explaining in detail her objections to communism and socialism, however, she joined in a group discussion of the upcoming election by making a very typical pro-PT speech.[83]

Other traditional women express some regard for the PT, but say that they consider each candidate individually. On those grounds, they are willing to vote for a range of political positions. Cleide, for example, said she rather liked the PT's candidate for governor, but thought she might vote for a wealthy center-right businessman. That individual was roundly criticized by many pastoral agents and CEB activists in the parish as the *patrão*, the "boss."

In contrast, all of the people-concerned and most integrated religionists interviewed supported the PT.[84] These two groups, however, generally do not share the same level of political analysis or political activism. Integrated religionists offer only the vaguest reasons for supporting the PT. They may say that it is a "small party," "a weak party," or that it is "on the side of the poor." They are unclear as to its objectives, but think of supporting it as a way in which the poor support the poor. After all, many PT candidates are workers, and thus the women believe they will have a more natural understanding of the problems of the poor. Integrated religionists (and some traditional women as well) often seem to favor the PT primarily because those around them, especially the CEB leaders, do. Maria Angela says, "We see that it is the party of the church."[85] As with the social movements, the impression given is one of a vaguely moral support, rather than support for a specific political position. Such support is clearly susceptible to erosion, especially as the Vatican increases pressure on the Brazilian church to lower its political profile.

Most integrated religionists limit themselves to voting for the PT. Their reluctance to become involved in politics again reflects the essentially moral nature of their political involvement. Chica, an active participant in the social movements and a declared PT supporter, nonetheless limits her electoral activities:

> I go to vote and all, you know? We have meetings with the women and I talk, no? But I don't really like politics. . . . And I have to say, it makes me nervous. I don't know how to talk about politics, because I don't like it. . . . People come and talk about those things, I get nervous. And people disagree, I get mad, and I don't like that. I go to some meetings because it's necessary, but I don't like it![86]

A distaste for political conflict and an approach to issues that springs from an ethic of love may combine to allow integrated religionists to view the PT as an appropriate political vehicle but to limit their politicization and partisan activism. Only one woman from this group has joined the people-concerned women in higher levels of involvement, like working the polls or distributing campaign literature in the neighborhood.

People-concerned women are unique in their degree of political understanding and involvement. They alone express relatively clear reasons for supporting the PT that go beyond moralism or its identification with the church. This group sees a socialist future as the only real hope for solving Brazil's serious social problems and recognizes the PT as a party committed to building socialism "from the bottom up." They are the most active partisans, devoting considerable time to electoral support work and organizing political meetings and rallies.

But the price of such activism for many of the people-concerned activists has been dear. Some are single, which facilitates their participation.[87] Others have limited their political participation because of family problems. Iracema explains her dilemma:

> With party politics, I still haven't liberated myself. I participate whenever I can. I'm a party member, but I don't have, you know, real "work." . . . But every time I say something, my husband gets scared, you know? I think if I enter in party politics, everything will be over! So I go very slowly. It's much more difficult than just participating in the church.[88]

A few have either separated from their husbands or live with them in a hostile truce.

Given their shared belief in the importance of women's role in the family, all of the women view such situations with dismay. Many of the traditional women, especially, privately criticize the people-concerned activists for neglecting their families.[89] Integrated religionists are sometimes more admiring of the activism, but are unwilling to make the sacrifices in their own families that they see being required of the people-concerned women.[90]

Successes and Failures of Political Mobilization

Through the CEBs, the church has brought thousands of women into the political process. It has made all three types of religionists more aware of and informed about politics—a not inconsiderable accomplishment when we consider the universality of the women's claim to have ignored politics before joining the CEB. Under any circumstances, their numbers would be too small for electoral effect. As the base of a social movement, however, they are strong. And they would still be available for mobilization if such a movement were presented in their frame of reference.

The CEBs have radicalized or conscientized only a few, however: the people-concerned religionists and, less uniformly and to a lesser extent, some of the integrated religionists. The social movements, especially, unite women with a fairly wide range of political positions because of their ethical cast. Women who see the movements as a crucial building block in achieving social justice, those who see them as an expression of love for the less fortunate, and those who see them as an extension of their traditional mothers' role have joined in a common cause. The fact that the social justice activists, the movement leaders, share the model and vocabulary of women's special role has surely facilitated incorporation of women with divergent political views. For the rest, a mobilization based on moral concerns is important but limited. For one thing, it is likely to mean that their active political participation will flare only when a particularly pressing local issue arises.

Ongoing mobilization for sustained electoral participation has been far less successful. Distant, of uncertain benefit to the community, divisive, and often corrupt, partisan politics do not appeal to the moral values of integrated or traditional religionists. Moreover, such politics often appear distressingly unfeminine to women who value a conciliatory female role. The people-concerned religionists alone have developed a sense of the political implications of their moral beliefs that is informed by liberation theology. They are unique in believing that the moral projects of the social movements are incomplete without a restructuring of Brazilian society.

The moral nature of most CEB members' participation means that their movements, and even many of their votes, cannot be interpreted in terms of political categories like "radical" or "conservative." Women who yesterday picketed the military government might well be willing to picket a PT government tomorrow if the same kinds of issues are at stake. Thus, the impact and meaning of the CEBs' moral politics will continue to derive from the context in which they are played out.[91]

CEBs and the Church in the 1990s

A variety of social and institutional factors will continue to limit the church's political role generally in the future. Even the role of CEBs specifically will be diminished by the difficulties of mobilizing their constituents for directed electoral activity. Weaknesses in the progressive church's ability politically to mobilize Brazilian society are compounded by the individual factors that influence the process of *conscientização* among those who are mobilized in the CEBs.

Having explored the political implications of religion in Brazilian CEBs, we can reverse the image and ask what challenges the CEBs, their militants, and especially their female leaders pose for the institutional church. One of the key areas in which the CEBs may complicate church strategy is in the competition with Protestant sects. Feeling the threat of evangelical encroachment among the urban poor and under pressure from the Vatican as well, many sectors of the Brazilian church propose a respiritualization and depoliticization of the CEBs, a strategic change Bruneau and Hewitt describe in Chapter 3.

It remains to be seen, however, whether such change would enable the CEBs to compete with Protestant groups for unaffiliated folk Catholics, a group which to date has been marginal in CEB formation in the cities. Evidence from Colombia suggests that poor urban women may be the basis of Protestant expansion, just as they are the core of the CEBs. Yet Protestant women converts are apparently seeking a different kind of moral structure and have a different construction of gender identity than many women in the CEBs. They seem to look to religion as a means of "taming" men and making them economically reliable, thus allowing women to fulfill their roles in the domestic sphere. Women in the CEBs, in contrast, have been encouraged to expand their wife-and-mother roles into the public sphere, even though their public action is often meant to shore up their ability to fulfill their domestic responsibilities toward children.[92]

A resacralization of the CEBs and a renewed emphasis on domestic issues and family morality might prove an effective way to attract unaffiliated folk Catholics, potential Protestant converts whom the CEBs have not reached. They would also be attractive to traditional religionists and at least some integrated religionists, two groups whose allegiance to the church is already fairly secure. These changes, however, would pose a different problem for the church. They would alienate the social justice activists who are the backbone of the CEBs, both religiously and politically.

People-concerned women, unlike most activist men, remain closely linked to their base communities and are often the organizer of catechism, liturgy groups, and religious ministries as well as political movements. They are an important part of the church's work force, and many threaten to withhold their labor if the church returns to strictly religious practice and discourages activism, or at least women's activism. Alienated by the more conservative turn of the diocese recently, people-concerned leaders in Santo Antônio decided to give up commitments at the regional and diocesan level.[93]

The church must accommodate women activists in another way as well. Many are becoming increasingly aware of the problems they face *as women*. The church encouraged their activism, but did not help them reconcile their domestic, religious, and political obligations.[94] Nor did it help them to understand sexism or to deal with the objections of husbands and children. Despite a growing literature by Latin American feminist liberation theologians, including Brazilians Ivone Gebara and María Clara Bingemer, there has been extremely little reflection on gender in the CEBs.[95] Activist women, however, concretely experienced the conflicts, stress, and fatigue that their new roles in both church and society evoked. Moreover, they began to wonder why they could have a voice in politics but not within the church they so devotedly served.

Women from Itaim Paulista have, as a result, begun to organize themselves as women to discuss their special problems. Their intent has never been to challenge the hierarchy, but the church's response to their organization has been cold.[96] The women's group was denied use of church facilities. Women were particularly hurt by their exclusion from organizing committees for the church's 1990 Lenten activities, the theme of which was "Women and Men: Image of God."[97]

Having awakened many laypeople to social activism through the CEBs in the 1970s and 1980s, the church has created its own dilemma for the 1990s. Strategies aimed at bringing folk Catholics into the sacramental fold and lowering the church's political profile are likely to alienate the very lay leaders the church created. Unless it can accommodate them and respect their independence and desire for a voice in the church as well as in society, the Brazilian church risks the loss of many of its hardest-working lay activists, particularly the women of the CEBs.

Notes

1. I use the terms CEBs, *comunidades de base*, and base communities interchangeably.

2. Ralph Della Cava, "The 'People's Church,' the Vatican, and *Abertura*," in Alfred Stepan, ed., *Democratizing Brazil: Problems of Transition and Consolidation* (New York: Oxford University Press, 1989), pp. 156–157.

3. Daniel Levine, "Religion, the Poor, and Politics in Latin America Today," in Daniel Levine, ed., *Religion and Political Conflict in Latin America*, (Chapel Hill: University of North Carolina Press, 1986), p. 14.

4. Teresa P. R. Caldeira, "Electoral Struggles in a Neighborhood on the Periphery of São Paulo," *Politics and Society*, 15, 1 (1986–1987), p. 44.

5. Thomas Bruneau, "Brazil: The Catholic Church and Basic Christian Communities," in Levine, *Religion and Political Conflict*, p. 120.

6. This point is eloquently made in Daniel Levine and Scott Mainwaring, "Religion and Popular Protest in Latin America: Contrasting Experiences," in Susan Eckstein, ed., *Power and Popular Protest: Latin American Social Movements* (Berkeley: University of California Press, 1989), p. 207.

7. Much excellent analysis has been devoted to the institutional level of analysis. See especially Scott Mainwaring, *The Catholic Church and Politics in Brazil, 1916–1985* (Stanford, Calif.: Stanford University Press, 1986); Della Cava, "The 'People's Church;'" and Thomas C. Bruneau and W. E. Hewitt, "Patterns of Church Influence in Brazil's Political Transition," *Comparative Politics* 22, 1 (October 1989), pp. 39–61.

8. Levine, "Religion, the Poor, and Politics," pp. 3, 16–17.

9. The analysis is based on a case study of CEBs in Itaim Paulista, a region of São Paulo's Zona Leste. São Paulo and the Zona Leste are in many respects atypical, because they are considered among the most politically sophisticated and religiously "progressive" regions in the country. It would not be possible to generalize from the São Paulo experience to all of Brazil. At the same time, however, given the region's advantages, any limits that we find there could be taken as the most fundamental forces shaping *conscientização* and the CEBs' political role.

10. Della Cava, "The 'People's Church,'" p. 148. See also Bruneau and Hewitt in Chapter 3.

11. Della Cava, "The 'People's Church,'" p. 149.

12. These included the Movimento de Custo de Vida (MCV), born in São Paulo's mothers' clubs in 1973. The MCV mobilized thousands of women to demonstrate for wage increases and price freezes. They eventually gathered more than a million signatures in support of these points, and the MCV spread nationwide. See Marianne Schmink, "Women in Brazilian *Abertura* Politics," *Signs* 7, 1 (1981), pp. 122–123. The church also turned out thousands of women in a movement for daycare centers in São Paulo's poor neighborhoods. Secular and middle-class feminist groups later joined the struggle, but the CEBs took the initiative. M. Gohn, *A força da periferia: A luta das mulheres por creches em São Paulo* (Petrópolis: Vozes, 1985), pp. 105–106.

13. E. J. Vasconcellos and Paulo J. Krischke, "Igreja, motivações e organizações dos moradores em loteamentos clandestinos," in P. Krischke, org., *Terra de habitação x terra de espoliação* (São Paulo: Cortez, 1984), p. 59. Mainwaring argues similarly for Rio de Janeiro; see Mainwaring, *The Catholic Church*, 204.

14. A. F. Pierucci, "Democracia, igreja e voto: O envolvimento dos padres

de paróqia de São Paulo nas eleições de 1982," Universidade de São Paulo, Ph.D. thesis, 1984, pp. 123–124.

15. Della Cava, "The 'People's Church,'" p. 156.

16. Ibid.

17. W. E. Hewitt, "The Structure and Orientation of Comunidades Eclesiais de Base (CEBs) in the Archdiocese of Sao Paulo," McMaster University, Ph.D. thesis, 1985, pp. 100–102.

18. Della Cava, "The 'People's Church,'" p. 155.

19. Bruneau, "Brazil: The Catholic Church and Basic Christian Communities," p. 119.

20. The pattern of CEB recruitment is discussed in Carol A. Drogus, "Religion, Gender, and Political Culture: Attitudes and Participation in Brazilian Basic Christian Communities," University of Wisconsin–Madison, Ph.D. thesis, 1991, ch. 5.

21. In 1984 the municipality of São Paulo's electorate numbered 4,542,546. Empresa Metropolitana de Planejamento de Grande São Paulo (EMPLASA), Sumário de dados de grande São Paulo 1983 (São Paulo: EMPLASA, 1984), p. 45.

22. Hewitt, The Structure and Orientation, p. 131.

23. Levine, "Religion, the Poor, and Politics," p. 14.

24. Pierucci, Democracia, igreja e voto, p. 288. Eighty-eight percent of Pierucci's respondents agreed that "the mission of the Church is to form the political consciousness of the people" (p. 287). This agreement conceals, however, a considerable disagreement about how such consciousness should be formed. For example, priests of different age groups varied considerably in their responses to questions designed to measure degree of political radicalism (p. 522).

25. Della Cava, "The 'People's Church,'" p. 143.

26. Pierucci, Democracia, igreja, e voto, pp. 369–370; Mainwaring, The Catholic Church, p. 202.

27. Pierucci, Democracia, igreja, e voto, p. 532.

28. Leonardo Boff and Clodovis Boff, "Comunidades: cristãs e política partidária, Encontros com a Civilização Brasileira 3 (Sept. 1978), pp. 15–17.

29. As reported in Latin America Weekly Report, September 14, 1989.

30. Hewitt, The Structure and Orientation, p. 120.

31. The lower figure is from Hewitt's survey of people attending mass in lower-class CEBs; Hewitt, The Structure and Orientation, p. 120. The higher figure is from a survey in my research area of people participating more intensively in the CEBs as members of grupos de rua, small prayer and reflection groups; "Aos animadores dos grupos de rua," São Paulo, mimeo, 1986, pp. 127–128.

32. Examples of tests of the hypothesized connection among religion, gender, and conservatism include Derek Urwin, "Germany: Continuity and Change in Electoral Politics," in Richard Rose, ed., Electoral Behavior: A Comparative Perspective (New York: Free Press, 1974), pp. 156–157; and Keith Hill, "Belgium: Political Change in a Segmented Society," in Rose, Electoral Behavior, pp. 92–93. Gary Marx found among blacks in the United States that women were more religious and, at the same time, less politically militant than men. Gary Marx, "Religion: Opiate or Inspiration of Civil Rights Militancy Among Negroes?" in B. Beit-Hallahmi, ed., Research in Religious Behavior: Selected Readings (Monterey, Calif.: Brooks/Cole, 1973), p. 385.

33. The educative function of the CEBs is stressed by Carmen Macedo, Tempo de genesis: O povo das comunidades de base (São Paulo: Brasiliense, 1986), p. 237.

34. Interview (C) 02-01.07.86.

35. Daniel Levine, "Popular Groups, Popular Culture and Popular Religion," Notre Dame University, Kellogg Institute Working Paper No. 127, 1989, p. 3.

36. This was true up to 1986. Since then the diocese has been separated from the archdiocese of São Paulo. Bishop Angélico Sândalo Bernardino was replaced in 1989, and many pastoral agents have been replaced with people widely considered more conservative and less committed to CEBs. There are indications that the diocese and parish are attempting to assert more control over the CEBs.

37. Interviews 45-04.04.86; 01-RM 04.01.84.

38. Interviews 20-29.10.86 and 26.07.86.

39. Interview 19-23.10.86.

40. The exceptions are themselves telling. One woman became disenchanted with the church when her father, in the wake of the changes wrought by Vatican II, forbade her to become a nun (interview 27-19.11.86). Another grew up in a nominally Catholic family but rarely attended church. Her passionate involvement in the CEBs began with her personal decision to make a belated first communion at thirteen (interview 23-20.10.86).

41. Michael R. Welch and David C. Leege, "Religious Predictors of Catholic Parishoners' Sociopolitical Attitudes: Devotional Style, Closeness to God, Imagery, and Agentic/Communal Religious Identity," *Journal for the Scientific Study of Religion* 27, 4 (1988), p. 546; Peter L. Benson and Dorothy L. Williams, *Religion on Capitol Hill: Myths and Realities* (New York: Oxford University Press, 1982), p. 137.

42. See Benson and Williams, *Religion on Capitol Hill.*

43. Interview 01-29.04.86.

44. Interview 25-18.11.86.

45. Interview 01-29.04.86.

46. Interview 20-19.10.86.

47. Interview 20-29.10.86.

48. Interviews 15-23.10.86, 13-21.11.86, and 34-25.09.86.

49. Interview 15-23.10.86.

50. Interview 08-22.06.86.

51. Interview 15-23.10.86.

52. Interview 15-23.10.86.

53. An interesting discussion of some factors that have led US Catholic feminists to reconcile themselves to the church despite their criticisms of its sexist practices is contained in Andrew Greeley and Mary G. Durkin, *Angry Catholic Women* (Chicago: Thomas More Press, 1984). I believe that a similar process is at work among traditional women in the CEBs.

54. Benson and Williams, *Religion on Capitol Hill,* p. 129.

55. Interview 11-11.11.86.

56. Interview 22-01.12.86.

57. Interview 11-11.11.86.

58. Interview 25-18.11.86.

59. Interview 21-16.11.86.

60. In the interview, the one clear exception to this pattern was a single, childless woman in her thirties who is a people-concerned religionist. Her activism is oriented primarily toward workers' issues rather than the more usual social movements. She has worked in a variety of factory and nonfactory situations and considers herself a trade-unionist.

61. Interview 39-29.11.86.

62. Interview 15-23.10.86.

63. Interviews 11-11.11.86 and 22-01.12.86.

64. Interview 01-29.04.86.

65. Interview 23-30.10.86.

66. Solange Padilha, "Características e limites das organizações de base femininas," in C. Bruschini and F. Rosemberg, orgs., *Trabalhadoras do Brasil* (São Paulo: Brasiliense/Fundação Carlos Chagas, 1982), pp. 199–200.

67. Ibid.; Ana Dias and Maria José Rosaldo Nunes, "A mulher, a igreja e processos da libertação," Série de Cadernos para Subsídios aos Movimentos Populares, mimeo, 1984, p. 31.

68. Welch and Leege, "Religious Predictors," p. 546; Benson and Williams, *Religion on Capitol Hill*, p. 148.

69. Interview 01-02.12.86.

70. Interview 11-11.11.86.

71. Interviews 09-07.08.86; 08-22.06.86.

72. Interview 34-25.09.86.

73. Interview (C) 05-20.08.86.

74. Interview 13-21.11.86.

75. Interview 15-27.05.86.

76. Interviews 18 and 39-03.12.86.

77. Interview 34-25.09.86.

78. Interview 13-21.11.86.

79. Interview 15-23.10.86.

80. Interview 34-25.09.86.

81. Interview 55-23.07.86.

82. Interviews 42-22.08.86 and 46-19.09.86.

83. Interview and field notes 34-25.09.86.

84. One woman expressed her intention to split her votes between the PT and the historical opposition party, the Partido do Movimento Democrático Brasiliero (PMDB) (interview 25-18.11.86).

85. Interview 11-11.11.86.

86. Interview 22-01.12.86.

87. Interview 38-29.05.86.

88. Interview 01-29.04.86.

89. Interview 13-21.11.86.

90. Interview 41-31.10.86.

91. Levine, "Popular Groups, Popular Culture, and Popular Religion," p. 12.

92. This interpretation is based on David Stoll's discussion of Elizabeth Brusco's research in Colombia, as described in David Stoll, *Is Latin America Turning Protestant? The Politics of Evangelical Growth* (Berkeley: University of California Press, 1990), pp. 318–319.

93. Interview 01-29.05.90.

94. Sonia Alvarez believes that this neglect occurs because discussion of the women's problems might quickly run up against questions of church doctrine. Sonia Alvarez, "The Politics of Gender in Latin America: Comparative Perspectives on Women in the Brazilian Transition to Democracy," Yale University, Ph.D. thesis, 1986, p. 273.

95. Dias and Nunes reached the same conclusion based on observations of CEBs in other areas of São Paulo. Dias and Nunes, *A mulher*, p. 27.

96. This lack of support may be part of the general tendency toward providing less support for CEBs and their activities that Bruneau and Hewitt describe in Chapter 3.

97. Interviews 01-29.05.90 and 59-29.05.90.

CHAPTER 5

The Church in Peru: Between Terrorism and Conservative Restraints

JEFFREY KLAIBER

In the past few years Peru, like Job, seems to have been smitten by more than its share of misfortunes. In the 1960s it was considered a "middle" country, behind Mexico and Brazil but far ahead of Bolivia and Haiti. But by the middle of the 1980s, compared to Peru, Bolivia seemed a model of economic and political stability. In the last two years of Alan García's term (1985–1990), the annual inflation rate was around 2,775 percent and the minimum monthly salary was less than $50. Nearly one-half of the working force of Peru's 22 million inhabitants belongs to the "informal sector," a blanket euphemism that covers millions of subemployed, nontaxpaying peasants, street vendors, and part-time workers, who by First World standards would be considered as simply unemployed. In spite of sweeping reforms carried out under the Juan Velasco military regime (1968–1975), 40 percent of the population still receives less than 10 percent of the nation's income. Health care is another sign of social erosion; the death rate for children under five is 53 percent. Peru, once considered a promising Third World test case for the Alliance for Progress, twenty years later displays many of the traits of a Fourth or Fifth World nation.

Rising and widespread violence is the other specter haunting the country. Since Peru's home-grown terrorists known as the Shining Path declared war in 1980, approximately 17,763 Peruvians have been killed by the terrorists (between the Shining Path and another group known as the Tupac Amaru Revolutionary Movement) or the army and the police, and another 3,000 have disappeared. The amount of damage to factories, roads, bridges, and farm cooperatives caused by terrorist attacks is estimated to be about $17 billion.[1] Close to 40 percent of the central Andes and jungle region have been declared emergency zones and are under the control of the military. The military left power in 1980, and Peru has since lived through two democratic administrations, Fernando Belaúnde in his second term (1980–1985) and the term of his successor, Alan García. Alberto Fujimori was elected in June 1990 with the hope of ending his term in 1995.

If poverty alone were the problem, Peru's frail democratic structures would have a chance of surviving. But under the double pressure of poverty and violence, the future of democracy is far from assured. The cocaine trade in the eastern jungles, corruption in the police and government, and constant social discontent that manifests itself in innumerable union strikes place additional strains on democracy. This is the general context and background for understanding the church in the decade since the military left power.

The Conservative Shift

The Peruvian church during the entire military regime (1968–1980) was considered one of the most progressive in Latin America. Under the leadership of Cardinal Juan Landázuri Ricketts, Lima's archbishop from 1955 to 1990, the church supported most of the military's measures, which included sweeping agrarian and educational reforms. ONIS (National Office of Social Information), the progressive priests' organization, took the lead in denouncing social injustices and in demanding further reform. Unlike the situation in other Latin American nations (Brazil, Bolivia, Chile, Argentina, Paraguay) where repressive right-wing military governments persecuted the church, the Peruvian church actively cooperated with the military. Although proponents of liberation theology and other more centrist church groups criticized the military, they felt by and large that Peru was changing for the better. A spirit of optimism was noticeably evident among church personnel who worked in the *pueblos jóvenes* ("young towns," the euphemism invented by the military to describe the squatter settlements ringing the coastal cities). New parishes that sprang up offered something close to a tabula rasa for applying the reforms of Vatican II to the Latin American reality in an atmosphere of general receptivity.

But the election of John Paul II, the Puebla Conference in 1979, and most of all the episcopal appointees' orientation since then have clearly signaled the end of the progressives' leadership in the hierarchy. By 1988 the conservatives achieved a majority in the national Episcopal Conference, which had 54 voting members. That year Cardinal Landázuri, who had been elected automatically president of the conference for years, did not present himself as a candidate, and Ricardo Durand Flórez, the Jesuit archbishop of Callao, won the election by two votes. Durand, who had attracted attention to himself by writing two books critical of liberation theology, symbolized the growing shift. Highly visible in the conservative block are seven Jesuits (out of eight in the country) and six Opus Dei bishops. When Landázuri stepped down as head of the archdiocese of Lima in January 1990, he was succeeded by one of the conservative Jesuits, Augusto Vargas Alzamora, thus making the conservative turnabout almost complete. Progressive church leaders such as Bishop José Dammert of Cajamarca still speak out, but their influence is noticeably weakened at episcopal assemblies. The majority of the bishops fall between the extremes, neither conservative nor progressive. But in their case, the powerful weight of Rome is the determining factor that inclines them to support the conservatives.

Many other signs have pointed to a conservative shift. In 1983 Cardinal Ratzinger, prefect of the Congregation for the Doctrine of the Faith, formally requested the Peruvian bishops to conduct an examination of liberation theology. During the annual national episcopal meetings of 1983 and 1984, liberation theology dominated the discussion. In September 1984 Ratzinger published the first formal Vatican document on liberation theology, and in October the bishops produced their own. The bishop's document, which contained the same general warnings about importing "ideologies foreign to the faith," nevertheless was more positive in tone. One reason was that the progressives were still dominant in the hierarchy. But another was the fact that the pope, in preparation for his upcoming 1985 trip to the Andean countries, had addressed two groups of Peruvian bishops. His stress on the need to speak out against injustice and to speak for the poor weighed considerably in the bishops' judgment.[2] But during his second visit to Peru in May 1988, John Paul warned the bishops again about the dangers of certain brands of liberation theology. This time the pontiff made no effort to point out the positive side of liberation theology.

The contrast between the two papal visits was eloquent proof that a major shift had indeed occurred in the Peruvian church. The first one, in February 1985, was characterized by enormous crowd spontaneity and affectionate rapport between the pontiff and the people. Most noticeable was the emphasis on justice and solidarity in the pope's addresses. But the return visit, made on the occasion of a devotional congress of some of the Andean countries emphasizing an otherworldly approach to religion, was tightly controlled by conservative groups, and the papal addresses lacked the stirring summons to address the realities of poverty and injustice that had characterized the 1985 visit. The conservative groups, most noticeably Opus Dei and Sodalitium Christianae Vitae (a lay-founded integralist association that has especially stood out for its attacks on liberation theology), appeared everywhere on organizing committees and advisory boards to the bishops.[3]

The conservatives, aided and supported by Rome, have also moved into areas not normally under their jurisdiction. For years most of the diocesan seminaries have as a matter of fact been under conservative bishops. But in 1987 Rome sent a visitor to investigate the seminaries, and the review extended to ISET in Lima (Superior Institute of Theological

Studies), run by the religious orders. When the "visit" was over, women religious who attended classes were forced to leave on the pretext that the institute was only for religious who were going to be ordained. In fact, they remained—but in a separate program for them, on the same property. Most important, Rome ignored the normal electoral process and maintained its own men in place by fiat.

The Progressives: In Retreat but Undaunted

In light of these and many other changes, subtle and not so subtle, a once highly progressive church has apparently been put under control; presumably with a few more episcopal appointments, it may soon disappear altogether. Nevertheless, there are many reasons for not arriving at too hasty a conclusion. Church realities are much more complex and the social and political sands in Peru are so shifting and uncertain that there is reason to doubt whether the new conservative fortress is built on solid ground. Conservative gains have been won by pressure from on high, not by acclamation from below.

The progressive church is very much alive and not likely to "disappear" for many years to come. There are three principal arguments to support this belief: the general missionary character of the Peruvian church that allows significant progressive enclaves to exist and even to flourish within a church dominated by a conservative hierarchy; the growth and strength of the progressive church since the influential Medellín Conference in 1968; and pressure from a society wracked by poverty and violence that can lead moderates and even conservatives to shift sides. It would be well at this point to define at least in general terms what is meant by the "progressive" church and then to focus on important characteristics of the progressive church and the church in general in Peru in order to understand why highly visible signs of change—episcopal appointees—do not necessarily signify real and lasting internal change.

The progressive church is made up of churchpeople—priests, nuns, laypersons—who are committed to the ideals of Vatican II and Medellín (reaffirmed at Puebla in 1979). In general this means that progressives have a twofold commitment: to encourage the growth of real lay participation in the church and to lend support and legitimacy to the popular movement. The first goal is clearly inspired by Vatican II, the second by Medellín. Although the progressives have been sympathetic toward the political left, that is not the key defining criterion. What is essential is their commitment to help empower the poor (*campesinos*, workers, women, youth, the mass of dwellers in the *pueblos jóvenes*) to build their own lives and to construct a democratic and just society from below.

In many ways the progressives have become, as one author termed them, "religious populists," who intersect the popular movement at many different levels: as advisers, members, and leaders.[4] The local parish in a *pueblo joven* may reach only a small percentage of the people by way of its sacramental action. Indeed, in Peru only about 10 percent or less of the population may be regular churchgoers. But the pastor and the team of pastoral agents who work with him will be very much involved in a great variety of community activities that reach far beyond those who regularly attend Sunday mass. Those activities range from promoting mothers' clubs, to supporting a march to demand water or electric power for the district, to arbitrating among a group of "invaders" (squatters), the mayor, and the police. In this sense, the popular or progressive church is very "political," although it is careful not to identity itself publicly with any political party. As the popular movement (which includes unions and communal civic organizations in the *pueblos jóvenes*) has grown in strength since the Velasco years, so too has the progressive church grown in numbers and in strength. In Peru, as in the rest of Latin America, laypersons of the lower classes have become both vocal political leaders and active and critical church leaders.

Thus, a conservative retrenchment at the level of the hierarchy, reinforced by conservative religious and lay groups, will not easily stem an entire social movement, which has increasingly influenced and conditioned the political atmosphere in Peru. This popular movement has been influenced by the new church, but it has also flowed back to invigorate the progressive tendency in the church. This does not mean that a defiant "popular church" has come into being. On the contrary, the vast majority of lay leaders from the popular classes are extremely respectful of the hierarchy, conservative or not. But they have also grown accustomed to their leadership role in the church. They will continue to be loyal to the church, but not on the same terms as before. As we shall see in the case of the Fujimori election, the conservative church has a very limited capability for influencing the popular classes in Peru today if it goes against political, social, and religious goals they consider important.

Beyond this more social consideration, there are certain basic ecclesiastical realities that limit the power not just of conservatives but of bishops and church authorities in general. In the first place, on the level of the clergy and religious women, the Peruvian church is still a mission church: the great majority of the clergy belong to religious orders, and 61 percent of all clergy are foreign-born, while slightly less than one-half of religious women are foreigners.[5] Thus, religious orders and missionary groups have an extraordinary presence and influence in the Peruvian church, not unlike the reality of many other Latin American churches. Bishops in many dioceses do not really have absolute control over the personnel of their own dioceses. Lima is a good example. Many of the city parishes in middle- and upper-class neighborhoods are under diocesan clergy, directly responsible to the archbishop. But the great majority of the parishes in the *pueblos jóvenes* (which comprise about half of Lima's 6 million inhabitants) are in the hands of foreign religious (some of whom are not strictly "religious," such as the priestly mission associations like the priests of Maryknoll, the Saint James Society based in Boston, or the Irish Columban priests). A change in the formal direction of the archdiocese of Lima will not immediately change their pastoral orientation, especially because it is the result of thirty years or more of work. Furthermore, given the scarcity of priests and the fact that the Peruvian church cannot support priests in the popular urbanizations, the bishops must accept the presence of the progressive foreigners in their dioceses, at least for some time.

This same fundamental fact of ecclesiastical life is true for many other parts of Peru. For years the most progressive region within the Peruvian church was the so-called southern Andean church, which comprised the dioceses of Cuzco, Puno, Juli, Sicuani, Ayaviri, and Chuquibambilla. Most of those dioceses grew out of prelatures administered by different religious groups (the Maryknoll Fathers, the French Sacred Heart Fathers, the American Carmelites, among others), who forged strong ties among themselves in the 1960s and lent support to peasant organizations. Up until his death in 1982, the archbishop of Cuzco, Luis Vallejo, was a staunch member of the southern Andean church. But his successor, Alcides Mendoza, who was chaplain to the armed forces and holds the rank of general, sought to undo all the pastoral efforts of his predecessor. He pulled his diocese out of the southern Andean church and sent his seminarians to the Opus Dei seminary in Abancay. He attempted to dislodge a group of French Dominicans who run a center of research for the region. Even though some of the Dominicans were suspended, they did not leave the diocese. Their center does not depend on the diocese financially. The Bartolomé de las Casas Rural Studies Institute continues to offer seminars and courses for researchers and lay church leaders from the region. The local diocesan clergy members, born in the area, are very conservative. But progressives have maintained a space of their own in the heart of the archdiocese, much to the displeasure of the archbishop.

There are other centers, dioceses, and institutionalized activities that for the near future will help to guarantee the progressive church the possibility of survival and even growth. The most celebrated activity of the progressive church is the summer course in theology organized by the theology department of the Catholic University in Lima. In the 1960s when the course was first offered, a few hundred attended. By the late 1980s the course drew close to 3,000 adult men and women and university students, mostly from the lower-middle and lower classes. The course, offered now both in the summer and winter, has over the years imparted a critical biblical-social consciousness to thousands of churchpeople, who come from all over Peru. Gustavo Gutiérrez is, without doubt, one of the main attractions, but the experience of ecclesial sharing is also one of the reasons for the popularity of the two-week course. The Bartolomé de las Casas Center founded by Father Gutiérrez in Lima holds seminars and training sessions for lay churchpeople who work in the *pueblos jóvenes* of Lima and other nearby dioceses.

In other areas, the Catholic University Students (UNEC) and the Christian Life Communities of the Jesuits, which is also university-oriented, hold annual seminars that draw up to 500 participants. In May 1990 the Christian communities (as they call themselves) at San Marcos National University in Lima organized a mass for peace. The mass was especially significant for two reasons: It symbolized an explicit repudiation of the Shining Path, which up until then had looked upon the university as its preserve, and it marked the coming of age of the progressive church in the midst of a university with a long laical and anticlerical heritage. The rector formally received the archbishop of Lima, who celebrated the mass. But far more important than the welcome given to a Catholic bishop at San Marcos was the presence of over 1,000 students who organized and attended the mass. Such a public Christian manifestation would have been unthinkable twenty years earlier. This and many other examples attest to the existence of a progressive church that is now far more widely based than when it consisted of the small core of priests and other religious activists who originally set out to create it.

This description of progressives and conservatives is somewhat simplistic and leaves out many important nuances. The lines between the two sides are not always so clearly defined. For example, not all conservatives are the same. Opus Dei bishops are perceived as somewhat clannish by other conservatives. In 1988 Archbishop Mendoza of Cuzco felt it necessary to restrict the pastoral duties of his auxiliary Opus Dei bishop, who apparently had attempted to import an Opus Dei contingent from Spain to run the seminary in the archdiocese. Vargas Alzamora was chosen to be Landázuri's successor in Lima in part because he was regarded as a more conciliatory conservative. In certain dioceses, progressives have learned to work with conservative bishops in order to resolve concrete pastoral problems. In areas especially affected by violence, conservative bishops have turned to progressives for help. Archbishop Emilio Vallebuona of Huancayo in the central Andes fit the description of the traditional Salesian, at least in Peru: few intellectual interests and no commitment to political or social change. But by the late 1980s the Shining Path had systematically attacked towns near the city and organized armed strikes (by which the whole population is ordered not to go to work or school at the risk of being killed) in Huancayo itself. Thoroughly alarmed, Vallebuona urged priests known for their progressive stance to organize peace marches and to work with the youth of the archdiocese.

Fujimori and the Religious Issue

The Fujimori election in June 1990 served to bring to light two of the phenomena touched upon here: the relative strength of the conservative church and the progressive church and the internal divisions between them. It also threw the spotlight in a most dramatic way on a third phenomena: the increasing influence of evangelicals and the "sects" in Peru. Protestants and other non-Christian religions make up approximately 5 percent of the population.[6] And evangelical Protestants (which include Pentecostals) make up the majority of that percentage. For several years evangelical pastors in Peru, as elsewhere in Latin America, had been questioning their traditional response to politics and social action. Ever-increasing levels of violence and poverty led some of them to see the need to take a political stance. In one dramatic incident in August 1984, six Presbyterian church members, accused of being "subversives," were killed by navy marines in a highland community.[7] On other occasions Shining Path attacks forced pastors to look for ways to defend their communities. In December 1989 a group of pastors who belonged to CONEP (National Evangelical Council of Peru) held a week-long session to discuss the relationship of politics to society. Many of the pastors came close to espousing some of the basic tenets of liberation theology. Among the participants were several who had already decided to organize themselves politically. Disenchanted with the corruption-ridden government of Alan García, young evangelicals formed a block to support the candidacy of Alberto Fujimori, whose themes of work, honesty, and morality attracted them.[8] Also, Fujimori identified himself as the man of the small entrepreneur. Some forty evangelicals ended up as candidates for congress on the list of Fujimori's new party, Cambio '90 (Change '90).

The presence of the evangelicals would never have attracted the attention it did were it not for the fact that Fujimori, a dark horse, won second place to Mario Vargas Llosa in the presidential elections held on April 8. Because neither candidate won a majority (Vargas Llosa, 27.6 percent and Fujimori, 24.62 percent) a runoff election, required by law, was set for June 10. When it became clear that Vargas Llosa had little chance of winning if all centrist and leftist groups threw their support to Fujimori, campaign strategists of FREDEMO (Frente Democrático), the electoral front for Vargas, groped in desperation for ways of galvanizing public opinion against their opponent. Given the fact that Fujimori identified himself with many of the neoliberal policies of Vargas Llosa, FREDEMO planners tried using more nonideological issues such as race and religion. The first backfired when it became evident that Fujimori, a first-generation Japanese, was popular in part because the lower classes identified with him racially. But religion had more potential. In the middle of the second electoral round, a mysterious flyer appeared that called upon evangelicals to vote for "our Pentecostal brother Fujimori" because he was "sent by Jehovah." The flyer also alluded to the superstitious practices of Catholics. Although it was evident to all critical observers that the flyer was forged by FREDEMO, and evangelicals denied any knowledge of it, the conservative bishops decided to hold processions in retaliation for the presumed attack on Catholicism.

Holding religious processions in the middle of an electoral process that had aroused passions throughout the country had the effect of infusing them with a political connotation. Although the bishops claimed that their interest was nonpolitical, their sympathies in favor of Vargas Llosa were only too well known. The bishops were no doubt sincere in their fears of growing Protestant strength in Peru, and they were especially concerned that the evangelicals with Fujimori would use political power to claim privileges for themselves. But they ignored or were unimpressed by the fact that Vargas Llosa was a nonbeliever and that Fujimori himself was a Catholic who enjoyed the support of the popular classes. The processions were held in Arequipa and in Lima (the Lord of Miracles, normally held only in October, was brought out in May), and warnings about the sects were made.[9] Bishop Bambarén of Chimbote, normally in the progressive camp, also published a pamphlet that underlined the dangers posed by the new religions. The pamphlet explicitly alluded to Fujimori and Cambio '90.[10]

If the bishops had hoped to dissuade the population from voting for a candidate with evangelicals, they certainly failed in their objective. Fujimori won 57 percent of the vote, Vargas Llosa 34 percent. In Chimbote, Cambio '90 won nearly 80 percent of the vote. In the meantime progressives, some of whom had supported Henry Pease, the Catholic candidate on the left, during the first round, openly sympathized with Fujimori—or at least looked upon him as more of the people's candidate than Vargas Llosa. Somewhat scandalized by the spectacle of holding processions during a political campaign, Bishop Dammert of Cajamarca declared emphatically that he was not about to write pamphlets or hold processions in his diocese.[11] After the election a group of bishops, including Vargas Alzamora, held a procession to congratulate Fujimori on his victory.

What hard and fast conclusions can be drawn from this entire affair are not clear. It did seem evident that the conservative bishops acted out of panic or fear, and at the very least, they acted imprudently. If they hoped to demonstrate their power to influence popular opinion, they did just the opposite. On the other hand, it cannot be demonstrated that the progressive church influenced public opinion in any important way either. If anything, the election revealed how little the conservative church was in touch with the popular classes, and how little the popular classes were concerned about episcopal opinions on politics and religion, especially when they seem to go against political and social objectives that the popular classes consider to be completely legitimate.

The Church and Sendero Luminoso

Conservative-progressive tensions in Peru have not unfolded in a vacuum. The shadow in the background that conditions all discussion in society and in the church is the worsening social situation of the lower classes and the rise of criminal and political violence—most of all the violence provoked by the terrorist groups, particularly the Shining Path. After ten years of incessant activity, the Shining Path, known in Spanish as Sendero Luminoso (or simply Sendero) has managed to win control over major areas of the central Andes and the Peruvian jungle. It also has bases in all major coastal cities, particularly in Lima. Numbering around 5,000 to 15,000, it is a highly clandestine organization. Its basic strategy and ideology are Maoist. By reason of its puritanical dogmatism, it has also been compared to the Khmer Rouge of Cambodia. Unlike other guerrilla groups in the rest of Latin America, it has shown no interest in attracting progressive or radical Christians. Although its symbols are infused with quasi-religious connotations (the leader is a mythical "Presidente Gonzalo," who may or may not be Abimael Guzmán, the founder), they have no reference either to Christianity or traditional Andean myths. Indeed, all signs indicate that Sendero is overtly hostile toward formal religious belief, which, in accord with classical Marxist lines, is viewed as a force that prevents Sendero from having total control over the people.[12]

Sendero originated in Ayacucho, a department located in the central Andes to the south of Lima. The region was not only isolated and poverty-stricken but dormant ecclesiastically. The city of Ayacucho was a tourist attraction in large part because of its many colonial churches, practically one on every block. But the living church also looked as though it had not changed much since colonial times. The clergy, like that in most of the highland communities, had little training, and many lived in concubinage. Their lack of culture, their conservative mentality, and the fact that some priests treated the people in a high-handed fashion made them very unattractive to the youth. Of the forty-six parishes in the archdiocese, twenty-three were unattended. The middle class sent their sons and daughters to one or another of the religious *colegios* in the city, but the schooling received there was so traditional that it offered them no preparation to deal intellectually with Marxism. While aging priests rushed through masses in the downtown churches, the Shining Path steadily built up a power base among the youth at the new university, founded in 1959.

Nevertheless, in the first few years after it initiated its own self-declared war, Sendero did not pay particular attention to the church. The conservative church in Ayacucho, which had not felt the winds of Vatican II or Medellín, simply offered no threat or challenge to its strategy. The most dramatic example that illustrates the ambiguous relationship between Sendero and the traditional church was the mass celebrated in the Ayacucho cathedral for Edith Lagos in mid-1982. Edith Lagos had graduated from the *colegio* run by the Salesian sisters, and by all accounts she was a model student in her religion class. But soon after graduating she was recruited by Sendero and shortly thereafter became a model leader: that is, a model terrorist. She was killed at the age of nineteen in a clash with the police. She was also perceived in Ayacucho as something of a heroine. The cathedral was filled, and thousands waited outside.[13] Archbishop Federico Richter-Prada, a Franciscan, having no clear thoughts of what to say about terrorism and no doubt fearful to express them in public, allowed the mass to be celebrated.

That incident helps to explain why Sendero apparently ignored the church in the beginning. In the first place, the church in Ayacucho, with no social doctrine or activity of its own, outside of traditional charities, posed no obstacle to Sendero's advance. In the second place, Sendero hoped to avoid unnecessarily alienating the peasantry by directly attacking religious symbols and persons that they esteemed. But as it spread out of the Ayacucho area, it did clash with two groups: Protestants and progressive Catholics. By the 1980s Protestants had founded numerous small churches throughout the central Andes. Although of a very conservative social and political mentality, they did impose new standards of morality in the villages. For that very reason alone they posed an obstacle to Sendero, which correctly sensed that villagers and peasants, armed with a new biblical consciousness, could not be easily won over. In 1984 Sendero drove a Pentecostal pastor and eighteen families out of their village located in Ayacucho.[14] But in many other cases, execution squads simply assassinated pastors and community leaders. One possible reason why Sendero singled out Protestants before coming down hard on Catholics was that the former stood out as more "alien" and therefore un-Peruvian. Although the vast majority of the Protestants attacked were in fact Peruvians, and a good number of Catholic priests and nuns are foreign-born, still, Catholicism was perceived as a religion more deeply wedded to Andean ways.

In the long run, however, progressive Catholicism represented a far greater challenge to Sendero. In order to achieve control over an area, the Shining Path first studies the terrain, then singles out the authorities and other leaders who could potentially summon the community to resist the takeover. An armed attack by Sendero usually involves "executing" the mayor, other town officials, and certain landowners or shopkeepers accused of being "exploiters" of the people. An essential part of its overall strategy consists of destroying all development projects that in any way signify dependence on the outside. To achieve this objective, the Shining Path has systematically attacked and destroyed training schools for peasants, experimental farms, and credit or technical assistance cooperatives throughout the Andes. Civilian engineers and development projects volunteers are usually warned in advance to leave the area. But when Sendero strikes, it is no more merciful to ordinary civilians than it is to government officials, police, or military. In December 1988 two French agricultural assistants were killed in Apurímac, a department to the east of Ayacucho. A year before that incident, a North American agricultural economist and his Peruvian counterpart were shot to death near Huancayo.[15] Because the church also runs many such developmental projects and schools in the highlands, it was only a question of time before the progressive church and Sendero came face to face.

One of the first Sendero attacks on a church project occurred in August 1981, when a group of masked and armed persons destroyed an educational center for the peasants run by the Maryknoll parish in Juli in the southern highlands. At the time it was believed that local landowners and others resentful of the progressive church were behind the assault. Since then many such incidents have occurred. In August 1987 in San Juan de Jarpa, a small town two hours' drive from Huancayo, a column of Senderistas attacked at night and burned down a building used by the church for training peasants. As though following a plan, the armed invaders did not touch the two Jesuits who were present. They did kill a man, however, whom they mistakenly believed to be the mayor of the town. Even more destructive was an attack in May 1989 on the Institute of Rural Education, run by the Sacred Heart Fathers in Ayaviri in the south.[16]

As the level of violence increased, Sendero began throwing caution to the winds. In December 1987 a group of Senderistas killed the first priest to fall victim to terrorism: Víctor Acuña, a diocesan priest in Ayacucho in charge of Cáritas. But that case was somewhat obscure: Whether Acuña was shot (while celebrating mass) because he was a priest or because Sendero perceived him as an exploiter of the people is not clear. In June 1989 a second priest was killed in a small town in Junín, but in this case he seemed to have been caught in the crossfire between the attackers and the police.[17] Finally, on September 27, 1990, a seventy-year-old Good Shepherd nun was executed along with several villagers in La Florida, in the jungle region of Junín in the central Andes.[18] This was the first case in which Sendero intentionally killed a Catholic religious person and for no other apparent reason than that she was a religious. A simple cook who was well-liked in the village, she could hardly have been accused of being an "exploiter" of the people. The killing of the nun signified that Sendero, or some groups within it, had now declared war not just on projects but on churchpeople. In dozens of villages throughout Ayacucho, Apurímac, Junín, and other affected areas, Sendero systematically harassed and threatened church personnel and in most cases succeeded in driving them out.

As Sendero moved out of the Ayacucho area, going south toward Puno or north toward Cajamarca, it encountered resistance and rejection on the part of the vast majority of peasants. The reason in part was that Sendero had not spent years building up bases of operation in those areas as it had in Ayacucho. But there were two other significant differences between the new areas and Ayacucho. In the southern highlands, quite poor like Ayacucho, the peasants had already gone through a politicization process since the late 1950s and were highly organized in peasant leagues or unions. Leftist parties were quite strong in the entire region. In addition, the progressive southern Andean church had built up a popular church throughout the area that harmonized with the new political consciousness. In 1969 the Maryknoll Fathers closed down their minor seminary in Puno, which had failed noticeably to produce priests, and set out to train adult catechists in the villages. Other religious groups in the area followed suit. More than twenty years later, IPA (the Andean Pastoral Institute), founded first in Cuzco but later relocated in Sicuani, had trained hundreds of lay leaders, many of whom were also community leaders in the villages. In October 1984 the first regional convention of Christian peasant "Animators" (one of the variant words used for "catechist" or "pastoral agent") was held in Puno. Some 550 Quechua- and Aymara-speaking peasants, men and women, attended, all armed with the Bible and the social teachings of the church.[19] These lay church leaders have spread the seeds of Medellín (and liberation theology) to their communities. In this situation the peasants have found religion to be a force that strengthens community cohesion and motivates them to work for community development. After the attack on the peasant training school in Ayaviri, thousands of peasants marched in protest to attend a mass of solidarity celebrated by the apostolic administrator, Francisco D'Alteroche.

In the diocese of Cajamarca in the northern central Andes, Bishop José Dammert has also promoted development projects and education for the peasants. The Opus Dei dioceses of Abancay and Cañete also operate projects for the peasants, but there is a fundamental difference in the orientation given the peasants in the two situations. In Cajamarca the emphasis in the training programs is on community action as opposed to individual advancement. Furthermore, the peasants are encouraged to stand up for their rights, a fact that led to tension between the military government and Dammert. Perhaps the best example of the link between peasant assertiveness and the church is the *rondas*, bands of armed peasants who organized themselves in 1976 in order to protect their herds from bandits. Many of the *ronderos* are catechists who look upon their nightly vigils as a form of community service. Because they are armed, it is evident that they also represent a potentially serious obstacle to Sendero. In an interview in 1989 Dammert stated, "*Rondas* are the best form of democracy in Peru."[20] In the context of the war being waged throughout the Andes and the jungle, that statement was a challenge to both the government and Sendero.

The concept of community self-defense, a virtual necessity in Peru where the armed forces and the police have proven to be ineffectual in the war against terrorism, has been taken up by individual towns in the Andes, by unions, and by other private groups. In Villa El Salvador, a vast *pueblo jóven* of Lima, Miguel Azcueta, the leftist mayor and an ex-seminarian with close ties to the church, has also favored organizing defense groups against terrorism. In the middle of the eastern jungle, an American Franciscan, Father Mariano, tried arming the Ashaninkas Indians to resist Sendero, but he was finally driven out of the area.[21]

But churchpeople have to wrestle with another problem: The armed forces and the police can be as brutal as the terrorists, and they violate human rights with virtual impunity. Everywhere military and police commandos, sometimes disguised as terrorists, have raided villages, conducted summary executions of suspected terrorists, pillaged the countryside, and dragged hundreds of young people off to military compounds or detention centers. A counterterrorist organization called Comando Rodrigo Franco, founded in 1988, has assassinated many union and student leaders presumably because they were sympathetic to Sendero. Frequently, the police, the military, and politicians on the right have accused the church of catering to subversives. In November 1987 the Aprista mayor of Puno accused the foreign clergy in the area of supporting the subversives. Bishop Jesús Calderón retorted that the church was only guilty of following out its "option for the poor."[22] The mayor himself was later assassinated by the Shining Path. In many highland communities, the church is held in suspicion by both the terrorists and the armed forces.

Leadership from Below

The church's response to violence has ranged from courageous to timid, from creative and energetic to totally ineffectual. The national Bishops' Conference has issued many statements on violence and the social situation in Peru since 1980. One of the most eloquent was entitled "Choose Life," published in April 1990.[23] The difficulty with these pronouncements, however well-written they were, was that the conservative attack on liberation theology and the generally timid support given by the bishops to human rights groups tended to diffuse their impact. Far more effective was a pastoral letter of the southern Andean bishops, "Sow Life to Harvest Peace," written in 1988 following a wave of attacks by Sendero.[24] In the letter the bishops announced the creation of vicariates of solidarity to aid victims of terrorism and to defend human rights. With the notable exceptions of these and certain other progressive bishops, the peace and human rights initiative has been promoted primarily by groups within the church, not the hierarchy as a whole.

The most energetic official agency of the bishops in this regard is CEAS, the Bishops' Commission for Social Action, founded in the 1960s. After presiding over the commission since the beginning, Bishop Luis Bambarén was succeeded in 1988 by Miguel Irizar, a Spanish Passionist who had been bishop of Yurimaguas in the jungle. Consisting of a team of about twenty lawyers, social workers, and volunteer activists, CEAS has become one of the main channels in Peru for funneling cases of missing persons and violations of human rights. CEAS is limited by the fact that it does not enjoy the full support of the conservative bishops. But Irizar, once labeled a conservative himself, has defended his commission against other bishops. Under Bambarén and Irizar, CEAS has become the single most influential body within the church affecting official church statements on peace and violence. The bishops in the jungle sponsor a similar agency called CAAAP (Amazonian Center for Applied Pastoral Anthropology) that promotes the natives' culture and speaks out against violations of human rights.

Beyond these official church organs are myriad human rights groups in Peru, many of them closely tied to the church. The National Coordinator of Human Rights, a central office that coordinates all other human rights groups in Lima and elsewhere, is led by committed Christians, both lay and religious. One of the attention-drawing activities of the human rights groups and other grassroots Christian organizations has been the holding of peace marches. In order to counteract an armed strike that Sendero had announced in order to disrupt the November 1989 municipal elections, the leftist candidate for mayor, Henry Pease, summoned the city to have a peace march in Lima on the day of the strike. Close to 200,000 people showed up.[25] Similar marches were held in Huancayo, Piura, and other cities. In all of these cases, progressive Christians played an important role in organizing and leading the marches.

Now, in the early 1990s, the mood in the Peruvian church ranges from gloomy pessimism to cautious hope. Conservative bishops either restrain or dampen efforts to respond creatively to Peru's crises. Many believe that a decade has been lost in useless debates over liberation theology. No doubt relations between conservatives and progressives will be strained for quite some time, especially given Rome's policy of promoting the former and snubbing the latter. Coexistence without dialogue seems to characterize relations between many in the two camps. Yet in other situations poverty and violence have drawn the two together to stand on a middle ground. When faced with the spectacle of terrorism at his doorstep, the bishop of Huancayo appealed to the progressives for aid, and the bishops, frequently uncertain of what to do, look to both CEAS and CAAAP for an agenda. For their part, the teams that make up CEAS, CAAAP, and the human rights groups have offered their full support to the bishops in their quest for some kind of response to violence and poverty. In some cases that support has been accepted; in other cases it has been ignored. In the meantime, as Peru stumbles from one crisis to the next, the emerging popular classes continue to look to the church for leadership and moral support. If they do not find that guidance and support in the church, they are more likely than at any other time in Peruvian history to look elsewhere.

Postscript

Since the writing of this chapter Sendero Luminoso has escalated dramatically its attacks on the church. In May 1991, a Senderista column killed an Australian-born nun, Sister Irene McCormack, in the department of Junín. On August 10th two Polish Franciscan Missionaries, Zbgniew Stralkowski and Michael Tomaszek, were shot and killed by Sendero in a town near Chimbote on the northern coast. And toward the end of August an Italian priest, Allessandro Dordi, was also killed in the same area.

Notes

1. "Perú, 1989–1990: Informe de la Coordinadora Nacional de Derechos Humanos," Lima, August 1990, mimeo, p. 1. The statistics cited in the report are based on a Peruvian senate investigation into the causes of violence in Peru.
2. For different analyses of the story behind the various liberation theology documents, see Jeffrey Klaiber, *La Iglesia en el Perú* (Lima: Pontificia Universidad Católica, 1988), pp. 430–433; Catalina Romero, "The Peruvian Church: Change and Continuity," in Scott Mainwaring and Alexander Wilde, eds., *The Progressive Church in Latin America* (Notre Dame, Ind.: University of Notre Dame Press, 1989), pp. 258–259. See also Luis Pásara's analysis of the radical clergy in Peru in Mainwaring and Wilde, *The Progressive Church*, pp. 276–327.
3. For a view of the conservative shift in Peru see John A. McCoy, *America*, June 3, 1989, pp. 526–530.
4. Charles A. Reilly, "Latin America's Religious Populists," in Daniel H. Levine, ed., *Religion and Political Conflict in Latin America* (Chapel Hill: University of North Carolina Press, 1986), pp. 42–57. See also Jeffrey Klaiber, "Prophets and Populists: Liberation Theology, 1968–1988," *The Americas* 46 (July 1989), pp. 1–15.
5. Klaiber, *La Iglesia en el Perú*, pp. 60, 458.
6. The figure of approximately 5 percent referring to Protestants and the

non-Christian sects is based on national census figures. See ibid., pp. 478–479. Samuel Escobar, a Peruvian Protestant pastor, accepts those figures: "Protestant Minority Reaches Political Significance in Peru," *Pulse*, July 27, 1990, p. 4. For one of the few studies on Protestantism and the new religions, see Manuel Marzal, *Los caminos religiosos de los inmigrantes en la gran Lima* (Lima: Pontificia Universidad Católica, 1988).

7. *Latinamerica Press* (Lima), November 9, 1989, p. 2.

8. This author was an invited guest at one of the sessions of the CONEP pastors held in December 1989 in Lima. Information also derived from private interview with Dr. Carlos García García, Baptist minister and second vice-president of Peru, Lima, July 5, 1990.

9. Jeffrey Klaiber, "Fujimori: Race and Religion in Peru," *America*, September 8–15, pp. 133–135.

10. Luis Bambarén Gastelumendi, *Sectas y política* (Lima: Empresa Editora Latina, 1990), p. 5.

11. Interview with Bishop José Dammert, *Página Libre* (Lima), Sunday supplement, June 3, 1990, p. B5.

12. For two accounts by specialists on the Shining Path and its origins, see David Scott Palmer, "Terrorism as a Revolutionary Strategy: Peru's Sendero Luminoso," in Barry Rubin, ed., *The Politics of Terrorism: Terror as a State and Revolutionary Strategy* (Lanham, Md.: University Press of America, 1989), pp. 129–152; and Cynthia McClintock, "Peru's Sendero Luminoso Rebellion: Origins and Trajectory," in Susan Eckstein, ed., *Power and Popular Protest: Latin American Social Movements* (Berkeley: University of California Press, 1989), pp. 61–101.

13. McClintock, "Peru's Sendero Luminoso Rebellion," p. 61.

14. *Latinamerica Press*, October 25, 1990, p. 7.

15. *Latinamerica Press*, January 26, 1989, p. 5.

16. *Latinamerica Press*, June 8, 1989, pp. 1–2.

17. *Latinamerica Press*, July 6, 1989, p. 2.

18. *Catholic News Service*, October 8, 1990, p. 10.

19. Klaiber, *La iglesia en el Perú*, p. 439.

20. *Latinamerica Press*, March 16, 1989, p. 5.

21. Gustavo Gorriti, "Terror in the Andes," *New York Times Magazine*, December 2, 1990, pp. 40–48, 65–72.

22. *La República* (Lima), November 26, 1987, pp. 1, 8; (*LADOC*), May/June 1988, pp. 19–21.

23. *LADOC*, September/October 1990, pp. 20–29.

24. *LADOC*, March/April 1988, pp. 21–27.

25. *News Notes* (Maryknoll Justice and Peace Office, Washington, D.C.), January/February 1990, pp. 23–25.

CHAPTER 6

The Catholic Church and Politics in Venezuela: Resource Limitations, Religious Competition, and Democracy

BRIAN FROEHLE

Venezuelan Catholicism, described in the 1930s as anomalous to its counterparts in the rest of Latin America,[1] today is not only a representative case but also suggestive of possible religious futures elsewhere in Latin America. The Venezuelan Catholic church has more than thirty years of experience operating within a political democracy as a respected member of civil society. It has long experience with limited finances and personnel and is conscious of the increasing inroads of religious competition arising from evangelicals and other religious movements of non-Catholic inspiration.

In this chapter I first discuss how the historically specific experience of the Venezuelan church has shaped its understanding of the world in which it operates and at the same time has led to the challenges it now faces. Second, I analyze the impact of limited resources and religious competition experienced by the church in Venezuela on a microlevel by bringing into focus the church of Caracas. Catholic and non-Catholic religious organizations are examined at their institutional and individual levels in order to portray contemporary Venezuelan religious reality and transformation at the community level. I conclude by considering the effect changing social and political realities have had on the framing of meaning within Venezuelan religious life. The emerging structures and meanings of the different religious groups promise potentially dramatic effects on the society within which they operate.

The Venezuelan Catholic Experience

The Historical Context

During three centuries of colonial rule, the Venezuelan church was neither as powerful as the churches of the major viceregal capitals of the empire such as Mexico City, Lima, or Bogotá nor as weak as those of the relatively declining Antillean region or the frontier areas of the southern cone. Rather, the Venezuelan church occupied a middle position, comparable to its counterparts in Central America—prosperous, expanding, and sufficiently financed and staffed, yet hardly in the luxurious situation of being located in the regions of vast wealth, political prominence, and cultural advancement characteristic of the former centers of the indigenous empires conquered by the Spanish.[2] Although it had fewer than half the priests of the more developed archdioceses of colonial Latin America, the extensive archdiocese of Caracas nevertheless did have the greatest income, as measured by the royal tithe, of any archdiocese in colonial Latin America by the end of the eighteenth century.[3]

A century later, the Venezuelan church had become one of the most marginal in Latin America in terms of its resources, institutional development, and political relevancy. The political program that led to the series of reversals the church experienced during the nineteenth century was inspired by Enlightenment thinking. It was largely based on French and Spanish revolutionary decrees designed to curtail powerful privileged social elements. However, Venezuelan civil society was weak, and the real power of the church hardly compared to the European models. The first and most encompassing piece of restrictive legislation was the 1824 Law of Patronage, whereby the state claimed the power to establish ecclesiastical divisions, appoint bishops, restrict activities of religious orders, and control migration of foreign priests. Anticlerical legislation continued, reaching its zenith in the 1870s during the regime of Antonio Guzmán Blanco, who found the church to be the only independent source of opposition, however weak, to his personal authority. He thus completed the already established anticlerical program in a particularly thoroughgoing way. The life cycle was completely desacralized. Births and marriages were secularized, as were cemeteries. All religious orders were expelled and their property seized. All seminaries were closed. Attempts were made to foster rival belief systems, and there was even talk of creating a national Venezuelan church separated from allegiance to Rome. By the end of his rule, the church was for all practical purposes nonexistent as a force in the life of civil society.

By the last decade of the nineteenth century, the process of rebuilding the Venezuelan church began, and not surprisingly the model followed was one exclusively religious, conscious of limitations within an inhospitable political climate. During the series of dictatorial governments that followed, the church carefully avoided political entanglements. It kept a low political profile and neither excessively committed itself to nor explicitly opposed any government. All the while it sought loopholes and advantages where it could, attempting in the process to rebuild and expand its institutional space.[4]

The nineteenth-century decline in the institutional presence of the church in society—a phenomenon by no means unique to Venezuela—is perhaps best measured by the decline in clergy and the number of unstaffed parishes resulting from this decline. During the height of the colonial period, priests had increased dramatically, from 456 in 1784 to 547 in 1810 and to 640 by 1820. In the aftermath of independence and civil wars, as well as ensuing restrictive legislation, their number decreased to 440 by 1847. Those remaining were for the most part old or infirm, and only 273 were physically able to attend parishes, leaving 40 percent of the parishes unattended. A few years later, in 1855, only 154 priests were left in the country, rendering some 68 percent of the parishes abandoned. By the census of 1881, conditions had stabilized, the number of priests had increased to 255, and 40 percent of the parishes were again staffed regularly.[5] Given that the boundaries of each parish were usually coterminous with those of the civil division in which it was situated, each unattended parish generally meant that inhabitants of a town of some size and its hinterland had no contact with the institutional church. The population, however, did not stop being Catholic. Rather, it substituted for orthodox practice and formation formerly offered by the priest the religious practices and formation within the family, chiefly that given by mothers and grandmothers from generation to generation. As a result, Venezuelan Catholicism has demanded lay initiative and been less clerical in practice. Accompanying this development, popular Catholicism became the religious norm in many areas of the country as religious practices and beliefs came to be increasingly unmediated by religious elites. Popular religiosity effectively replaced official colonial Catholicism as a form of civil religion.

Institutional Strategies and Class Alliances

The Venezuelan church's almost complete lack of class or institutional allies put it in a somewhat different position from other Latin American churches during the nineteenth century.[6] The particular form of plantation economy used in cacao production during the colonial period, the key industry of the time, had effectively discouraged the development of a "traditional" landholding aristocracy favoring the church. Use of imported, replaceable slaves in place of indigenous labor mitigated the need for a religious ideology that would produce a docile labor force. Further, the rationalist, agricultural capitalist class that emerged was highly dependent on the Caribbean trade routes of the Dutch and English, the traditional source of Enlightenment ideas in the Americas. Not surprisingly, the Venezuelan colonial elite was among the most enlightened and anticlerical of the continent. After independence, Venezuelan institutions such as the army were at best indifferent to the problems the church experienced and often were led or controlled by precisely the same persons who directed an unfriendly state. Civil society remained weak, the result of the colonial heritage, continuing political upheavals, endemic civil wars, and a dislocated, unproductive plantation economy.

Insofar as church personnel also came from the national period of the enlightenment, they influenced the local intellectual environment, and in the early years of independence, many priests were among those who attacked the privileges of the church. By the end of the nineteenth century, however, church leaders and ordinary clergy alike had become ardent supporters of the papacy as a result of their definitively weak position vis-à-vis the state. Under the impetus given by the first Latin American Bishops' Conference of 1899–1900, the first conference of Venezuelan bishops in 1904, and the International Eucharistic Congress celebrated in Caracas in 1907,[7] the church began to develop organizationally and increase its social projection. More parishes were served than ever, clergy increased, and the bishops began to have regular consultations with each other and issue joint pastoral letters.

The lack of class or institutional allies continued to be a pressing problem for the church. In this regard, the decision made during the early twentieth century to adopt the heavily institutional program followed in most of the Catholic world at the time had a special role in Venezuela. The building and promotion of educational institutions soon became by default the major rebuilding strategy of the Venezuelan church. This policy permitted the church to develop a constituency that could be counted on to identify its interests with those of the church.

Precisely during the time when Catholic schools began to expand dramatically, the incipient urban professional class was in a very fragile position. Although these middle sectors aspired to play a leading role in the transformation of Venezuela from a backward plantation society to an industrial, urbanized one, they were unable to reproduce themselves without education and were confronted by a notable absence of government schools. Their invaluable ally thus became the expanding, vigorous Catholic school system of low-cost, imported European teachers recruited from religious orders and congregations. By 1944, half of all students in secondary schools were in Catholic schools.[8] Once the state became more committed to education, this number would decrease significantly, but Catholic schools would continue to have a special place in the life of the urban middle classes. The relationship was mutual, and the church came to expect that it could rely on this group for defense when necessary. Precisely such a moment came when the government attempted to nationalize aspects of the church's school system in 1946 and 1947.[9] Threatened with the loss of its patient, arduous work of the previous half century, the church desperately committed its resources to what became virtually a crusade for survival that can only be understood in light of its previous losses. The church spearheaded a countermovement against the "communist and atheist" government—and for the first time found itself on the winning side in a confrontation with the state. Indeed, when the existing government collapsed in 1948, a myth developed that it had failed largely because it had opposed the church.[10] In fact, the victory came about more through a coup led by military officers interested in eliminating the "radicalism" of the civilian government.

The shared preoccupation with communism characteristic of the church and succeeding military regimes during this period resulted in relatively more acceptance and freedom of action than had been the rule previously. With the definitive establishment of a democratic regime in 1958, church and state were also able to find common ground in their rejection of communism and interest in political stability. The leading party of the democratic transition—precisely the despised adversary of the educational struggle a decade earlier—had since purged itself of radical and anticlerical elements and sought the support of the church and its middle-class allies in shoring up the regime against guerrilla attacks and alleged Cuban infiltrations as well as conservative, antidemocratic opposition. For its part, the church came to accept its former enemies as preferable to what had occurred in Cuba. The church was able to increase its political prestige between the end of the dictatorship and the rise of democracy, confident that its declarations, no less than the forces it had mobilized, largely through the schools, had been key players in the successful birth of a new era of democratic politics.[11] Reflecting the new cordiality in church-state relations was the elimination in 1969 of the Law of Patronage, which was replaced with a definitive ecclesiastical status negotiated with the Vatican to the satisfaction of both parties.[12]

Implications of the Institution-Building Program

By the 1960s the strategy of building the church through the development of a school system for urban middle-class youth came to present three major contradictions.

First, this strategy solved the problem of the shortage of personnel, but only in the short term. The schools founded were run by European, chiefly Spanish, religious orders. This situation continues: More than 70 percent of the Catholic schools in the country remain in the direct control of religious orders and congregations, and only 10 percent are controlled by the parishes.[13] By the 1960s, these religious groups had created Venezuelan administrative subdivisions, thereby promoting more local planning and administration. However, insufficient new adherents to vocations emerged to change the imbalance between foreign-born (often naturalized) religious and their native recruits. In terms of personnel, this is a long-term problem that will not be fully felt until the last of the imported religious of the 1960s pass their productive years.

Second, dependence on religious orders for church personnel has promoted the decentralization of church resources and reduced the role of the local diocesan church as a coherent unit. Foreign religious congregations had relatively plentiful supplies of personnel until about 1965, and the Venezuelan bishops, not unlike their counterparts throughout the continent, saw no other way to staff the new parishes made necessary by accelerating population growth. The local church came to depend excessively on foreign priests, particularly foreign-born members of religious orders.[14] As a result, once religious-order priests began to enter the country in substantial numbers by the 1930s, the number of total priests per inhabitant remained steady until the 1960s in spite of rapid population growth. In 1912, there were 5,600 inhabitants per diocesan priest, at that time virtually the only priests in the country. By 1960, there were 5,500 persons per any type of priest in the country, including religious-order priests, who by then represented 55 percent of the total number of priests. At the same time, the number of persons per parish was rising sharply. In effect, the relative social projection of Catholic church personnel had shifted dramatically away from parish work because religious priests most commonly were to be found in the schools.[15] Today, religious-order priests still constitute 55 percent of the total number of priests, but diocesan clergy have been increasing relatively more rapidly. Although growth rates for both are positive, they are considerably less than the population growth rate. In the 1980s, the population increased by 2.5 percent annually, and priests by 1.2 percent.[16]

The presence of religious priests in parish life in Latin America relative to Europe or North America underlines their special role in the region. Very few European countries have more than 10 percent of their parishes conducted by religious orders, and no more than some 15 percent of parishes in the United States and Canada are so administered. Of twenty Latin American countries, however, seventeen have more than 20 percent of their parishes in nondiocesan hands.[17] Venezuela is at the Latin American average, with 28 percent of its parishes administered by religious orders or congregations.

The presence of religious, religious parishes, and foreign-born priests relative to their native counterparts tends to reduce the ability of the local hierarchies to control Catholic activity in their dioceses. This is all the more so when the foreign diocesan and religious priests staffing the parishes come from cultural perspectives and historical traditions significantly different from those of local church leaders.[18] Further, religious orders and congregations of priests and sisters more commonly identify with progressive political and ecclesial positions than do bishops and diocesan priests. The independent resource and formation networks of religious priests and sisters remove them from direct communication lines with the hierarchy and thus from conservative tendencies stemming from local church policy and Vatican influences. Many religious are also involved in pastoral work in poor neighborhoods, which in itself promotes isolation from specifically ecclesiastical issues while widening concern for social problems and political issues. As a result of these factors, although over time church organization has become more complex at the top, the church's ability to control those at the bottom remains limited. Leadership remains possible but difficult, and the role of the bishops has therefore typically been to bless initiatives after they have been shown successful rather than to set priorities and invest their limited resources in possibly risky new programs.

Third, a focus on institution building has implied that resources were to be committed not only in the short term but over the long term, thereby sacrificing a certain degree of flexibility. The schools that the religious communities conducted fit well with the ecclesiology of Christendom that prevailed until the aggiornamento of the 1960s. They were a closed universe, a fortress of Catholicism where students would be prepared to go out and do battle with an indifferent society that must in the end follow the lead of Catholicism. Such a worldview had a certain affinity with the prevailing model of religious life common at the time. If not "cloistered," then at least the model was for these groups of religious to live and teach on-site in their institution and devote themselves to their students and their spiritual development. This model found itself questioned as the "signs of the times" were read during the 1960s and Catholic leaders throughout the world reconsidered the direction of their past efforts. The effects of such reconsiderations would be all the more powerful in a country where such a single-minded effort had been devoted to the development of the schools, which until that moment had been an absolutely uncompromisable rebuilding strategy.

Indicative of the shifting outreach characterizing Catholic education since the post-Medellín period, a survey of Catholic educators in 1974 found some 81 percent in favor of orienting Catholic education toward the poor and reducing the overall effort spent in education of the rich.[19] In 1991, however, the Venezuelan Association of Catholic Schools (AVEC), the umbrella organization of Venezuelan Catholic schools, was still planning how to "popularize" the schools to a greater degree, proposing that those in poor areas more fully integrate themselves into the local community and that schools in rich areas preferentially admit poor students from nearby neighborhoods.[20] The most common response of the religious congregations to the dramatic postconciliar changes in orientation was to keep the existing schools open but to open no more, gradually shifting religious personnel from education to pastoral work in the dramatically expanding shantytowns of the major cities. In itself, this has been a most challenging task and, given institutional commitments, impossible to ex-

ecute rapidly. Religious groups made little progress in detaching themselves from their educational institutions in the late 1960s and early 1970s,
but by the early 1980s this process had advanced considerably.[21] Between
1978 and 1984 alone, the percentage of religious dedicated to educational
activities declined from 51 percent to 28 percent.[22]

Tendencies in the Church Today: Quiet Cacophony

The change from an eminently institution-centered ministry to one involving more open-ended pastoral work in the barrios was not made to create
a new class clientele for the church, but rather derived from a new
understanding of the gospel and the role of Christian ministry. Since then,
church personnel have contributed considerably to popular organizations,
nongovernmental social services, and informal education in poor neighborhoods. The social and political impact of this shift has been notable
and began precisely when the urban popular sectors were expanding most
dramatically. Just as the institutional strategy to develop education
resulted, somewhat unexpectedly, in an alliance of mutual interests between the middle class and the church, so too the response to the
"preferential option for the poor" cultivated a new social constituency.
Nevertheless, one must be cautious in coming to any strong conclusions
regarding this new focus of church activity. Although political understandings have changed in some sectors of the church, and organization
of the poor by Catholic activists has increased, spillover effects are relatively limited because this phenomenon has never been characteristic of
the institutional church as a whole but rather of an activist minority. At
the same time, though the poor are a key political sector by virtue of sheer
numbers, one cannot expect this new relation to have the same effect as
the older ties with the middle classes, which brought significant social
resources to their alliance with the church.

The impact of the new social orientation of the postconciliar church
was perhaps even more profound in internal church politics. In the wake
of the new emphasis on serving the poor, increasing discord developed
between those who favored the newer, explicitly political agenda and
those who preferred to continue the earlier program of internal institution
building. As has been the case throughout Latin America and the church
in general, this turn toward the social gospel has changed the discourse
with which church members and leaders relate to and understand politics.
One notable example in Venezuela was the turn made by the Jesuits who
published the magazine *SIC*, created during the 1930s as the organ of the
interdiocesan seminary and dedicated to internal church issues. In the
1960s, the magazine was reoriented toward national and international
social issues, and its content strongly questioned the traditional, cautious
politics practiced by church leaders and urged more radical options from

within the framework of a church dedicated to the poor.[23]

By 1972, conflicts in the Venezuelan church between conservatives and progressives reached a point of crisis. These developments occurred when they did for several key reasons. First, the conflicts with the church took place during a stable democratic regime hospitable to the church. Thus, there were no strong external threats to encourage internal church unity. Second, institutional memory of difficult church-state relations precluded any interest the hierarchy might have had in new external commitments that could risk its institutional gains. Third, the lack of personnel and resources made it seem unwise to take on new commitments when the ongoing project of institution building had been so promising. As such, the conservatives, fearful of losing their hegemony, moved effectively to prevent any change in direction at the organizational level.[24]

The immediate conservative response appeared definitive. Progressive institutes were closed, movement organizations were dissolved or stripped of their church affiliation, and progressive church leaders were transferred to nonthreatening positions or simply fired. Yet after conservative elements of the hierarchy assured themselves of formal institutional control and progressives conceded their losses in exchange for autonomous action within their own spheres, hostilities mellowed. The country and the population are simply so vast relative to the limited human and material resources of the church that virtually any form of Catholic ministry is usually, by necessity, either accepted, bargained with, or blithely ignored by the hierarchy. To be overly ideological at the expense of a compromising, pragmatic spirit would simply sacrifice too much for either side. The hierarchy cannot afford to lose the already minimal presence of the church in most social sectors and innovators would rather expend their limited energy on their projects than on the ecclesiastical battlefield. An indication of the notable success of the progressive project twenty years after its supposed defeat may be measured by the progressive Inter-Religious Theological Seminary in Caracas, established in 1980 as the chief advanced training ground for religious in the country. This institute forms part of a network that connects religious activists with social and pastoral work while serving as a space for the development of their theological and ecclesial perspectives. In the final analysis, the Venezuelan church simply goes in many directions at once, and the most compelling result of the struggles between conservatives and progressives has been that both the winners and losers are stronger than ever today. The Venezuelan hierarchy instinctively articulates a "chord" of explicit cautiousness and orthodoxy combined with an implicit spirit of compromise and coexistence. At the same time, many Venezuelan religious orders and congregations, among others, have adopted a notably progressive chord, creating durable networks of institutions and contacts while explicitly cultivating a peaceful coexistence with the institution and implicitly accepting their nondominant status within the larger church community. Only the future will tell whether these chords will be able to be articulated from cacophony to symphony in order to meet common goals.

The Postconciliar Catholic Project and Religious Competition

New Challenges

The contemporary Venezuelan church, like many other Latin American churches, may be characterized as an understaffed, underfunded institution with relatively few strongly committed members. Unlike European Catholic countries that average between 2,500 to 5,000 persons per parish, Latin America in general averages over 18,000 persons per parish and Venezuela has some 20,055 persons per parish.[25] Using the average size of churches and chapels in Caracas and the average number of weekly masses celebrated in them, I estimate that 2,000 persons at maximum are able to attend mass within an average parish over the course of a year, at least on a sporadic or standing-room basis. This indicator suggests that over 50 percent of Europeans in Catholic countries have an opportunity formally to practice Catholicism and participate in parish life, whereas only from 2 to 19 percent of Latin Americans do, depending on the country. About 10 percent of the Latin American population as a whole, and a similar percentage of Venezuelans in particular, may thus be expected to participate in local parish life. The situation is reversed north of the Rio Grande: Subtracting out the protestant majorities in North America leaves as few as 3,675 Catholics per parish in the United States and Canada. That is, over 50 percent of North American Catholics but less than 10 percent of Latin Americans, Venezuelans included, may be touched by parish structure and personnel.

The challenge for the Latin American Bishops' Conference in 1992, the so-called "new evangelization" proclaimed by the bishops and the pope as the conference theme, has perhaps even further-reaching implications than those of the Medellín conference in terms of the long-term future of the Latin American church. In large part, of course, the impact of this new agenda will depend on just how "evangelization" is interpreted.[26] At the beginning of Lent 1990, in order "to prepare for the fifth centennial of the evangelization of America," a catechism was distributed free in every newspaper purchased in the greater Caracas metropolitan region. This catechism was a reprint of one written by Caracas Archbishop Rafael Arias Blanco in the late 1950s and is a virtual twin of the Baltimore catechism, presented in a question-and-answer, true-false fashion.[27] There was no observable impact of this effort, and this particular booklet, in spite of its enormous dissemination, seems to have lasted no longer than the editions of the newspapers that accompanied it.

Should a more serious commitment on the part of the bishops' conferences and the church in general be made to evangelization, profound consideration of the dynamics behind the notable expansion of the evangelical churches will have to be made. Between 1967 and 1980, the Venezuelan evangelical movement began to grow spectacularly, increasing from some 47,000 to 500,000 members.[28] Simple explanations of this as a passing phenomenon created by politically motivated foreign sponsors and resources do not account for the dramatic, growing numbers of enthusiastic adherents of these new religious movements. Indeed, although Venezuelan evangelical churches grew out of British and North American mission efforts dating back to the end of the nineteenth century, the great majority of these churches are now completely independent of the original missions and fully national in terms of their financial and personnel resources.[29] Proportionally, the number of nonnative evangelical pastors today is insignificant. In contrast, the available data for Catholicism present a different situation. A 1984 study found that 984 of 1,077 Catholic religious order priests, or 94 percent of the total, were not born in Venezuela.[30] In Caracas, 68 percent of all parish pastors (53 percent of the diocesan ones and 90 percent of the religious) are foreign-born. At the very least, such data make relative the "foreign factor" cited by many Venezuelan Catholic church officials as being a principal cause for the continuing development of evangelical groups[31] when precisely such a factor accounts even more for the continuing vitality of Venezuelan Catholicism and much of Latin American Catholicism in general.

In order for the Venezuelan Catholic church to initiate a process of reevangelization, a better understanding of the emergence and dramatically increasing appeal of the evangelicals is required. In any such explanation, consideration must be given to the changing ideas and meanings given to religion as Latin American societies completed the transition from a rural plantation society to an urban service economy. In the new urban environment, the traditional Catholic approaches no longer work, and newer ones have proved insufficient to prevent the increasing consolidation of the religious alternative represented by evangelicals. At the same time, the extraordinary deficits of Catholic personnel and infrastructure relative to the population and the rapid and unproblematic expansion of evangelical pastors suggest a far-reaching challenge to the future of Catholicism.

Caracas: Religious Change and Competition

During the 1950s and 1960s, urban popular sectors in Latin America began to grow dramatically, and those of Caracas were no exception. Between

1958 and 1962 alone, its impoverished sectors grew by some 200,000 additional residents.[32] These were also the decades of the first dramatic expansion in evangelical and other non-Catholic religious movements. In 1967, there were 75 evangelical churches and 233 Catholic places of worship in Caracas. By 1990, Catholic churches or chapels where weekly worship was conducted numbered 217, whereas evangelical sites of weekly worship alone numbered 239, and other non-Catholic sites of Christian worship may be estimated as an additional 30.

In early efforts to counteract these developments, Catholic church leaders in Caracas commonly pursued a strategy based on the Christendom mentality of providing institutional fortresses to combat "the threat every day more manifest of sectarian infiltration, as much protestant as communist."[33] By the late 1960s, difficulties in erecting sufficient institutional fortresses, combined with new ways of thinking after the Vatican Council and the Medellín conference, led the Caracas archdiocese to develop two new forms of providing ministry to the expanding neighborhoods of the urban poor: religious vicariates and evangelization centers.

Religious vicariates owe their existence to post–Vatican II changes in canon law that permitted religious congregations of women to administer portions of parishes; evangelization centers are an invention of the archdiocese. These centers developed from post–Vatican II initiatives of a variety of religious congregations and orders that attempted to share the living conditions characteristic of the impoverished majority without formally constituting parishes.[34] The first centers were created when Maryknoll was turning over its parishes to diocesan control and redirecting efforts toward nonparish, pastoral work in the poorest neighborhoods with teams of priests and lay volunteers. Because these centers are typically composed of priests, they tend to involve more sacramental activity than the vicariates and offer relatively fewer community services and outreach than vicariates.

In many ways, these new forms of local church life are not particularly different from parishes in popular areas. The emphasis remains one of youth groups, catecheses, and community resources. The intent, nevertheless, is to present a ministry closer to the community and less institutional than the traditional parish. These organizations have enjoyed slow but undiminished growth, increasing from 8 in 1972 to 24 by 1990.[35] Because only 22 of the 104 traditional territorial-based parishes of the archdiocese are located in similar social sectors these pastoral centers are a key part of the Catholic presence in those social sectors that comprise over half of the city's population. These new forms of local church life nevertheless remain affiliated with a mother parish and often dependent on it for sacramental services. These experiments have ensured a continuing Catholic presence in the popular sector, but by no means have they reduced the threat to the Catholic religious monopoly presented by the

Table 6.1 Relative Social Locations of Religious Organizations in Caracas, 1990 (percentages)

Social Range of Population	Evangelical Churches	Catholic Religious	Catholic Parishes
Upper 19	18	44	37
Middle 38	54	44	52
Bottom 44	28	13	12

Source: Survey by Brian Froehle, 1990.
Note: Columns may not total 100% due to rounding.

dynamic new non-Catholic churches.

The data on the social strata in which Catholic and evangelical groups are found indicate a tendency of Catholic institutions to be located in middle and upper sectors, and a contrasting tendency of evangelical organizations toward location within middle and lower portions of the population (see Table 6.1). The relatively rich presence of Catholic organization in privileged social sectors may explain why the evangelical newcomers have concentrated on less privileged areas. Such a division may also have to do with the considerably greater indifference institutional Catholicism has traditionally encountered in the popular sectors.[36] The evangelical presence in such areas may also reflect certain affinities underprivileged classes have for salvational, congregational religion.[37] In any case, these data underline the relative difficulties the Catholic church has had in keeping up with population growth and evangelical competition, particularly in the rapidly growing popular classes.

Although evangelicals in general and Pentecostals in particular have a strong presence in the lower classes, to locate the social prospects of the evangelicals in the "uprooted and marginal," as many have argued,[38] is not confirmed by the evidence in Caracas. Case studies of evangelical churches and interviews of their members indicate that they are hardly marginal to economic and political life and no more "uprooted" than their nonevangelical neighbors. Further, although more present in poor areas than Catholic organizations, evangelical and Pentecostal churches are relatively less present among the poorest. Only 28 percent of the evangelical churches of Caracas are located among the poorest 44 percent of the population. In a social ranking in which 1 represents the most affluent areas and 10 the least affluent,[39] the locations of the 166 Pentecostal evangelical churches average a ranking of 7, and those of the 73 non-Pentecostal evangelical churches a 5.

Table 6.2 A Sample of Neighborhood Religious Activity by Social Strata

Social Range of Population	Religion	Average Number of Churches	Founding Date	Percent of Total Attendance Per Religious Group
Upper (19%)	Catholics	5	1824	59
	Protestants	3	1961	14
Middle (38%)	Catholics	16	1952	28
	Protestants	24	1977	74
Lower (44%)	Catholics	8	1969	13
	Protestants	8	1978	12

Source: Survey by Brian Froehle, 1990.

In order to understand more clearly the religious activity charac-teristic of individuals in relation to their social strata, I collected detailed data on all public places of regular worship within a stratified random sample of socially homogeneous areas in Caracas. In the sampled areas, 45 percent of all the places of public Christian worship are Catholic. Of those persons who attend any weekly worship in a given week in these areas, 68 percent attended Catholic places of worship, 26 percent evan-gelical ones, and 6 percent churches of denominations traditionally out-side the evangelical mainstream such as the Jehovah's Witnesses or Seventh-Day Adventists.

Presented in Table 6.2 are the number of churches, their average founding dates, and the percentage of total attendance for Catholics or non-Catholics found in each social strata of the sample. The data indicate an overwhelmingly strong Catholic presence in the most affluent portion of the population where it has traditionally been established. The upper and upper-middle classes have long been closely affiliated with institu-tional Catholicism through their ties to Catholic schools and social tradi-tion. Some 59 percent of all Catholic attendance on any given Sunday occurs within the upper 19 percent of the population. In contrast, only 14 percent of non-Catholic attendance is found in these strata. Nevertheless, it was within these areas that Protestantism first established itself. The oldest, most traditional evangelical churches are located here. The middle range of the sample was found to contain the highest relative concentra-tion of evangelicals. In fact, in absolute numbers, more non-Catholics than Catholics attend churches within this middle range. Evangelical activity in these areas is of a considerably more recent nature than its Catholic counterpart and on average dates to the 1970s. The Catholic churches and chapels within these areas trace their roots to the 1950s when large numbers of fresh foreign recruits so invigorated the institutional expansion program of the time. Finally, although the number of churches is the same, there are more persons in attendance at Catholic churches than non-Catholic ones in the poorest areas of the sample. However, the evangelical movement seems to be making its most recent gains here. The moment when Catholic pastoral activity began to be focused on the needs of the poorest in the late 1960s was also the time when the number of persons called to vocations plummeted; thus, available recruits to carry on a program of vigorous, expanding Catholic ministry in difficult environments dramatically decreased. In any case, this portion of the sample remains the least touched by institutional religion—only 13 percent of those who are in any church on any given Sunday may be found within the kinds of areas where the lower 44 percent of the population lives.

Individual-Level Data: The Urban Population in General

Available data on individual religious behavior, although limited, are helpful in identifying what kinds of people are more likely to attend weekly services and how often this practice occurs in the population. Individual-level data are also helpful in understanding relative Catholic and evangelical dynamics and suggest how profound the social impact of contemporary religious transformation may actually be.

In a random survey I conducted, 88 percent of those persons surveyed identified themselves as Catholics. Sixteen percent of those, or 14 percent of the total sample, reported attending mass during the previous weekend. Of the Protestants, 7 percent of the sample, 71 percent reported that they had attended services. This difference is quite impressive in itself, but there is reason to believe that Catholic attendance is even lower than actually reported. Archival data on Catholic places of worship, seating space, and the numbers of available celebrants within the territory that today comprises the archdiocese of Caracas suggest that the proportion of the population that could have attended Catholic mass on any particular Sunday dropped from 13 percent in 1950 to 8 percent by 1990. Attendance figures collected from priests at every place of Catholic worship in the archdiocese for 1990 indicate that no more than 6 percent of the entire population actually attended Catholic worship on any particular Sunday that year. During times when there may be a greater general interest in attending, such as Christmas or Easter, the churches may of course be filled, though overall the percentage of the population in attendance does not dramatically change. In any case, such low percentages of regular weekly mass attendance are by no means unheard of within the Catholic

Table 6.3 Social Characteristics of Persons Reporting Attending Mass in Caracas, 1989

Social Characteristics		Percentage Attending Weekly
Gender:	Female	61
	Male	39
Age:	15–24	29
	25–44	26
	45+	45
Education:	Primary	26
	Secondary	29
	Superior	45

Source: Encuesta sociopastoral de Caracas: Resultados globales (Caracas: Centro de Investigación en Ciencias Sociales [CISOR], 1989)

world. According to available studies, less than 10 percent of the population attends weekly mass in such European cities such as Florence,[40] Pisa,[41] Paris,[42] and Brussels.[43]

The social characteristics of those likely to attend Catholic services are suggested by a 1989 pastoral survey of Caracas conducted for the archdiocese.[44] In accord with traditional cultural patterns, a majority of those persons who report attendance are women (see Table 6.3). Further, although the national age distribution is concentrated in the younger ages, attendance is skewed toward the older age groups. Consistent with its middle-class character, the church draws a plurality of attendees from among those who have completed advanced levels of schooling, a characteristic at the same time more common in the younger generation. This suggests that there may be two contrasting poles in the church around which group life and a common discourse may develop, one of older women and another of relatively well-educated young adults.

Underlining the importance Catholic schools have had in building commitment to the Venezuelan Catholic church is the fact that 55 percent of those who reported attending mass at least once a month also reported having attended Catholic schools, although such schools have had less than 10 percent of the school-age population for decades. This echoes Greeley's studies on the impact of US Catholic education on Catholic practice and commitment.[45] In terms of sacramental practice, 44 percent of those who described themselves as practicing Catholics reported that they never or almost never receive communion when they attend mass. Such a separation between the laity and the sacred is found neither in folk Catholicism, with its emphasis on sacred objects and rites within the reach of all,[46] nor in evangelical Christianity, which often highlights the direct accessibility of a personal God through prayer, Holy Spirit–filled experiences, and the Bible.

Shifting Frames in Changing Contexts

Like any social movement, religious groups must be able to attract members, cultivate commitment, and reproduce themselves. What makes religious movements particularly interesting is that in addition to offering their publics incentives of social goods, such as social networks, schooling, and social services, they offer spiritual incentives, in the process giving a code of conduct and a sense of meaning to people's lives. Both the social and spiritual dimensions of religion are key to understanding why individuals are more drawn to one group or another or to any at all.

The long-standing affinity in Venezuela between the Catholic church and the more affluent social sectors is a case in point. The social goods the church offered, particularly the schools, fit the social needs of the middle class. At the same time, the traditional message of affirmation the Catholic church offers found a certain resonance in the spiritual environment of this social sector. In contrast, evangelicals project a frame centered on conversion—the notion that one needs to work out one's salvation following behavior patterns that often starkly contrast with those of one's peers. Such a countercultural yet profoundly personal message implies a different audience in terms of class and personal experience. As interviews indicate, many of those who find this frame appealing have undergone some sort of personal crisis and seek the support that can often only be found in small, highly committed religious groups. The tendency of Pentecostal groups to be located in relatively poorer areas than traditional evangelicals suggests that an emphasis on the power of the Holy Spirit, outside the control of the recipient, makes more sense to people for whom control is seldom an option.

In a climate of religious competition, religious movements are influenced by their competitors, both consciously and unconsciously, no less than by their social environment. In stable and relatively more affluent areas, where evangelical competition has been relatively limited, the Catholic church largely continues to emphasize its traditional themes, whereas within popular sectors, there has been more experimentation with congregational styles of ministry and organization. The religious vicariates and the evangelization centers previously mentioned are two examples of this, as are the socially oriented CEBs and the internally focused neocatechumenate groups. These latter two types of organizations are designed to produce small grassroots groups in order to heighten in a communitarian, congregational way the role of the Scriptures in members' lives.[47] The charismatics, originally a middle-class phenomenon, have become increasingly characteristic of lower-class parish life and bring in new orientations toward spontaneous prayer and fervent, animated worship, including an emphasis on divine healing and speaking in tongues.[48]

The change has been significant. Traditional devotional groups, such as *cofradías*, accounted for some 35 percent of all Catholic parish groups in 1967 and only 24 percent of all groups in 1990. Centrally organized church groups, such as Catholic Action, the Cursillo movement, and the Christian Family Movement, declined from 24 percent of all Catholic parish groups in 1967 to only 7 percent in 1990. In contrast, the more congregational-style groups, which were nonexistent in 1967, such as charismatic groups, CEBs, and neocatechumenate communities, now constitute 10 percent of all parish groups. Correspondingly, youth groups, which also place relatively greater emphasis on group dynamics than do traditional devotional groups, increased from 7 percent of all groups in 1967 to 20 percent by 1990. Indeed, locally based, communally focused, and relatively highly committed groups form the most dynamically growing sector of parish organizations. Although they share notable similarities with their evangelical counterparts, none are slavish imitators and all have a distinctive Catholic flavor.

Evangelical groups are no less influenced by Catholicism, though perhaps more so by popular Ibero-US Catholicism than by institutional Catholicism per se. Ever since the relative decline in social presence of the Catholic church during the social dislocations of the nineteenth century, popular forms of Catholicism have remained the dominant form of actual Catholic practice and belief in Venezuela. Such religiosity is notable for its powerful sense of the sacred within a focus on the immediate problems of everyday life. In this environment, spiritual mediators before the supernatural powers that can dominate one's life have a particularly important role. Spiritual healings from disease are often seen as more permanent and efficacious than merely physiological ones. In this sense, the particular form Pentecostal Protestantism has taken represents not so much a rejection of traditional religiosity as a systematization of it. For example, Pentecostal churches emphasize the devil and the rejection of the devil, thus highlighting the power of the Holy Spirit to save one from evil spirits and cure both physical and spiritual ailments. The personal encounter with Jesus so central to the evangelicals is often understood as a kind of spiritual possession by the Holy Spirit. The idea of using holy water, common in Latin American popular Catholicism, is frequently not eliminated outright, but instead the water is replaced with an oil of anointing considered even more efficacious. Such oil is commonly used in praying for the sick or exorcising demons from the disturbed. Often even the pulpit may be referred to as an altar and considered a sacred space through which only the most worthy—pastors and their closest associates—may pass.

Future Prospects

Analysis of the contemporary Venezuelan church experience suggests some possible futures for Latin American churches as recent democratic transitions come to a conclusion and the churches confront a difficult era of relatively declining resources and increasing religious competition. One phenomenon of interest in this sense is that after thirty years of operating under democracy, the Venezuelan hierarchy has not fundamentally changed its traditional, undynamic character. Under dictatorial regimes, the hierarchy was cautious in order to survive and grow under hostile governments with a minimum of state interference. Under democracy, the church is no longer so compelled to respond to state pressures, but its need to appeal to all, particularly its middle-class allies who provide the resource base for the church, has tended to perpetuate the cautious, conservative nature of the bishops. Although the Venezuelan state under democracy has retained some of its traditional legal power over the bishop—for example, it may reject episcopal candidates deemed unsuitable on political grounds and provides a portion of their income in the form of annual subsidies—such formal power has not been especially necessary to ensure the reproduction of an undynamic, cautious hierarchy. Rather, the hierarchy reproduces its established, traditional character through internal processes, instinctively practicing a sort of self-censorship. Clerics not disposed to play by the unwritten rules are hardly likely even to begin to climb the ladder of church appointments. In Venezuela this serves all the more to reinforce the conservatism of the native clergy because according to the modus vivendi of 1964, only Venezuelan-born priests may be appointed bishop. Given the limited number of native Venezuelan clergy, a high proportion of their number may become bishops. This allows the existing hierarchy to offer them very tangible rewards for conforming to the established leadership patterns.

Such a situation underlines a wider problem. Each bishop acknowledges and accepts the national Bishops' Conference, but jealously guards his local autonomy of action. Yet local autonomy is considerably limited by the role of nonnative clergy, the preponderant presence of religious orders and congregations relative to that of the dioceses, and the limited resources at a bishop's disposal.[49] Given that the bishops do not exercise a particularly active leadership role at the local diocesan level, it should not be surprising that little decisive unity is evident at the national level. Such tendencies are reflected in public pronouncements on social issues—statements are made more when it is clear that something must be said in order not to lose credibility as a participant in civil society rather than to serve as a catalyst for action. These patterns may change under the more activist bishops who have recently come into leadership positions. However, given the kinds of countervailing pressures stemming from the hierarchy's need for resources, its middle-class allies, and its internal formation process, profound changes are hardly likely. Given such pressures, there has been little need for external papal tinkering with episcopal appointments. The only notable interventions, in fact, have been in those cases when retiring bishops have recommended close associates who are otherwise largely unqualified.[50]

In 1972, the Venezuelan Catholic church faced a crossroads as the gulf between the conservative and progressive sectors widened in the wake of reduced external threats and the multiple political options resulting from the democratic transition. In the final analysis, however, the conflicting sectors came to coexist quietly with each other rather than make the unacceptably costly moves necessary to eliminate their opponents. Thus, in a church characterized by a traditionalist, conservative hierarchy, activists are permitted and even encouraged. Under democracy, there is no longer a need to preserve unity for the sake of a united front before a hostile, dictatorial state. Yet religious competition is a new, perhaps even more compelling force for peaceful coexistence between the hierarchy and activist elements. Because the latter are working precisely in popular areas, where competition is fiercest and the institutional presence of Catholicism weakest, the hierarchy cannot negate or ignore their importance within the church.

Catholicism continues to have immense institutional staying power and remains a continuing source of cultural identity, within both the upper and lower classes. Nevertheless, the level of upper-class commitment to the church is not likely to increase. Both the absence of new imperatives for Catholic commitment and the continuing lack of sufficient human and material resources preclude such a possibility. Among popular sectors, newer forms of religious practice and organization, such as the congregational and charismatic groups, are likely to increase as continuing social crises promote a greater reliance on mutual support and meaningful systems that enable such support. The relative and continuing shortage of Catholic personnel will significantly slow such possibilities of growth, but the momentum of evangelical groups is not likely to be lost. Their structure permits rapid expansion, the social sectors with which they have been associated are increasing, and their message provides islands of meaning and support in a time of increasing social crisis.

Conclusion

The prospects for religion cannot be predicted by static institutional analysis. Rather, dynamic ideas and meanings are the essence of religion and religious change. Analysis of the frames out of which Catholicism and Protestantism operate leads to compelling ways of thinking about the interaction of religion and society. Such dynamics within Catholicism and the evangelical movement suggest that religious change in Venezuela is not simply an issue of the growth of one group relative to another but the reflection of cultural shifts based on social dynamics that affect all social institutions, including religious ones. To understand the prospects for religious groups and religion in general in Venezuela, one needs to consider possible societal futures no less than the changing agendas within religious movements themselves. A full consideration of possible societal futures and their impact on religion is outside the scope of this chapter, though I have tried to indicate possible effects of some phenomena, such as the long-term operation of democratic politics and the shifting role of different class groups. One of the clearest immediate social prospects is the increasing prominence of non-Catholic Christianity within social life. This socioreligious transformation promises to negate the traditional myth that Latin America is Catholic in an institutional sense. The net result for institutional Catholicism must eventually be a recognition of fundamentally new rules of the game within the sphere of religion itself.

At the same time, religion is not simply a passive recipient of social change. The new religious phenomena of a multifaceted Catholicism and a militant evangelical movement must inevitably have repercussions within social life in general. In a context of a traditionally weak civil society with few participatory alternatives in daily life, the expansion of religious options of a congregational, communitarian type promises to deepen not only religious pluralism but cultural pluralism as well. As such, these changes are significant not only in terms of religious change but also in their potential effect on the politics of the society in which they operate.

Notes

Special thanks to Edward Cleary, Thomas Depew, Susan Eckstein, Mary Froehle, Alberto Gruson, Daniel Levine, Jochen Streiter, and Luis Ugalde for their helpful criticisms and comments.

1. See Mary Watters, *A History of the Church in Venezuela: 1810–1930* (Chapel Hill: University of North Carolina Press, 1933). Her work remains a classic among research on the Venezuelan church and on the historical development of religion and politics within Latin America in general.

2. For corroborating this point, I am indebted to Hermann González Oropeza, director of the Center for Venezuelan Church History.

3. Watters, *A History of the Church*, p. 35.

4. Alberto Micheo and Luis Ugalde, "El proceso histórico de la iglesia venezolana," in *Historia general de la iglesia en América Latina: Colombia y Venezuela* (Salamanca, España: Ediciones Sígueme, 1981), p. 623.

5. Watters, *A History of the Church*, pp. 34, 90, 156.

6. This interpretation was first suggested in ibid., p. 220, based on comments by the turn-of-the-century Venezuelan literary critic Laureano Vallenilla Lanz in his *Críticas de sinceridad y exactitud* (Caracas: Imprenta Bolívar, 1921), p. 401. However, the detailed interpretation I present here is my own, inspired by the kind of political economic analysis suggested by Jeffrey Paige, *Agrarian Revolution* (New York: Free Press, 1975); Barrington Moore, *The Social Origins of Dictatorship and Democracy* (Boston: Beacon Press, 1966); and Maurice Zeitlin, *The Civil Wars in Chile* (Princeton, N.J.: Princeton University Press, 1984).

7. Hermann González Oropeza, *La liberación de la iglesia venezolana del patronato* (Caracas: Ediciones Paulinas, 1988), pp. 130–136.

8. Daniel Levine, *Conflict and Political Change in Venezuela* (Princeton, N.J.: Princeton University Press, 1973), p. 71.

9. For a full account of these events, see ibid., pp. 64–73.

10. See ibid., pp. 88–92; and Micheo and Ugalde, "El proceso histórico," p. 627.

11. For more on this theme, see Levine, *Conflict and Political Change*, p. 109; and González Oropeza, *La liberación*, pp. 141–146.

12. See González Oropeza, *La Liberación*, p. 146; Levine, *Conflict and Political Change*, p. 109; and Irene Casique, *Relaciones entre la institución eclesiástica y el estado venezolano a partir de la firma del modus vivendi (1964–1985)* (Caracas: Escuela de las Ciencias Sociales de la Universidad Católica Andrés Bello, 1989), pp. 39–52. Casique's work is an undergraduate thesis that focuses on the changes in church-state relations brought about by the modus vivendi.

13. See *Boletín estadístico: 1989–1990*, a compilation of the most recent statistical information on the Venezuelan Catholic school system, issued by Asociación Venezolana de la Educación Católica (AVEC), in 1990.

14. Daniel Levine, among others, has traced out this theme, a common reality in many Latin American churches during this period. See Daniel Levine, *Religion and Politics in Latin America: The Catholic Church in Venezuela and Colombia* (Princeton, N.J.: Princeton University Press, 1981), p. 72.

15. For a detailed comparative, statistical study of two very different Latin American countries that received a considerable influx of Spanish-born clergy during the immediate postwar period, see Isidoro Alonso, Merardo Luzardo, Gines Garrido, and José Oriol, *La iglesia en Venezuela y Ecuador* (Bogotá: Oficina Central de Investigaciones de FERES and Madrid: Centro de Información y Sociología de la Obra de Cooperación Sacerdotal Hispanoamericana, 1962). The statistics cited in the text are given on p. 55.

16. For population data, see Oficina Central de Estadística e Información (OCEI), "Nueve años de cambios demográficos," in *Tiempo de Resultados*, 1, 1 (Febrero 1991), p.4. For information on Catholic clergy, I used the time series data available in the *Annuarium statisticum eclesiae* (Rome: Vatican Secretary of State, 1987).

17. See the data presented in *Annuarium statisticum ecclesiae*, esp. ch. 1, pp. 17–70.

18. See Micheo and Ugalde, "El proceso histórico, pp. 630–631. Alberto Gruson also covers this problem in his *Area urbana de Caracas: Ecológica del personal ecclesiático católico* (Caracas: CISOR, 1970). CISOR was founded in 1966 by Father Alberto Gruson, at the request of the Venezuelan Bishops' Conference, as the Centro de Investigaciones Socio-Religiosas (CISOR). By 1970 its mission had widened; it therefore was renamed the Centro de Investigación en Ciencias Sociales, but retained its original acronym.

19. See Alberto Gruson, *La problemática de la educación católica en Venezuela: Primeros resultados de la consulta a los educadores católicos* (Caracas:

CISOR, 1974), pp. 89–105.

20. Asociación Venezolana de Educación Católica (AVEC), "Los pobres nos necesitan," Caracas, 1991. This was a policy statement of AVEC signed by Father Ramón Requeiro Salgado, the president of AVEC, for the organization.

21. Micheo and Ugalde, "El proceso histórico," p. 630; and *Los religiosos en Venezuela: Informe descriptivo de respuestas a la encuesta a los religiosos y religiosas de Venezuela* (Caracas: SECORVE, Secretariado Conjunto de Religiosos y Religiosas de Venezuela, 1978).

22. See *Los religiosos en Venezuela: Informe Descriptivo;* and *Los religiosos en Venezuela: Levantamiento sociográfico* (Caracas: SECORVE, 1984).

23. Juan Carlos Navarro, *Contestación en la iglesia venezolana (1966–1972): Contribución al estudio de los movimientos sociales* (Caracas: Escuela de las Ciencias Sociales de la Universidad Católica Andrés Bello, 1981), p. 119. Navarro's work is an undergraduate thesis that focuses on the period of open infighting within the Venezuelan church, relating the events to a Tourainian perspective on social movements.

24. Ibid., pp. 169–179.

25. *Annuarium statisticum ecclesiae*, pp. 33–41.

26. See, for example, "La nueva evangelización," *ITER* 1, 1 (Enero–Junio 1990). *ITER* is a biannual journal produced by the Instituto de Teología para Religiosos.

27. Rafael Arias Blanco, *Catecismo de iniciación cristiana* (Caracas, various newspapers, 1990).

28. Jacinto Ayerra, *Los Protestantes en Venezuela* (Caracas: Ediciones Trípode, 1980), p. 26.

29. Ibid.

30. *Los religiosos en Venezuela: Levantamiento sociográfico*, p. 23.

31. See the pastoral letter of the Venezuelan bishops, *La instrucción pastoral del episcopado venezolano sobre el fenómeno de las sectas* (Caracas: SPEV, Secretariado Permanente del Episcopado Venezolano, 1988), p. 16. Typical of the interpretation of the growth of evangelical Christianity in Venezuela commonly heard from Catholic clergy are the comments of Nicholas Espinoza, rector of Holy Trinity Chapel, interviewed November 15, 1990.

32. Kenneth Kartz, Murray Schwartz, and Audrey Schwartz, *The Evolution of Law in the Barrios of Caracas* (Los Angeles: UCLA Latin American Center, 1973).

33. Rafael Arias Blanco, "Arzobispo coadjutor de Caracas al señor director de urbanismo," letter written April 27, 1954, and found in the archdiocesan archives.

34. This information was provided by Hector Maldonado, chancellor of the archdiocese of Caracas, interviewed September 15, 1990.

35. *ADSUM: Directorio de la arquidiócesis de Caracas.* (Caracas: Archdiocese of Caracas, 1972, 1990). Although religious vicariates appeared as early as 1970, the first directory of the archdiocese to contain them was not published until 1972. See *Vicarías en acción: Boletín informativo, 1970* (Archives, CISOR).

36. Based on data in CISOR's archival collection of hundreds of interviews with Catholic parish priests in the archdiocese of Caracas between 1967 and 1977. The complete collection includes interviews, surveys, and documentation from virtually every parish in Venezuela during this period.

37. Max Weber, *Económia y sociedad: Tomo I* (Mexico City: Fondo de Cultura Economica, 1974), pp. 366–367.

38. For example, John Coleman, "Will Latin America Become Protestant?"

in *Commonweal*, 118, 2 (1991), pp. 59–63, esp. p. 62; Bryan Roberts, "Protestant Groups and Coping with Urban Life in Guatemala City," in *American Journal of Sociology* 73 (1968), pp. 753–767; and Christian Lalive D'Epinay, *El refugio de las masas: Estudio sociológico del protestantismo chileno* (Santiago: Editorial del Pacífico, 1968).

39. The data used in the social rankings consist of 639 sociologically homogeneous divisions of the metropolitan area of Caracas identified, categorized, and ranked between 1985 and 1990 by CISOR. This ambitious task was undertaken in order to permit future stratified random sampling by socially homogeneous areas. As an associated researcher at CISOR, I was able to use these data in the random sample surveys conducted in the course of my research as well as in the analyses of social rank of religious organizations in the Caracas metropolitan area.

40. Paul Furlong, "Authority, Change, and Conflict in Italian Catholicism," in Thomas Gannon, ed., *World Catholicism in Transition* (New York: Macmillan, 1988), p. 121.

41. Ibid.

42. Henri Madelin, "The Paradoxical Evolution of the French Catholic Church," in Gannon, *World Catholicism in Transition*, p. 61.

43. Karel Dobbelaere, "Secularization, Pillarization, and Religious Change in the Low Countries," in Gannon, *World Catholicism in Transition*, p. 96.

44. The preliminary results of the pastoral survey have been published by CISOR under the title *Encuesta socio-pastoral de Caracas: Resultados globales* (Caracas: CISOR, 1989).

45. On this point, see Andrew Greeley, *Religious Change in America* (Boston: Harvard University Press, 1989).

46. Angelina Pollack-Eltz, "Magico-Religious Movements and Social Change in Venezuela," *Journal of Caribbean Studies* 2, 2 and 3 (1981), pp. 162–180; and "Pentecostalism in Venezuela," *Anthropos: International Review of Ethnology and Linguistics* 73 (1978), pp. 462–482.

47. Daniel Levine, "Popular Groups, Popular Culture, and Popular Religion," *Comparative Studies of Society and History*, 32, 4 (1990), pp. 718–764.

48. See, for example, María Diaz de la Serna, *El movimiento de la renovación carismática como un proceso de socialización adulta* (Mexico: Cuadernos Universitarios, Universidad Autonoma Metropolitana Iztapalapa, 1985), esp. p. 49. Angelina Pollack-Eltz, an Austrian-Venezuelan anthropologist whose specialty is the study of popular religious cults, such as that of María Lionza, has long been interested in charismatic religious phenomena within the established churches in Venezuela. Her article "Pentecostalism in Venezuela" related her observations of Pentecostal worship services, and in an interview with the author on May 21, 1991, she shared her observations of the Catholic charismatic movement over the past twenty years, particularly of the yearly Pentecost celebration held in Caracas.

49. Báltazar Porras, *El episcopado y los problemas de Venezuela* (Caracas: Ediciones Trípode, 1978), p. 285.

50. For this information, as well as the intellectual and personal support given throughout my research, I am grateful to Luis Ugalde, university president and professor of sociology at the Universidad Católica Andrés Bello.

CHAPTER 7

The Limits of Religious Influence: The Progressive Church in Nicaragua

PHILIP WILLIAMS

The historical significance of the Nicaraguan revolution cannot be over-stated. It represented the first time that a Marxist-inspired revolutionary movement had come to power with the support of significant sectors of the Catholic church. The revolution was heralded as a major breakthrough by Marxists and Christians alike, a unique opportunity to join together believers and nonbelievers in a project of national reconstruction.

In this chapter I focus on the progressive church in Nicaragua, arguing that since July 1979 its influence within the institutional church has declined significantly. The reasons for this decline are several. Besides the counteroffensive launched against it by the Catholic hierarchy and the Vatican, the progressive church had difficulty finding its role within the revolutionary process after Anastasio Somoza was overthrown. This "identity crisis," in addition to fueling disillusionment within the base community movement, sometimes led the progressive church to pursue strategies that were counterproductive to its development and consolidation. The extent to which each of these various factors limited the construction of a grassroots church is discussed in the first part of the chapter. In the second part I assess the future prospects for the progressive church, especially in the wake of the opposition victory in the February 1990 elections. On the one hand, the changed political landscape will present new challenges for the progressive church, but on the other hand, it may bring a new sense of purpose and dynamism lacking in recent years.

The term *progressive church* refers to that sector of the institutional church dedicated to building a grassroots church in Nicaragua.[1] In contrast to the traditional hierarchical notion of ecclesiastical authority, the grassroots model advocates the decentralization of church decisionmaking and authority, with *comunidades eclesiaies de base* (CEBs) serving as the fundamental organizational units in the church. According to this communitarian notion, clergy in the grassroots church exercise their functions as copartners within the CEBs, rather than simply presiding over the CEBs.

Besides restructuring ecclesiastical authority within the church, this alternative grassroots model also seeks to transform the church's traditional relationship with civil society. Rather than seeking its "social insertion" by way of alliances with dominant economic groups, the grassroots church seeks its place amid the dominated and oppressed classes in society. This "preferential option for the poor" is seen as necessarily having political implications. In the context of revolutionary Nicaragua, the church's option for the poor translated into supporting government programs that benefited the poor and encouraging Christians to participate in them. Such collaboration with the government was rooted in an interpretation of the gospel message that equates serving the poor with organizing people for their own benefit. Accordingly, it was only natural to support those government projects that advanced the cooperation and organization of the people. Simply put, by giving the revolutionary process its critical support, the church was fulfilling its mission of serving the poor.

The progressive church in Nicaragua is not an entity separate from the institutional church, and few progressives would advocate such a formal separation. Nevertheless, many of its activities take place "at the margin" of the institutional church (i.e., without the hierarchy's explicit approval). Finding it increasingly difficult to promote change from within the official structures of the church, the progressives have sought to provide an alternative Christian discourse to compensate for the hierarchy's silence on a number of issues. Not surprisingly, some of the bishops have viewed these activities as an attempt to form a breakaway church.

The Crisis in the Progressive Church

After Somoza's overthrow, the progressive church was confronted with several challenges. One of the most serious of these was the radically different political context after July 1979. Before Somoza's fall, the burning issue within the Nicaraguan church was its relationship vis-à-vis the dictatorship. During the late 1960s, progressives began pressuring the hierarchy to break its silence concerning government human rights abuses and socioeconomic injustices. As the brutal nature of the Somoza regime became increasingly apparent during the 1970s, a consensus emerged within the church on the need to speak out publicly against the dictatorship. With Somoza's overthrow in 1979, the question was no longer whether to speak out but to what end. Should the church become the "moral conscience" of the revolution, pointing out deviations from the revolution's original goals and criticizing government abuses of power? Or should it be more concerned with awakening people to the benefits of the revolution and encouraging their active participation? Related to this was the question of whether the church should actively collaborate with the Sandinista-led government in the tasks of the revolution or whether it should assume a less activist role so as not to jeopardize its political autonomy.

Progressives were inclined to collaborate with the new government in some form, but even so, their responses varied. Elsewhere, I have identified three distinct positions within the progressive sector of the church: direct participation, active collaboration, and passive collaboration.[2] Here, I will only summarize.

The first group included those priests and religious who took up positions in the government.[3] They considered their participation in the government a manifestation of their obedience to God, viewing the project of the revolution as consistent with the gospel message. As long as the revolution was under threat from external aggression, they saw their presence in the government as a necessary sacrifice to defend the revolution. Moreover, this presence ensured the church an active role within the revolutionary process, which could prevent it from becoming anti-religious. In response to the bishops' ultimatums that they leave the government, these priests and religious adopted a position of "conscientious objection," insisting upon their loyalty to the church hierarchy, but affirming that their duty to serve the poor was more important than retaining their ecclesiastical status. If anything, over time they became more determined than ever to continue in their posts, despite being sanctioned by the bishops in late 1984 and early 1985.[4]

The second group, of which the majority were foreign religious, corresponded to priests and religious actively collaborating in the tasks of the revolution. Their support for the revolutionary process was based on the belief that its objectives were in basic agreement with the gospel message. Their activities included assisting in various government programs, especially health and education, encouraging Christian participation in mass organizations, and providing an alternative Christian discourse supportive of the revolutionary process. Although their activities were criticized as being overly politicized, these priests and religious maintained that the church cannot and should not divorce itself from politics. They argued that Christ's own option for the poor had political implications, and that the church, as follower of Christ, should carry out his project regardless of the political repercussions.

After 1982, because of confrontations with the hierarchy, this second group undertook a reevaluation of its objectives and strategies. Recognizing the futility of conflict with the bishops (which led to the removal of a number of priests and religious from their parishes), some members of this group became more prudent in their criticisms of the hierarchy and went out of their way to demonstrate their loyalty to the church. They no longer referred to themselves as the Popular Church because this term was exploited by conservative sectors of the church to accuse progressive clergy of attempting to form a breakaway church.

The third group was characterized by a posture of passive collaboration. Although generally in agreement with the revolution's objectives and fairly supportive of government programs, priests and religious within this group tended to be more critical of what they considered unnecessary government abuses and less inclined to participate directly in government projects. Although respecting those priests and religious who collaborated actively in the revolution, this group was more wary of such political identification. Drawing a distinction between politics in the general sense of the word and partisan politics, priests and religious in this group argued that the church can never divorce itself from the former, but that it should try not to involve itself in the latter.

Within this group, in addition to a handful of Nicaraguan secular priests, were several foreign religious who served as parish priests. After initially assuming a posture of active collaboration, they had to curtail their public identification with the revolution because of tensions with their bishops.[5] With the hierarchy's growing opposition to the revolutionary process, many found it impossible to sustain a position of active collaboration.

From this brief discussion, it is clear that a key issue distinguishing these three groups from one another was that of partisan politics. There was some disagreement as to whether the progressive church, by identifying with the Sandinista National Liberation Front (FSLN), was pinning its future to a political party and thereby endangering its influence in civil society. What happened, for example, if the FSLN's popularity began to wane; would this damage the progressive sector's credibility among the populace? The concerns over the church's partisan identification reflected the subtle differences within the progressive church.

There are some interesting parallels with the progressive church in Brazil. There, the changing political landscape during the 1980s presented the church with a whole new set of issues. After years of struggling against government abuses and repression, the church was suddenly faced with a process of political liberalization. The most pressing issue became the progressive church's relationship with opposition political parties, which had been strengthened by the political *abertura* (opening). Whereas some grassroots activists were highly suspicious of traditional political parties and shunned any formal contact, others "devoted themselves principally to partisan politics."[6] For those who chose greater political involvement, the issue of which party to support also became important.

Although there are many parallels between the two cases, it is important to point out some differences. In the Nicaraguan context, it was in a sense logical for progressives to identify with the FSLN after 1979. During the insurrections of 1978 and 1979, the urgency of the situation brought many church activists into close collaboration with the Sandinistas, whom they saw as the only real alternative to Somoza. The FSLN's credentials to speak on behalf of poor Nicaraguans undoubtedly were enhanced by the presence of a handful of Catholic priests within its ranks. In short, strong links already were forged and a pattern of collaboration established before the Sandinistas assumed power. This contrasts with the Brazilian case in which formal contacts between Catholic grassroots groups and political parties before the *abertura* were minimal. Until the creation of the Workers' Party (PT) in 1980, most Brazilian parties were viewed as essentially elitist and not representative of popular interests. Consequently, partisan political involvement was a much less obvious choice than in the Nicaraguan case.

A good example of how the issue of partisan politics affected the progressive church was the decline of the CEB movement. The crisis became so serious that in 1987 a progressive Christian magazine asserted:

> In fact, currently in the cities there are not many dynamic or creative CEBs, but rather only some groups or remnants of groups. . . . There scarcely exist CEBs that include men and women who live out their faith within the revolutionary process. . . . Instead what one sees are groups of men and women who come together because of their traditional religious sentiment.[7]

The reasons behind the CEBs' decline were several. On one level, CEBs had difficulty in redefining their evangelizing role. Unfortunately, before the revolution, CEBs did not focus on their future role within a revolutionary Nicaragua. Instead, the emphasis was on more immediate concerns such as denouncing human rights abuses and political repression. Before the triumph, the CEBs served as the only channels for political expression and grassroots organization. With Somoza's fall, however, the possibilities for political participation were greatly expanded, as people could take part in popular organizations, trade unions, and political parties. In some neighborhoods, CEBs became almost redundant, because their composition and activities differed little from that of the *comites de defensa Sandinista* (CDSs).[8] To avoid becoming merely another mass organization, the CEB movement needed to develop its own separate identity within the revolutionary process.

Efforts by the base community movement to carve out a space for revolutionary Christians were not very successful. Because of the lack of coordination at the national level, CEB members tended to participate in the revolutionary process in a personal capacity, not as part of an organized movement that could serve as an effective interlocutor for its rank and file. Given the CEB movement's dispersed nature, the FSLN made little effort to incorporate it into the revolution in a more organic manner. Consequently, instead of advocating the interests of revolutionary Christians in a programmatic fashion, CEBs acted in a more conjunctural manner, responding to periodic crises that threatened the revolution. The lack of coordination also complicated the efforts to develop a national plan for the training of new pastoral agents and for the reactivation of idle CEBs, goals fundamental to the movement's growth and consolidation.[9]

The identity crisis also manifested itself in the efforts of some CEB members to rediscover the spiritual dimension of their faith. During the insurrection, the urgent tasks of the armed struggle permitted very little time for any serious theological reflection; as a result, CEBs came to function more like political action groups than Bible reflection groups.[10] Even after 1979, many CEBs continued to focus primarily on sociopolitical issues. This led some CEB members to turn to such movements as the *catecumenado* (intense religious instruction), in hopes of rediscovering the spiritual element that seemed to be lacking in their base communities.[11]

Reintroducing this spiritual element was essential if the CEB movement was to maintain its identity within the revolutionary process. As Levine points out in his paper, "the most durable and successful" grassroots groups tend to be those that "have a vital and continuing religious message, and manage to keep religious practice and discussion at the core of their activities."[12] The Brazilian case would seem to confirm this. In Brazil, CEBs have been relatively successful in maintaining their religious character and avoiding explicit partisan involvement. Instead of focusing primarily on issues of national political import, Brazilian CEBs have tended to concentrate on local issues. Also contributing to their vitality has been their enduring linkage with the institutional church. Support from the hierarchy, though possibly limiting the autonomy of CEBs, has been essential to their growth.[13]

In contrast, CEBs in Nicaragua maintained a highly tenuous relationship with the institutional church. Even before 1979, CEBs, particularly in the archdiocese, had weak ties to the hierarchy. Rather than constituting a key component of the archdiocese's pastoral strategies, they were regarded as isolated pilot projects, tolerated by the archbishop. After 1979, when the hierarchy became preoccupied with asserting its authority over the institution of the church, CEBs increasingly were seen as being overly politicized and a threat to the bishops' authority.

The hierarchy's less tolerant attitude toward the CEB movement fueled tension. In some parishes, CEB members occupied churches to protest the hierarchy's removal of priests and religious supportive of the revolution and publicly criticized the bishops' more controversial pastoral letters. Instead of focusing on redefining their role within the revolutionary process, the CEBs devoted much of their energy to an ideological struggle against the hierarchy. Because of their criticisms of the hierarchy, some of the bishops no longer considered CEBs to be in communion with the institutional church. Although CEBs insisted on their loyalty to the bishops, some found it difficult, if not impossible, to maintain their ecclesial identity. On an individual level, this led to a feeling of isolation and confusion on the part of some members. Consequently, many CEB members no longer felt themselves accepted as part of the church.[14]

Because most of the bishops refused to support the CEB movement, its activities took place largely on the fringe of the institutional church. This, of course, presented it with a number of problems. First of all, the CEB movement lacked access to the resources that the institutional church could obtain. Also, without the official blessing of the hierarchy, its credibility was questioned by some of the faithful. And finally, the potential for conflict with the hierarchy was great, with serious repercussions for the progressive church. Tension escalated during 1981 and 1982, when criticisms of the hierarchy were converted into a personal struggle against the archbishop. As a result, the progressive church lost sight of its primary objectives and instead devoted much energy to its conflict with archbishop Miguel Obando y Bravo. This was at a time when it should have been consolidating its accomplishments and elaborating its new role within the revolutionary process.

Another challenge facing the progressive church was the problem of "membership drain." After the triumph, many of the best lay leaders who were involved in the armed struggle gave up their pastoral duties to become local leaders in the FSLN or to take up positions in the government. In fact, there was a much diminished participation in pastoral activities in general, as many Catholic were involved full-time in other activities (e.g., popular organizations, adult education programs, militia duties, and production brigades). This was especially true in the case of CEBs, which lost many of their most dynamic members. After 1984, the situation was compounded by the deepening economic crisis. In a typical Nicaraguan family, family members had to work two or three jobs simply to make ends meet, which left little time for other activities.

Catholic youth groups also were hard hit because many of the most capable student leaders were involved in Sandinista youth organizations and were constantly being mobilized for militia training or crop harvesting. Large numbers (of young males) were called up for their two-year military service. The war greatly exacerbated the membership drain. In northern departments, many lay leaders were kidnapped or assassinated by the *contras*, and those working in conflictive zones were in constant danger.[15] They were targeted by the *contras* because of their participation in the struggle to overthrow Somoza and their support of the revolution.

The membership drain presented the progressive church with a curious dilemma. On the one hand, it welcomed the participation of Catholics in the government and mass organizations, because this involvement guaranteed the church a Christian presence within the revolutionary process.[16] On the other hand, the loss of such dynamic pastoral agents was a setback to the efforts to build a grassroots church in Nicaragua. The question, then, was whether the institutional interests of the church should be put before the interests of the revolution. Most progressives were inclined to point to the positive aspects of the phenomenon, but it served as an important limitation on their influence.

Undoubtedly the most serious challenge for the progressive sector was the neoconservative offensive launched by members of the Nicaraguan hierarchy and the Vatican, who blamed progressive clergy and religious for the divisions within the church and for attempting to create a popular church outside the authority of the bishops. According to the church hierarchy, internal unity and stability were threatened by the political activities of priests and religious in support of the revolution. One of the clearest statements of this view was contained in the bishops' April 6, 1986, pastoral letter entitled "The Eucharist: Source of Unity and Reconciliation."[17] In it, the bishops denounced a "belligerent group" of progressive priests and religious for trying to undermine the unity of the church "with acts and postures of open rebellion" against the hierarchy. They also accused the group of attempting to damage the hierarchy's credibility by linking the bishops with the "imperialist plans of the United States" and portraying the pope as "*ejecutor* of said plans." Resting total responsibility for the church's divisions with this group of priests and religious, the bishops called on them "to reconsider their errors" and rectify their situation with the church hierarchy. The bishops did not mention dialogue or a healthy diversity of views as facilitating unity. Rather, uniformity—"one single mentality and one single judgment"— was considered the best guarantor of unity.

One example of the hierarchy's efforts to undermine the progressive sector was the removal of several priests and religious from their parishes. The archbishop of Managua, Cardinal Obando y Bravo, pursued a strategy aimed at purging the archdiocese of progressive clergy. Between 1980 and 1982, fourteen priests and twenty-two sisters supportive of the revolution were transferred from their parishes or had their official pastoral authorization suspended.[18] Although a large number of progressive priests and religious still remained, only a handful were authorized to engage in pastoral work. Generally, the replacements were priests loyal to Obando, who attempted to undo the pastoral strategies of their predecessors. This fueled tensions in a number of parishes, particularly those where the CEB movement was strongest.

The removals were not confined to the archdiocese. In the diocese of Estelí, for example, twenty-eight priests and religious (of a total of sixty-six) were removed from their parishes between 1983 and 1987. The majority of these did not even receive an official explanation from the bishop.[19] Furthermore, the purges extended beyond the clergy to lay leaders. For example, in September 1984 the bishop of Estelí, Monsignor

Rubén López, sent out a circular informing priests that any Delegates of the Word not trained in courses expressly authorized by the bishop no longer had the authority to carry out pastoral work.[20] The bottom line was that hundreds of Delegates of the Word were no longer recognized by the bishop as legitimate lay leaders. Such strategies no doubt were aimed at undermining the pastoral work of priests no longer considered to be in communion with their bishops.

The Vatican also publicly expressed its support for the bishops and its distaste for the progressive sector of the church. For example, during his March 1983 visit to Nicaragua, the pope blamed progressive clergy and religious for divisions within the church and ordered them to respect the doctrinal and pastoral directives of their bishops, so as to preserve the church's internal unity. Likewise, in a December 1985 letter to the Nicaraguan bishops, the Pope applauded the hierarchy's efforts to achieve national reconciliation, alluding to the bishops' April 1984 pastoral letter that called on the government to begin talks with the *contras*. The pope also lamented recent "difficulties in pastoral work," implying that the church was being persecuted by the government.[21] An even more significant affirmation of support for the Nicaraguan episcopate was the pope's appointment of Obando y Bravo as cardinal in April 1985, the only one in Central America.

Besides public expressions of support for the bishops, the Vatican adopted other more subtle strategies in its offensive against priests and religious who identified with the Sandinistas. One such strategy was to modify the statutes of the Association of Nicaraguan Clergy (ACLEN) and the National Conference of Religious (CONFER), both of which were known to take a line independent of the bishops with regard to the revolution. By revising these organizations' statutes, the Vatican was able to alter significantly their political configuration and to bring them under control of the local hierarchy and regional superiors.[22]

Another strategy was the appointment of bishops who were loyal to the Vatican line. Besides having ultimate authority over these appointments, the Vatican, through its papal nuncios, ensured that nominees were properly conservative and noncontroversial. Although such a strategy can never be foolproof (as the case of Archbishop Oscar Romero would indicate), recent appointments in Nicaragua should not alter the increasingly conservative nature of the bishops' conference. In 1988 two new auxiliary bishops were named for the archdiocese. Both are conservative and have close ties to Obando. In the case of Monsignor Abelardo Mata, his relationship with Obando seems to have been more important than his pastoral experience in Nicaragua, where he has spent very little time during the past twenty years. In fact, one of the bishops confided that before seeing the list of nominees, he had never heard of Mata.[23] Such strategies may serve the short-term interests of the Vatican in its offensive against the progressive sector, but in the long run they may weaken the church's ability to respond dynamically to social change.

Undoubtedly, the influence of the progressive sector within the institutional church has been greatly weakened since 1979. This does not mean, however, that its influence among the faithful is no longer significant. Opinion surveys, in fact, demonstrate quite the opposite. For example, an August 1988 poll taken among Managua's youth (ages 16–24) revealed that 44 percent identified with the "popular" current of the church as opposed to 31 percent who identified with the "traditional" current.[24] Although its influence among younger Nicaraguans does not carry over to the population as a whole—a June 1988 opinion poll revealed that 18 percent of Managuans identified with the popular current versus 47 percent with the traditional—the figures are nonetheless significant.[25] According to Roger Lancaster's study of popular religion in working-class barrios of Managua:

> A substantial majority of the population in Managua's popular barrios affiliates with, identifies with, or supports the activities of the Popular Church to one degree or another. Various observers . . . have commented on the "weak social base" of the Popular Church. . . . But in fact the strength lies less in its activism at the base community level and more in its relative hegemony over popular religious ideology.[26]

Thus, although the progressive sector may no longer hold much sway over the institutional church, it still maintains a considerable degree of influence within civil society as a whole. It is this continuing influence, in addition to its relationship with the Sandinistas, that so much concerns the church hierarchy. The question is whether the new political landscape in Nicaragua will serve to limit yet further the religious influence of the progressive church.

New Challenges in the 1990s

The National Opposition Union (UNO) victory in the February 1990 elections has presented the progressive church with a whole new set of challenges. On the one hand, these challenges may reduce even further the influence of the progressive church; on the other, they may bring a new sense of purpose and dynamism that was lacking in recent years. The future of the progressive church will depend largely on (1) the extent to which the elections contribute to the emergence of a consensus within Nicaraguan society; (2) the way in which the progressive church defines its role within the new political context; and (3) its relationship with the institutional church. These three factors are, of course, closely related to one another. For example, the progressive sector's vision of the church's mission in society will be affected by the particular political context within which it must operate. Similarly, their relationship with the institutional church will depend in part on how they define their mission and the strategies they adopt. Finally, the degree of consensus in society will be influenced to some extent by the church's efforts at internal reconciliation.

One factor that will be important in determining the future of the progressive church is the extent to which the February 1990 elections contribute to the emergence of a consensus among the key political actors in the country. For this to happen, however, there needs to be an agreement as to the ground rules of the political game. The prospects for such a consensus emerging are mixed. On the positive side, the Sandinistas carried through with their commitment to administer a democratic electoral process and to respect the results. This, in addition to Daniel Ortega's conciliatory gestures immediately after the elections, paved the way for a transition agreement between the FSLN and the government-elect of Violeta Barrios de Chamorro in March 1990.

Although the transition agreement may have contributed positively to the emergence of a consensus, several caveats are worth mentioning. First of all, the agreement was very exclusive in nature. Only the FSLN leadership and Chamorro's personal advisers participated in the discussions. Neither UNO political leadership nor COSEP (Superior Council for Private Enterprise) was consulted during any stage of the process. The danger of marginalizing such groups was illustrated during the July 1990 general strike, when leaders from UNO and COSEP displayed an unwillingness to play by the agreed-upon "rules of the game."[27] Rejecting accommodation with the Sandinistas, these groups have tried to cultivate support among demobilized *contras*—another group marginalized from the transition negotiations—by supporting their demands for land, credit, and technical assistance. The Chamorro government's failure to deliver on its promises has led to widespread disaffection among former *contra* soldiers. In the months after the elections, bands of ex-*contras* staged land invasions, often with the support of right-wing UNO politicians. Beginning in January 1991, a number of former *contras* took up arms against the government because of the slow pace of the proposed land distribution program. Sporadic violence, involving both ex-*contras* and former members of the Sandinista military continued throughout 1991.[28]

Maintaining a consensus depends not only on the willingness of leaders to abide by the terms of agreements but also on their ability to control the demands of party faithful. Given the deteriorating economic situation, it is uncertain whether the FSLN can or will enforce discipline over its mass organizations. The FSLN's support for the workers' demands during the strikes of May and July 1990 reflected its unwillingness to cooperate with the government's stabilization and structural adjustment program, especially given the program's impact on living conditions of lower-class Nicaraguans. Furthermore, without access to state resources, the FSLN's ability to restrain the demands of Sandinista-affiliated mass organizations has declined. This no doubt has been compounded by the party's internal crisis, which has resulted in a less coherent leadership and a generalized sense of disorientation among the rank-and-file.

Despite these setbacks, during the first two years of the Chamorro government there has been a growing degree of collaboration between it and the FSLN leadership. Lacking a cohesive political party with links to organized interests in civil society, the Chamorro government increasingly has looked to Sandinista leaders to play an intermediary role that would facilitate implementation of its stabilization and structural adjustment program. For example, in October 1990 talks were held to hammer out a socioeconomic pact between the government, labor, and employers. At the same time, the FSLN leadership engaged in behind-the-scenes lobbying to persuade the government to abandon the more "explosive" elements of its program. These parallel conversations, which produced compromises on both sides, removed important obstacles that otherwise may have precluded an agreement in the public negotiations.[29] Since then, despite outbreaks of violence and disaffection among more-radical elements of the UNO coalition and the FSLN, Sandinista leaders have maintained a working relationship with the Chamorro government.

A second factor which will shape the future of the progressive church is the way in which it views its mission within the new political landscape. During the two years since the elections, progressives have dedicated their efforts to defending the "social conquests" of the revolution and searching for new strategies to improve the conditions of poor Nicaraguans. This commitment to defend the accomplishments of the revolution in the areas of agrarian reform, education, health care, and women's rights probably has led to tensions with the Chamorro government and continuing tension with the hierarchy. The level of conflict has been limited somewhat by the FSLN leadership's success in moderating the government's structural adjustment program. Nonetheless, the deepening economic crisis has led to growing demands by mass organizations, at a time when the government's capacity to respond to these demands has diminished. In the future, the majority of progressive clergy and religious can be expected to continue to support the demands of mass organizations. Whether this will lead to an increase in tensions with the government ultimately will depend on the government's success in improving the conditions of poor Nicaraguans.

The last factor is the progressive sector's relationship with the institutional church. This relationship will be influenced both by the new political context and the way in which each side defines the church's mission. As mentioned above, as long as progressives view the church's role as that of defending the accomplishments of the revolution on behalf

Nicaraguans, conflict with the more conservative bishops will be likely, given their contrasting vision of the church. These bishops see the church's mission as mediating between God and humankind—personal salvation must be mediated through the church—and this view, of course, connotes a hierarchical conception of decisionmaking and authority, with the bishops as the ultimate authority. Not surprisingly, efforts by progressive clergy and religious to decentralize the church, are seen as an obstacle to the church's completion of its mission. Furthermore, in line with established church tradition, the conservative bishops oppose revolutionary political change and favor a "third way" between communism on the left and capitalism on the right. They object to progressives' partisan identification with the FSLN, viewing it as a threat to the church's political autonomy. According to these bishops, the church should foster reconciliation between conflicting interests rather than taking sides.

Immediately following the elections, the conservative bishops, including Cardinal Obando y Bravo, sought a relationship of active collaboration with the new government. Although the hierarchy adopted a formally "neutral" position during the electoral process, it was no secret where Obando's political sympathies lay. The coincidence of political positions between the most conservative sector of the church and political opposition groups before the February 1990 elections has been well documented.[30]

A clear indication of the hierarchy's identification with the new government was its June 1990 pastoral letter calling on Nicaraguans to close ranks behind the government in support of its economic recovery plan.[31] This was followed by another letter in August, in which the bishops warned workers against staging politically motivated strikes that could lead to "the paralyzing of all socioeconomic life"—an obvious reference to the July general strike.[32]

On a symbolic level, church leaders, particularly Obando y Bravo, have been present at state occasions, as have government officials at important religious ceremonies. This public support for the new government has not gone unrewarded. For example, soon after her inauguration, President Chamorro promised to assist the archdiocese with the construction of a new cathedral, a long-held dream of the cardinal. Even more significant was the appointment of Sofonías Cisneros, member of the archdiocesan secretariat and a close associate of the cardinal, as minister of education, thereby guaranteeing the church hierarchy considerable influence over the planned reform of school curriculum. In an interview in July 1990, Vice Minister of Education Humberto Belli (another Obando confidant) stated that the government intended to introduce an "education with Christian values," echoing similar statements made by Cardinal Obando.[33] Finally, the government has provided the church with free space on the state television station to broadcast Obando's regular Sunday mass.

Since the summer of 1990, the more conservative bishops have become increasingly critical of the Chamorro government, adopting public positions similar to those of UNO's right wing. In November 1991, for example, the Bishops' Conference issued a pastoral letter criticizing the government's failure to take a hard line against Sandinista militants implicated in violent disturbances that same month. According to the bishops, instead of bringing those responsible to justice the government continues to justify its inaction in the name of peace and reconciliation. Echoing the demands of UNO's right wing, the bishops also called on the government to sharply reduce the defense budget, given that the country is no longer involved in a military conflict.[34]

The degree of identification between the conservative sector of the church and the right wing of UNO will have an important impact on the bishops' strategies toward the progressive church. Refusal to accept a relationship of peaceful coexistence with the Sandinistas can only complicate efforts to reconcile divisions within the church. Consequently, it is doubtful that the conservative bishops will tolerate the pastoral initiatives of the progressive clergy and religious. Rather, they will continue to view such initiatives as politicized and as a threat to their authority within the church.

There are, of course, limits to how far the conservative bishops can go in their efforts to undermine the progressive church. Given the relative scarcity of pastoral agents in the country, a continued offensive against progressive clergy and religious could lock the hierarchy into a dangerous conflict which ultimately will be counterproductive to the institutional church. Over the years, progressive clergy and religious have been effective in training lay leaders, especially in rural parishes where the ratio of parishoners to priests can reach as high as 20,000 to 1. Their removal would further weaken the church's presence in such areas. Even in urban parishes, the church has been stretched thin of late—partly the result of the numerous removals discussed above and the massive influx of war refugees. For example, in the urban parish of Matagalpa current levels of church personnel are insufficient to attend the thousands of new parishoners that have flooded into squatter settlements in recent years.[35] The problem of insufficient personnel has been compounded by the bishop of Matagalpa's refusal to implement pastoral strategies, such as the promotion of CEBs, that might otherwise have strengthened the church's presence in marginal towns. However, the success of evangelical sects in winning hundreds of new converts in squatter settlements may have tempered Bishop Santi's fear about CEBs becoming excessively politicized. Recently, the bishop has been considering the adoption of new pastoral strategies, including the formation of CEBs, to check the influence of evangelical sects in these areas.[36]

The challenge posed by the growing influence of evangelical sects is a concern to both progressives and conservatives within the church. In February 1990, the spokesman for the archbishop's office, Monsignor Bismark Carballo, denounced a media blitz undertaken by the Christian Broadcast Network as "trafficking with the hunger of the people."[37] Members of the base community movement seconded his objections. The $3-million campaign targeted Guatemala and El Salvador as well as Nicaragua and was expected to win more than 2 million converts. The continued growth of evangelical sects challenges the influence of the institutional church as a whole, but it may present opportunities for future collaboration between formerly antagonistic sectors of the church.

Conclusion

Faced with these new challenges, progressive clergy and religious will find it necessary to develop strategies which enable them to work within the official structures of the church. In recent years, their activities at the margin of the institutional church have made them an easy target for the bishops, who could accuse them of "parallel magisterium." It may be in the interests of the progressive church to repair its strained relations with some of the bishops, but this will be possible only within the context of national reconciliation. The emergence of a consensus whereby the country's principal political actors agree to work together in a project of national reconstruction would have a beneficial impact on the church's efforts toward internal reconciliation. A reduction in tensions within the church and in civil society in general may lead to a more tolerant attitude on the part of some of the bishops. In a less politically charged atmosphere, grassroots pastoral initiatives may not be seen as having such serious political implications. This, of course, would enable progressives to re-establish the ecclesial link between such initiatives and the institutional church.

As noted above, the prospects for such a national consensus emerging are mixed. Even if a consensus is forged in the near future, the possibilities of reconciliation within the church continue to be problematic in the archdiocese. Obando's unwillingness to tolerate diversity among his clergy is not likely to change. Although in the future he may view the progressive church as less of a political problem, it is almost certain that he will continue to regard it as an internal church problem. An indication of this was Obando's decision to deny the Dominicans' provincial superior a vote in the upcoming 1992 Church Council, purportedly because of an ongoing political feud with the Dominicans.[38] In other dioceses, which suffer from an acute personnel shortage and where internal divisions are nowhere near as severe, the prospects for internal reconciliation are much better. For example, on the Atlantic Coast the bishops have been more tolerant of different political positions and pastoral orientations. As a result, progressive clergy and religious are assured a greater degree of flexibility with which to implement grassroots pastoral strategies. It may be that the seeds of a revitalized progressive church will take root in isolated rural parishes. The challenge, however, will be to project such pastoral experiences on a national scale.

Despite the limitations on the progressive church in the wake of the opposition electoral victory, the changed political landscape may present new opportunities in the future. In the context of the Chamorro government, progressive clergy and religious may have an easier time defining their role within civil society. While the question of partisan identification with the FSLN and Sandinista-affiliated mass organizations will continue to serve as a source of some disagreement, opposition to UNO attempts to roll back programs that benefit poor Nicaraguans may provide a focus for unity. By defining its new role in terms of defending the social conquests of the past ten years, the progressive church may succeed in energizing that sector of the church committed to the empowerment of poor Nicaraguans. In short, the new political context may enable the progressive church to finally overcome the identity crisis which has limited its ability to influence civil society in recent years.

Notes

1. For an excellent discussion of the main features of the progressive church in Latin America, see Scott Mainwaring and Alexander Wilde, eds., *The Progressive Church in Latin America* (Notre Dame, Ind.: University of Notre Dame Press, 1989), pp. 4–34.

2. See Philip Williams, *The Catholic Church and Politics in Nicaragua and Costa Rica* (London: Macmillan, 1989), pp. 68–79.

3. Immediately after the triumph, two priests, Ernesto Cardenal and Miguel D'Escoto, became minister of culture and foreign minister respectively. Fernando Cardenal became director of the Sandinista Youth and then minister of education, and Edgar Parrales was appointed minister of social health, later to become Nicaragua's representative to the Organization of American States (OAS). A number of other priests and religious took up technical and advisory positions within various government ministries and institutions.

4. Fernando Cardenal was removed from the Jesuit order in December 1984, and Ernesto Cardenal and Miguel D'Escoto were sanctioned in January 1985. Edgar Parrales asked to leave the priesthood about the same time. Those priests sanctioned refrained from public priestly functions as long as they were in office.

5. Unlike other religious, who teach at universities, technical colleges, and schools (and who are not engaged in pastoral work), these priests are responsible to both their local bishops and their religious superiors.

6. Scott Mainwaring, "Grass-Roots Catholic Groups and Politics in Brazil," in Mainwaring and Wilde, *The Progressive Church*, p. 173.

7. *Amanecer*, no. 50 (June–July 1987), p. 22.

8. CDSs were organized at the urban block level and functioned as political decisionmaking bodies concerned with production, distribution, health, education, militia organization, and neighborhood security.

9. Interview with Rafael Aragón (provincial superior of the Dominicans in Central America), July 12, 1990.

10. *Amanecer*, nos. 7–8 (March–April 1982), p. 13.

11. Interview with Domingo Gatti, May 17–18, 1985, Juigalpa.

12. Daniel Levine, "Popular Religion and Political Change in Latin America," paper prepared for Latin American Studies Association International Congress, December 1989, pp. 9–10.

13. Mainwaring, "Grass-Roots Catholic Groups," pp. 154–158.

14. Rosa María Pochet and Abelino Martínez, *Nicaragua: Iglesia— Manipulación política o profecía?* (San Jose: Editorial DEI, 1987), p. 60.

15. In the El Jícaro parish (Nueva Segovia), for example, nine Delegates of the Word had been assassinated by the *contras* through 1984. Interview with Alfredo Gundrum (parish priest in El Jícaro), December 7, 1984, El Jícaro; for a collection of firsthand accounts of *contra* atrocities against Catholic lay leaders, see Teófilo Cabestrero, *Blood of the Innocent: Victims of the Contra War in Nicaragua* (Maryknoll, N.Y.: Orbis, 1985).

16. Interview with Bernard Wagner (parish priest in Wiwili and Quilali), November 20, 1984, Managua; interview with Ramón Pardina (parish priest in San Juan del Sur), January 10, 1985, San Juan del Sur; interview with Enrique Coursol (parish priest in Totogalpa), December 2, 1984, Totogalpa.

17. Conferencia Episcopal de Nicaragua (CEN), "Carta del episcopado nicaragüense sobre la eucaristía, fuente de unidad y reconciliación," Managua, April 6, 1986.

18. *Nuevo Diario*, November 4, 1983.

19. *Amanecer*, no. 51 (June–July 1987), pp. 7–9.

20. Rubén López Ardón, "Instrucción diocesana 'eminente vocación' sobre los delegados de la palabra," Estelí, September 24, 1984. Although the bishop of Estelí is one of the more moderate bishops, as the only Nicaraguan among this group, he is under constant pressure from the hard-line bishops (most of whom are Nicaraguan) to adopt a tougher stance. Consequently, he has assumed a highly ambiguous position. On the one hand, he has sought to consolidate his authority within the diocese of Estelí; on the other, he was the only bishop to greet Miguel D'Escoto during the February 1986 "March for Peace."

21. *Envío*, November 1987, p. 32.

22. For more on this, see Williams, *The Catholic Church*, pp. 60–62.

23. Confidential interview.

24. *Envío*, March 1989, pp. 30–40.

25. *Envío*, December 1988, pp. 10–23.

26. Roger Lancaster, *Thanks to God and the Revolution* (New York: Columbia University Press, 1988), pp. 86–88.

27. During the strike, representatives from UNO and COSEP formed the National Salvation Committee, charging that Chamorro was incapable of dealing with the national emergency. The committee began organizing and distributing arms to paramilitary brigades, directly undermining the Chamorro government's political authority. See *Central America Report*, July 13 and 20, 1990.

28. For an excellent assessment of the postelection reconstruction period, see Laura Enríquez, et. al., *Nicaragua: Reconciliation Awaiting Recovery* (Washington Office on Latin America, April 1991).

29. Interview with Comandante Luis Carrión, November 23, 1990, Managua.

30. See Williams, *The Catholic Church*, pp. 88–95, and Ana María Ezcurra,

Agresión Ideológica Contra la Revolución Sandinista (Mexico City: Ediciones Nuevomar, 1983).

31. CEN, "Comunicado de la Conferencia Episcopal de Nicaragua" (Managua, June 4, 1990).

32. CEN, "Mensaje de la Conferencia Episcopal de Nicaragua" (Managua, August 15, 1990).

33. *Envío*, July 1990, p. 17.

34. *La Prensa Gráfica*, "La Iglesia Nicaraguënse Demanda Reducir Gasto Militar," November 25, 1991, p. 63.

35. Since the beginning of the war, the city's population has mushroomed from about 40,000 to slightly over 70,000.

36. Interview with Monsignor Benedicto Herrera, vicar general of Matagalpa, February 21, 1990, Matagalpa.

37. *Central America Report*, April 6, 1990, pp. 101–103.

38. The Dominicans were particularly outspoken in their support for the revolutionary process. At one point Obando tried to pressure the Dominican superiors to withdraw the entire order from Nicaragua. Interview with Rafael Aragón, (provincial superior of the Dominicans in Central America), July 12, 1990, Managua.

CHAPTER 8

(Still) Waiting for John Paul II: The Church in Cuba

JOHN M. KIRK

> I believe we are in a process in which shortcuts are not easily taken, a
> process that must take its course. . . . [W]e go from situations that seem
> to be of rupture and misunderstanding . . . and later, little by little, there
> is perhaps a long period in which there is an atmosphere of trust where
> we must try to eliminate all the previous prejudice. . . . I believe the period
> in which talks can begin and problems can be posed has arrived, and we
> get closer and closer to a situation in which Christians can assert them-
> selves as such.
> I believe we are now in this progressive stage. . . . I believe that the
> steps have been gradual, but have been taken in the right direction.
> —*Monsignor Jaime Ortega,*
> *archbishop of Havana, August 1988*

The controversial and hotly debated visit of John Paul II to Cuba
(proposed in 1989 and at the time of this writing, November 1991,
postponed indefinitely) is a fascinating benchmark from which to examine
the Catholic church in Cuba. It appears clear that both the country and its
church are an anomaly in modern times and therefore present quite a
different case history from the other cases presented in this book. For
example, not only is Cuba one of only a handful of Marxist countries not
to follow Poland's example in the giddy rejection of the communist system
by the erstwhile Soviet bloc (Cuba's leader, Fidel Castro, has also joked
about Cuba becoming the "Albania of the Caribbean"), but it is also very
much a Latin country—yet one with only approximately 2 percent of its
population currently practicing their religion. The church too is a paradox:
Unlike other churches in the mainland countries of Latin America, it was
scarcely affected by the liberation theology that spread like wildfire in the
1970s (preferring instead to pursue a theology of reconciliation), and
although there has been a form of institutionalized discrimination against
practicing Christians since the advent of the revolution, the violence that
has been directed against the church in other countries of Latin America

has fortunately been missing. There have been no death squads or disappearances, but in Cuba—unlike in other parts of the mainland—the church has not needed to be the voice of the voiceless.

Cuba is a unique case, then. Its political leader is also a paradox: He is Latin America's only Marxist leader, yet he was educated by the Jesuits for many years in their exclusive (and now nationalized) Belem school. Indeed, Fidel Castro is much given to showing his formidable knowledge of the New Testament and in 1985 sat down with Brazilian Dominican Frei Betto to talk for twenty-three hours about things religious. The end result, *Fidel y la religion* (published by the Council of State in 1985) is a tour de force, treating a plethora of church-related topics. For its part, the church has seen its "social acceptability" steadily increase over the last decade—with an especially impressive increase in baptism rates—though it is still regarded with some suspicion by the revolutionary government, particularly in the wake of events in Eastern Europe. Archbishop Jaime Ortega, who was imprisoned in the notorious labor camps (UMAP) in the 1960s, has emerged as an articulate and respected church leader—pushing firmly for an improvement in the church's status, yet seeking to avoid the triumphalism found in the church in Poland and Czechoslovakia, for example.

It is appropriate that this study of the Catholic church begin with a quotation from the archbishop of Havana, because it hints at both the unique situation of the church and the difficult balancing act that it has to perform in order to develop within Latin America's only Marxist-Leninist society. On the one hand, the church has to pursue its mission of evangelization and of seeking social justice; on the other, it must avoid alienating the government, which of course possesses tremendous influence and power. Moreover, the church must seek to extend its influence above and beyond the small nucleus of practicing Catholics (approximately 100,000–200,000), but it must remember that its radius of support is distinctly limited, in both financial and political matters. Finally, the church has to atone for its sins of omission in the past while projecting an image of relevance and pragmatism within Cuba's revolutionary society. As can be seen, this complex situation makes for parameters that are unique in Latin America. It has also provided some difficulties for the church in overcoming its identity crisis and determining precisely what its role is in this context. (And this challenge does not take into account the effect of the major political changes taking place in the erstwhile Soviet bloc, which obviously have had a major impact on the body politic of revolutionary Cuba.)

Speaking in 1988,[1] Archbishop Ortega explained well the current trajectory of church-state relations and referred to the strengthened position in which Christians currently find themselves in Cuba. Indeed, when compared with its situation of a decade or even five years ago, the church has made startling progress in reasserting itself within Cuban society. The visit of John Paul II, provided it can be realized in a constructive and harmonious fashion, will be an important culmination of this process, barely ten years in its development. Yet regardless of whether the pontiff visits Cuba, the church in Cuba will continue to seek its own aggiorna-mento and to demand that it be taken more seriously by the government.

Church and government representatives alike, when pressed for an assessment of the current rapprochement, are understandably diplomatic: Phrases often heard are "gradual period of normalization of relations," "beginnings of a meaningful dialogue," and the like. At the same time, however, hints are frequently dropped, particularly from church sources, that the pace of dialogue is not as swift as it should be, that a policy of token improvements has been emphasized, and that significant develop-ments—such as allowing church members to have guaranteed access to the media or to run their own schools—are consistently neglected. (Often heard too throughout the 1980s was a demand that practicing Christians be allowed to participate actively in Cuba's only political party, the Communist Party. Traditionally, the revolutionary government politely ignored such demands, claiming that this would be desirable but in essence doing little about it. The Fourth Party Congress, however, which took place in October 1991, finally enacted legislation to allow this develop-ment, which was long overdue in Cuba).

On the other side of the ideological divide, concerns are aired by government representatives about according the church more authority than its membership warrants, while some party members refer to its traditionally conservative role in prerevolutionary Cuba and wonder aloud whether the progressive direction taken by the Cuban church is merely a tactical approach to attain greater political power. Indeed, in a major address to Brazilian Catholics in March 1990, Fidel Castro issued his strongest public criticism in recent years of the church leadership in Cuba:

> The hierarchy of the U.S. Catholic Church wields a lot of authority over the hierarchy of the Cuban Church, while official government policy in the United States also influences the Church hierarchy there.... In Cuba the Catholic Church never identified itself with the revolutionary process. Instead it has been lying low, waiting for the Revolution to encounter difficulties in order to act against it.[2]

Church and state thus have a somewhat uneasy relationship, one in which both sides have yet to develop mutual trust and respect but have established cordial and formal ties. (One has only to examine the conflic-tual nature of these ties throughout the 1960s to realize the nature of this progress.) This process of rapprochement is particularly difficult in the current international political climate generated by momentous events, such as the electoral defeat of Cuba's closest ally in Latin America, the Sandinista government in Nicaragua; the fall of the Berlin wall; the ouster of communist governments behind the iron curtain (which is now itself an anomaly); the virtual dismantling of the Council for Mutual Economic Assistance (COMECON); and widespread division and polarization within the Soviet Union itself. This has led Cuba to question where its trade and aid will proceed from, an issue that has understandably become the revolutionary government's major preoccupation.

This concern has acted as a filter through which the Castro government sees all important foreign policy decisions, including the planned visit of John Paul II to Cuba. The pope's visit to Czechoslovakia in April 1990 (where he spoke of the "tragic utopia" represented by communism and waxed eloquent at the way "communism had crumbled like the tower of Babel")[3] only served to underscore the Church's formidable political influence—and thus its potential opposition. In the case of the papal visit to Cuba, this concern held by the government was accentuated when the pontiff's spokesman explained to media representatives (without first consulting with Cuban officials) that John Paul II might travel to Cuba earlier than expected, possibly by late 1990. Coming on the heels of what some government sectors perceived as an objectionable pastoral letter calling for greater openness and democratization in Cuba issued by the Cuban bishops, this unilateral suggestion by the Vatican was rebuffed immediately by Havana. It was interpreted as the pope rushing to pursue the impetus for change that was emanating from Eastern Europe and to seek to foment it actively in Cuba. Coupled with the rather triumphalist nature of his comments in Czechoslovakia on the demise of Marxism, it served to cool noticeably the incipient church-state dialogue. Truly, as the quotation by Archbishop Ortega at the beginning of this chapter highlights, shortcuts have not been a feature of this relationship: There are clearly limits to the desirability of rapprochement.

It is true that old prejudices (for the church and party alike) die hard, but it is also true that at the level of both hierarchies, a policy of incipient dialogue has been studiously developed, and has progressed significantly. Moreover, it is quite clear that in pursuing this accommodation with the revolutionary government, the church has also gained significant benefits, both in material terms (repair of church buildings, visas for foreign clergy to work in Cuba, access to telecommunication and printing facilities, travel abroad for Cuban clergy) and in intangible benefits (including far greater social prestige and respect, a remarkably favorable treatment in the government-controlled media, and occasional praise from President Fidel Castro). When viewed from a balanced perspective, it is a remarkable success story, particularly given the early stormy relationship between the church and the revolutionary government. And although there have been occasional incidents and confrontations—as seen in the planning around

John Paul's visit to Cuba—a broader historical interpretation would indicate that over the course of these three turbulent decades, significant progress has indeed been realized in setting the church-state relationship on something resembling a firm footing.

In this chapter I outline the nature of these gains and analyze their significance. My perspective is based upon a thesis that such gains, though limited in scope, are indeed important and have been extremely beneficial for the church, despite claims to the contrary from certain sectors of the Cuban community in exile. The objective, then, is to trace the development of this process over the last years and to present a portrait of the church as it awaits the pontiff's visit. First, however, it is crucially important to appreciate the departure point for this development because, as emphasized earlier, the Cuban case is unique.

The Historical Background

As I have discussed elsewhere,[4] just over a decade ago the likelihood of any form of meaningful dialogue between the Communist Party of Cuba and the church was quite improbable, largely because of the extremely conservative ideological bent of the church in Cuba and its outspoken objections—and at times strenuous opposition—to the reforms enacted by the revolutionary government. It should be remembered that the islands of Cuba and Puerto Rico were bastions of avid *españolismo*, remaining as colonies nearly eighty years after the Latin American mainland was liberated. Add to this a church hierarchy that with very few exceptions traditionally supported the de facto rulers, including Fulgencio Batista, and that had clearly decided to support the prerevolutionary status quo.

On the eve of the Cuban revolution, a profile of the church was far from flattering. Admittedly, the private Catholic schools were highly regarded by the bourgeoisie (ironically, Fidel Castro and several Central Committee members attended them), and there were some 700 priests, yet beneath this superficial success lay grave problems and some disquieting statistics. A 1955 report of the hierarchy, for instance, showed that there was a disastrous rate of native vocations—an excellent yardstick of the church's well-being—in Cuba. Only 95 of the 200 priests belonging to dioceses and 30 of 461 priests belonging to religious communities were Cuban. Indeed, fully one third of all priests belonging to religious communities, 90 percent of the teaching brothers, and two-thirds of the nuns worked in Catholic schools.[5] The vast majority of the clergy were from Spain, trained—significantly—during the rise of General Francisco Franco, and were fearful of government attempts at any kind of liberal reform.

Even the much-vaunted private schools could be taken as reflecting the church's imbalance in its evangelical priorities. Indeed, fully a third of all *religiosos sacerdotes*, 90 percent of *religiosos laicales*, and two-thirds of nuns worked in 200 Catholic schools, almost all of which were private. As a result, the church was held in high esteem by the urban middle classes who sent their children to church schools, but in rural areas the minds and the souls of Cubans were deliberately neglected.[6] By comparison with the other churches of Latin America, the Cuban church was clearly among the weakest and most conservative. Remarkably few Catholics attended mass on a regular basis, and the rural sector received little attention.

The two decades between the victory of the *barbudos* (revolutionaries) in 1959 and that of the Sandinistas in Nicaragua in 1979 witnessed great changes in the church throughout the world. Landmark developments emanating from Vatican II (1962–1965) and the CELAM meetings of 1968 in Medellín (and, to a lesser extent, Puebla in 1979) as well as a host of spin-off developments (including liberation theology, the concept of *comunidades de base*, the increasingly vocal political role played by the church in the face of right-wing state terrorism, and the church's revived preferential option for the poor) all converted the Latin American church of the last decade into a progressive force for change. This did not happen in Cuba, where the church leadership was slow to grasp—much less appreciate—the momentous changes of Vatican II. The tragedy for the church in Cuba was quite simply that there the revolution took place fully nine years before the concept of the preferential option for the poor was widely accepted at Medellín. Had the Cuban revolution taken place after the Second Vatican Council or the CELAM meetings, perhaps the bitter invective of the early 1960s could have been avoided. For most of Cuba's Catholics, Vatican II arrived too late.

Unfortunately, the first two formative years of the church's role in revolutionary Cuba were marred by a forceful opposition to the government's reforms, culminating in the involvement of three Spanish priests in the April 1961 Bay of Pigs invasion. The invasion itself was presented among many Cubans as a religious crusade, complete with a cross as the official insignia and a religious proclamation composed by one of the priests involved in the invasion, Father Ismael de Lugo. In the wake of protests at the May 1, 1961, nationalization of all private schools—which of course destroyed the very raison d'être of many clergy—the government moved, deporting in September some 135 priests (estimated at about one-half the remaining clergy). This stormy year of confrontation was followed by a period of withdrawal and reflection by the church (1962–1969) and an eventual coming to terms with its mission in a socialist society (1969–1979). During this time, the church's constituency steadily decreased as the Cuban bourgeoisie, the principal supporters of church activities, headed increasingly for life in exile. Reduced to approximately one-quarter of its clergy, stripped of its private schools, and with its supporters increasingly in Miami, Caracas, and Madrid, the church slowly—

and not without great pain and introspection—came to terms with its situation. When seen in this light, it is no exaggeration to claim that the church in Cuba saw itself decimated within three short years, with the vast majority of its members living in exile and only a fraction of its supporters left on the island.

The decade between 1969 and 1979 was extremely important in the development of the church's mission in Cuba. Two key pastoral letters released in 1969—after several years of self-imposed silence—set the tone for the need to reassess the church's role in a revolutionary society, a task admirably assisted by the Medellín conference. Of particular importance was the contribution of papal emissary Monsignor Cesare Zacchi, who struggled for many years to bring about the necessary aggiornamento within the church. Increasingly, church officials sought to show the relevance of the church to Cuba's development, and although they were rewarded by words of encouragement from Fidel Castro (particularly in talks given in Chile, 1971, and Jamaica, 1977), little benefit accrued to the church as an institution.

A major influence on the Cuban revolutionary process occurred in 1979. The impact of the Nicaraguan revolution in Cuba was quite profound, not only because of the substantial economic, social, and military aid Havana gave but also because of the moral example provided by Managua. The experience rekindled memories of the *barbudos'* own revolutionary struggle against apparently invincible odds and won the imagination and support of Cubans in all walks of life. This psychological impact was also felt in religious matters because many respected Nicaraguan revolutionaries showed they could also pursue an active religious life—a fact underlined by the inclusion of four Catholic priests in the Nicaraguan cabinet. This in turn strengthened the church's conviction to accompany the people in their daily toil and to show skeptical party cadres that revolutionary and Christian ideals could happily coexist.

This was a lesson some Cuban church leaders had gradually been coming to terms with since 1969. Prodded by Monsignor Cesare Zacchi and encouraged by Fidel Castro's comments on the need for a strategic alliance between the church and the revolutionary government, the leadership of the church in Cuba came to terms with its limitations and its potential and has been gradually transforming the role and the nature of the church. This process has been particularly apparent during the last decade.

Changes in the Church, 1979–1991

The most significant development during this period is that the "church in Cuba" has gradually become the "Cuban church." This interpretation is not meant as some bizarre linguistic game; rather, it is intended to underline the effective manner in which the transformation into a distinctive church body has taken place, with the institution reflecting an effective national identity and truly Cuban concerns. This can be seen most clearly in official pronouncements on international questions (on which church statements largely coincide with those of the government), in the nature of constructive criticism leveled at government policies, and perhaps most important, in developments within the church itself.

In comparison with the fiery broadsides of the early 1960s condemning the social reforms introduced and Cuba's reopening of diplomatic relations with the Soviet Union, official pronouncements in recent years by church representatives have changed dramatically. Now, rather than show support for Washington (as the former archbishop of Santiago de Cuba, Enrique Pérez Serantes, had been prone to do in the early 1960s), the church is often critical. A series of official documents roundly criticized the Reagan administration for its policies toward Central America and the Caribbean, condemning the invasion of Grenada, calling for the US blockade of Cuba to be lifted, and condemning the development of the neutron bomb. Bishops have taken part in official meetings to condemn the international debt crisis,[7] have negotiated the release of political prisoners, and have rarely adopted a position in international affairs that is different from that of the government. Significantly, whereas bishops counseled Cuban Catholics to leave the island in the early 1960s, they now encourage Cubans to stay and work for the development of their church and their country. It is a remarkable about-face, unprecedented in recent church history in Latin America. To appreciate the extent of this shift in policy, one would need to imagine something akin to Nicaragua's Cardinal Obando y Bravo condemning US funding of the *contras*, agreeing with the Sandinistas' attempts at social reform, and urging Nicaraguan Catholics to work within the socialist revolutionary process.

Lest it be thought that the church has been co-opted by the Communist Party of Cuba—bought off for a handful of permits to import a handful of automobiles or have a church roof repaired—it is worth remembering that official church documents and pronouncements have also contained clear criticism of government policies. One can cite, for example, the criticism of current Cuban society issued by the vicar-general of Havana, the highly regarded Carlos Manuel de Céspedes. Speaking in November 1988 at a service to celebrate the second centenary of the birth of Cuban nationalist (and priest) Felix Varela, de Céspedes pronounced a detailed critical analysis of the current situation in Cuba:

> Our present situation is not an easy one, and indeed is full of ambiguity—both in regard to its immediate future and subsequent developments. . . . We are going through a difficult economic period, and the predictions

are not encouraging. The apparently monolithic socio-political structure here cannot conceal tensions, actual and potential divisions, and frustrations.... Of course these many complex problems cannot be resolved by simply ignoring them, or by repeating slogans and rhetorical phrases, or by proposing goals that meant something twenty years ago, but which now say little to the new generations—and not much more to those who accepted them as valid two decades ago.[8]

In the landmark church conference of 1986 known as the Encuentro Nacional Eclesial Cubano (ENEC), it was clear that the nearly 200 delegates meeting shared common concerns about some of Cuba's more pressing social problems. Although extremely complimentary about many of the social benefits that had resulted from the socialist revolution,[9] the extensive (more than 200 legal-size pages) final report also criticized several aspects of contemporary Cuban society. A certain moral stagnation was noted[10] in a manner that is particularly relevant in light of the tragic Ochoa Case, in which one of Cuba's war heroes, a top general, was connected to narcotics smuggling with Colombian drug interests in 1989; the decline of the family unit and personal relations—largely because of the demands on members' time—received particular attention;[11] and the continued discrimination against practicing Christians (who are still in effect denied membership in Cuba's Communist Party) was also noted.[12] The ENEC document also criticized the dogmatic educational system (and requested the opportunity to participate in Cuban schools)[13] and state control of the media.[14] Castro's negative reaction to the report—"In other words, the years went by, they produced a light self-criticism, and that's all"[15]—is rather unfair because the document clearly outlined, openly and objectively, the strengths and weaknesses of both the church and of Cuban society.

It is clearly within the church itself, however, that truly remarkable developments have taken place. A series of visits to the United States by Cuban bishops (including a retreat for Hispanic priests conducted in 1984 by Havana's Archbishop Jaime Ortega), closely paralleled by various visits to Cuba in recent years of US church leaders (a trend initiated in 1985 by the visit of the president of the US Bishops' Conference, James Malone), helped bring Cuba within the mainstream of international church currents. Other North American church representatives, including Cardinal Bernard Law of Boston, who visited the island twice; Archbishop Patrick Flores of San Antonio; Monsignor Daniel Hoye (general secretary of the US Catholic Conference); Cardinal John O'Connor of New York; Archbishop Theodore McCarrick of Newark, New Jersey; and Archbishop James Hayes of Halifax (president of the Canadian Bishops' Conference), traveled to Cuba on official church business during this time. Also extremely important was the visit of Reverend Jesse Jackson, which helped to prepare the way for visits by higher-ranking Catholic clergy. Moreover, many other highly influential church leaders from around the globe have visited Cuba in recent years, often meeting with Fidel Castro. Among these have been Bishop Jean Vilnet (president of the French Episcopal Conference), Reverend Hans Peter Kolvenbach (superior general of the Jesuits), Archbishop Fiorenzo Angelini (co-president of the Pontifical Commission on Health), Bishop Karl Lehmann of Mainz (president of the West German Episcopal Conference), Cardinal Roger Etchegaray (president of the Pontifical Commission on Justice and Peace), Archbishop Adolfo Suárez (president of the Mexican Bishops' Conference), and Mother Teresa of Calcutta, who has opened four missions in Cuba.

Without any doubt, though, the single most important development within the Cuban church since 1959 has been the February of 1986 ENEC conference. The objective of this extraordinary meeting was to define the church's role in its unique, revolutionary reality, to provide a "Puebla in Cuba," as organizers noted. Cognizant of the church's traditional shortcomings (summed up concisely in what was termed a "worrisome severing of connections between religious practice and our reality"),[16] the church delegates also prepared an outline for the nature of the church they needed to develop. In his opening address, Monsignor Adolfo Rodríguez, president of the Cuban Episcopal Conference at that time, explained the goals church members had to set themselves. Above all, he emphasized, was the need for the church to insert itself into the "real world," and he therefore called for

> a Church that wants to be a missionary Church, since otherwise it would be merely a sect heading directly for a hypocritical cult, it would cease to be the Church. . . . The Cuban Church has to be, of necessity, the Church of openness, of dialogue, the Church of participation, the Church with its hand extended and its doors opened.[17]

At the level of church leadership there have also been some noteworthy changes. The old-guard members of the church hierarchy have gradually been replaced by a younger generation of bishops, educated in state schools, who are infinitely more attuned to the realities of revolutionary Cuba. (Conversely, most of the leaders of the Communist Party were educated in private Catholic schools.) The Vatican's role should of course not be underestimated. Since the departure of Vatican nuncio Zacchi in 1974, after more than a decade of extremely successful service at a critical time for the church, some extremely able nuncios have worked in Cuba. It is too early to say how the appointment in early 1989 of the new pronuncio, Faustino Sáinz, will affect the church, but it is clear that with his wide range of diplomatic experience and comparatively young age (he is in his early fifties), his influence will be great.[18]

Church-State Relations

Over the course of the past decade, remarkable changes in the church-state relationship have taken place. These of course are the result, in no small degree, of changes within the church itself. From sending seminarians to cut sugarcane alongside members of the Unión de Jóvenes Comunistas[19] to praising educational and health reforms enacted by the government, the church has clearly sought to establish that it in no way represents a threat to the Communist Party of Cuba or to the socialist revolution. At the same time, it is worth mentioning that in pursuing such a course, the church has also caught up with the magisterium of Vatican II and Medellín. If friction has occasionally occurred between leaders of the revolutionary government and the church, this perhaps stems more from the international context—and its worrisome impact upon Cuba's future prospects—than from any deliberate attempt by the church to seek to overturn the revolutionary process.

One must also recognize the efforts made by the revolutionary government to reciprocate these gestures of goodwill and in some cases to take diplomatic initiatives. The flurry of meetings between Fidel Castro and church leaders in the mid-1980s (after more than a decade of his studiously ignoring their requests to meet) are but one manifestation of an enlightened government policy toward the church. It is unfortunate that in recent years, these meetings have once again been dropped, apparently because of government disinterest. Also important is the extremely positive media treatment accorded the church in the government-controlled media. Compared with the early 1960s—when an extremely negative approach to these "thugs in priest's dress" was commonplace—it is now virtually impossible to encounter a negative interpretation.

Similarly, official pronouncements on the church in various party congresses have shifted in tone dramatically since the mid-1970s[20] as a distinctly more conciliatory tone has been steadily emphasized by the party leadership. Significantly, the "Convocatoria" for the 1991 Fourth Congress of the Communist Party of Cuba referred to the need to struggle for a more just and open society and to eradicate all vestiges of discrimination, including in religious matters.[21] Speaking to the Cuban Ecumenical Council two weeks later (in a significant meeting that was subsequently broadcast on state television), Fidel Castro again emphasized the need to end religious discrimination and hinted that Christians might soon be able to become members of the Communist Party—both concepts being conditional, he explained, on a position of allegiance from the Christian sector. The 1985 inauguration of an Office of Religious Affairs attached to the secretariat of the party's Central Committee under the able leadership of José Felipe Carneado was a further step in that direction.[22] Carneado is close to retirement, though, and much will hinge upon the approach of his successor.

Other important gestures are worth noting, among them the authorization in 1988 to import 30,000 Bibles (after 20,000 were authorized in 1986) and to import both a large printing press (funded largely from Germany and the United States) and a telex system to connect the seven dioceses with abroad. A further new development was the government's permission in 1988 to thirty priests and fifty religious to come to Cuba. Between 1985 and 1988, by comparison, only seven priests were authorized to enter Cuba. Indeed, Fidel Castro, who on several occasions has held up the dedication and commitment of women religious as a model for "socialist emulation," recently offered to grant as many as 10,000 visas to religious—so much does he respect their contribution to society.

A final development—in its own way as important as the 1986 ENEC—should be noted, because in many ways the role played by President Fidel Castro has been the major catalyst for this change in climate. His excellent working relationship with Vatican envoy Zacchi from the early 1960s to 1974 set the tone for subsequent pronouncements on religion. In particular, the publication by the Council of State in 1985 of *Fidel y la religión* was a major event in signaling government determination to coexist fraternally with the church. Immediately a best-seller (the first runs of 200,000 copies were sold out, and now more than a million copies have been sold in Cuba alone), the book's central theme revolves around the compatibility of Christianity and Marxism.[23] Its publication signified the official imprimatur on the policy of dialogue that has evolved in recent years. Moreover, despite the occasional frustration Castro has expressed (as in his angry address to Brazilian Catholics), the dominant note has been one of seeking a constructive commitment with the Christian sector.

The Cuban Church in the 1990s

In light of these recent developments, one question still remains to be answered: Precisely what type of church can one expect to encounter in the Cuba of the 1990s? From the perspective of the Vatican, the situation of the Cuban church must appear encouraging on various levels. From the perspective of what could be called the macrocosm—as the pope expressed with great exuberance in Czechoslovakia—it must be pleasing to see the fall of communist governments in Eastern Europe. Moreover, it must be a logical conclusion for the pontiff to hope (and to pray) that Cuba would follow a similar fate, bringing in a Western-style multiparty democracy, mixed economy, and increased role for the church.

On the level of the microcosm, there are many encouraging signals for the church. In addition to the newly arrived clergy, there has been a noticeable increase in native vocations: More than half the clergy are young Cubans ordained since the revolution. Between 1970 and 1984, some 102 new priests were ordained. Unofficial figures given in November 1991 indicated 35 students at the Havana seminary, and another 10 seminarians joining. Although the numbers represent a decrease from prerevolutionary times, it is nevertheless clear that there is a solid, if relatively small, body of competent native clergy on whom the church's future rests. The average age of seminarians increased from 21.4 (1971) to 26.5 (1982), and many of them have brought a solid professional background to their theological studies. The low dropout rate of 15 percent must also be encouraging.[24] It is of course important to bear in mind that this has transpired in an atypically Latin American environment, where educational opportunities for young Cubans are extensive and where the chances for social mobility and advancement through church membership are limited indeed. Moreover, in light of traditional skepticism toward religious life and of Cuba's unique political context, the statistics represent a comparatively high level of priestly vocations.

With regard to the actual number of practicing Catholics, most reliable estimates indicate 1–2 percent, compared with an average of 5–8 percent in prerevolutionary times. Official church figures of nominal Catholics are highly inflated and need to be treated with great care. Popular religiosity, however—particularly when seen in the various blends of Catholicism and Afro-Cuban religions—has always been deeply rooted and continues to be an underappreciated phenomenon. Its influence can be seen in the annual procession to the San Lázaro shrine outside Havana, in which some 100,000 persons participate. The importance of this *mestizaje* (blending of popular religious influences) is extremely great, and although it was referred to briefly in the 1986 ENEC, it needs to be addressed more deeply by church leaders, who often tend to ignore the problem and seem notably wary of dealing with it.

The numbers of Cubans attending and participating in religious ceremonies has been increasing over the past fifteen years and particularly during the last decade. It is claimed, for example, that approximately 50 percent of Cubans request a religious ceremony to accompany burials at Havana's Colón cemetery—a remarkable number in a society where religious education is strictly limited to the church buildings.[25] The most promising figure for church leaders, though, has to be the growth in baptism. The rates for those baptized actually doubled between 1979 and 1985 (when 15,000 people were baptized).[26] Unofficial figures given in fall 1991 indicate that this trend continued to grow in subsequent years. Moreover, compared with births nationwide, the percentage of infants baptized increased from 15–20 percent in the late 1970s to 25–30 percent in the mid-1980s, clearly an encouraging trend for church members.[27]

This growth of course has taken place in a society where being a practicing Christian is accompanied by traditional skepticism and some distrust. Institutionalized discrimination in certain professions continues to exist against Christians, membership in Cuba's only political party was denied practicing Christians until October 1991, and promulgation of the Christian message at schools and through popular media is not permitted. These factors should in no way be glossed over, because for three decades active Christians were essentially denied access to educational and employment possibilities solely on account of their religious preferences. Unable to specialize in certain areas, forbidden membership in the only political party on the island, and clearly limited in regard to employment opportunities because they were regarded as some sort of security risk, Christians were—despite Fidel Castro's consistent admonitions to party members—victims of a widespread form of institutionalized discrimination. When seen in this light, the growth rates in religious practice are quite noteworthy.

As the economic difficulties and potential for political insecurity grow (particularly in light of the widespread political instability in the former Soviet Union), the church can expect to see an increase in its membership. The manifest economic problems facing the island and—for the first time in three decades—the shortage of food will also add to the growing social unrest. The church must be careful, however, to avoid being perceived as a bulwark for anticommunism and by extension as the de facto political opposition. This occurred in the early 1960s and was largely the reason why the church became marginalized from the sociopolitical mainstream. Indeed, although significant progress was made in developing a warming trend between the government and church hierarchies in the mid-1980s, it is clear that in the 1989–1991 period this relationship cooled quite noticeably—a development that probably resulted in no small measure from the government feeling increasingly beleaguered.

As the effect of the stringent economic measures introduced by the government in the wake of the disintegration of the Soviet Union is felt in Cuba, and as the "special period" of shared adversity outlined by Fidel Castro is introduced, it clearly behooves the church to maintain a low political profile in this difficult period. To do otherwise would be to court political disaster, particularly because the government will be increasingly aware of where its allies are to be found. Indeed, it may well lie in the church's best interests to come down from its somewhat distant perch and declare its support for some of the government's attempts at reform, a policy the church largely overlooked in 1991.

The Cuban church, when compared with other Latin American bodies, is in many ways a fledgling institution; it has only recently discovered its identity and has learned to pursue its mission in a revolutionary socialist society with some difficulty. Much progress has been made in the past decade, however, particularly in terms of determining its specific goals in a unique setting. Without the context of the international crisis affecting Marxism-Leninism, it is quite likely that the church would have continued to experience slow, if unspectacular, growth in Cuba. Regardless of the political crisis in Cuba, the church will gradually build up a base of popular support and slowly develop the unquestionable popular religiosity that exists in Cuba. Yet the church needs to pursue its goals slowly and at all costs must avoid falling into the trap of believing itself to be more powerful and influential than it actually is. Its potential for growth is thus difficult to assess, largely because of political uncertainty throughout the world and of a range of variables on both national and international levels. The church needs to articulate its position on these difficulties more definitively and to make its voice heard because it basically refrained from commenting in 1990 and 1991.

What is quite clear is that Cuba is at the most difficult point of its national development since the missile crisis of October 1962. The "special period" to which Fidel Castro has consistently alluded will undoubtedly mean much hardship for the Cuban people; more depressing than anything for Cubans is the fact that there is no apparent end in sight. ("Option zero"—the next stage should the "special period" fail—must at this juncture appear a most disturbing development indeed.) What is abundantly clear in light of the demise of the Soviet Union and the continuing conflicts in the Commonwealth of Independent States is that Cuba is now totally alone in world politics. The Cuban revolutionary process is thus at a major crossroads, and it is uncertain which direction it will pursue.

Given the ongoing climate of uncertainty in Cuba and the sweeping social measures that will be undertaken by the government to keep the revolutionary process afloat, the church too is faced with difficult decisions. One possible course of action would be to support the joyful, triumphalist approach of John Paul II in singing the praises of the liberation of the East and the downfall of communism. Another possibility would be to continue its present course—straddling an ever-widening chasm between support for the (revolutionary) status quo and an increasing frustration that it is not taken seriously enough. A third course—of openly supporting the Castro government, and pledging church support for the revolutionary process—will almost certainly be discounted, although a vocal minority of church members would certainly support such a step. (Ironically, the mainstream Protestant churches, which are members of the Consejo Ecumenico Cubano, have consistently been more supportive of the revolutionary government and as a result have frequently been promoted by Fidel Castro as the models for Catholic leaders. Understandably, this is not appreciated by some Catholic clergy, who

believe their Protestant counterparts are engaging in unbridled opportunism.

This chapter was originally intended as a piece that would assess the
nature of the church awaiting Pope John Paul II on his planned trip to
Cuba. The visit was discussed by Vatican and Cuban diplomats at some
length, and despite a last-ditch attempt to save it, the trip is clearly now
postponed indefinitely. This unfortunate development provides abundant
evidence of the intransigence to be found on both sides of the ideological
divide. The depths of the crisis affecting Cuba in the wake of the Soviet
Union's awesome difficulties, combined with a lack of sensitivity on the
part of Rome, make the trip an unlikely development for the foreseeable
future—until the crisis is resolved in some fashion. There are at present
simply too many uncertainties on the political chessboard for either side
to force the issue of a papal visit at this time; as a result, procrastination
would appear to benefit both protagonists.

Yet the pope will, sooner or later, arrive in Cuba. This of course begs
the question of how the pontiff's visit will impact both the church and the
body politic of Cuba. The record shows that in the wake of the fanfare and
show-business nature of John Paul II's frequent international sorties,
comparatively little changes: There is neither generally any major upsurge
in religious conversions nor any massive return to the faith of lapsed
Catholics, for example. This will probably be the case in Cuba; John Paul
II and Fidel Castro—both of them consummate world-class political
leaders—are fully aware of the potential and limitations for organized
religion there. A slow, steady growth in religious life will of course
continue (particularly in light of government support and church initiatives), the outcome of the church's consistent efforts to come to terms with
its unique reality and to seek to develop within that reality. Should
economic difficulties continue to increase, however, it is more than likely
that a significant—albeit somewhat superficial—growth in religious interest will occur. Already in fall 1991 the increased number of crosses and
crucifixes being worn by people in Havana was noticeable.

Within the context of revolutionary Cuba, then, it is unfortunate that
the visit of John Paul will not be made for the foreseeable future. This is
a disturbing development because the trip would have helped to solidify
the gains made by the church (not without much soul-searching and some
difficulty) over the past three decades. Nevertheless, the future for this
unique church remains bright, in no small measure because it has steadily
come to appreciate more practically its own limitations and potential for
growth. It is therefore all the sadder that the pope's visit, which would
have brought spiritual joy to many and a clear identity resulting from the
necessary government recognition, was postponed. Speaking in July 1989,
Carlos Manuel de Céspedes, vicar-general of Havana, emphasized that
the visit of a statesman of the caliber of the pope should have benefits for

all Cubans: "I think it will be a positive visit for all, leading to greater unity and understanding, a step towards dialogue to help resolve any differing views and rejecting all forms of confrontation and rifts among the people."[28]

That "greater unity and understanding" will have to wait, however, for happier times. The church will continue its process of slow but steady growth—and the gradual steps "taken in the right direction" (Archbishop Ortega's phrase noted at the beginning of the chapter) will thus continue for many more years—as the Cuban church rejoins the mainstream of the Latin American church and in so doing discovers its true mission.

Notes

The author gratefully recognizes the advice provided him by Carlos Manuel de Céspedes, vicar-general of Havana, and by Thomas Quigley, Department of Social Development and World Peace of the US Catholic Conference. There are areas of basic disagreement between the author and these two church representatives, yet their contribution and interpretation have been much appreciated and have been the source of a more rigorous questioning. Their assistance is gratefully acknowledged.

All translations from the Spanish are by the author, who assumes full responsibility for their accuracy.

1. See Mireya Castañeda, "Cuba's Seven Bishops Go to Rome," *Granma Weekly*, August 21, 1988, p. 5.

2. See "Respuesta de Fidel en torno a la posibilidad de que los creyentes puedan ingresar al partido," *Granma Resumen Semanal*, March 25, 1990, p. 11.

3. See Clyde Haberman, "Pope, on Sweep Through Prague, Sees a United Europe," *New York Times*, April 22, 1990. This might be a somewhat simplistic interpretation of the pope's talk. For the complete text, see "Overcoming the Tower of Babel," *Origins*, vol. 19, no. 48 (May 3, 1990), pp. 797–799.

4. See John M. Kirk, "Ante el volcán: La iglesia en la Cuba prerevolucionaria," *Revista Latinoamericana de Teología*, año V, 13 (April 1988), pp. 67–84; and Kirk, *Between God and the Party: Religion and Politics in Revolutionary Cuba* (Gainesville: University Presses of Florida, 1989), ch. 2.

5. See "Resumen de las respuestas del episcopado de Cuba al cuestionario de la S. Congregación Consistorial para la Conferencia de Latinoamérica en Río de Janeiro," March 30, 1955, Havana, mimeo, p. 8.

6. See Kirk, "Ante el volcán," pp. 74–80; and Mateo Jover's insightful analysis, "The Church," in Carmelo Mesa-Lago, ed., *Revolutionary Change in Cuba* (Pittsburgh: University of Pittsburgh Press, 1974), pp. 399–426. Two well-publicized studies undertaken in 1954 and 1957 by the Agrupación Católica Universitaria in Cuba pointed out substantial differences between rural and urban Catholics. In the first survey, for instance, although 72.5 percent of those interviewed claimed to be Catholic, in the countryside this fell to 52 percent (there, 41 percent claimed indifference to any religious affiliation). The 1957 survey—taken in the countryside—confirmed these impressions; indeed, some 53 percent claimed they had never even seen a priest. See Kirk, *Between God and the Party*, pp. 45–47.

7. In summer 1985, for example, at a meeting held in Havana to discuss

international debt issues, more than 100 religious figures from Cuba (including representatives of the Cuban Episcopal Conference) and abroad participated.

8. See his sermon, reproduced in *La religión en Cuba*, no. 14 (1988), pp. 13–14.

9. Among the benefits noted in the report were the following items:

> Socialist society has taught us to:
> —possess a greater appreciation of our fellow humans;
> —acquire a greater awareness of the social dimension of sin, especially with regards to different forms of injustice and inequality (such as racial and economic). It has taught us how to give out of a sense of justice, when before we gave because of charity;
> —better appreciate the role of labor, not only as a means of production, but also as a means of developing oneself;
> —understand the need for structural change in order to bring about a better distribution of wealth and services such as education and health care;
> —to give more of oneself in order to show solidarity with others.

See the *Documento final, Encuentro Nacional Eclesial Cubano* (Havana: Conferencia Episcopal Cubana, 1986), pp. 118–119.

10. Ibid., p. 119.
11. Ibid., p. 178.
12. Ibid., p. 173.
13. Ibid., p. 139.
14. Ibid., p. 126.
15. See "Respuesta de Fidel," p. 11.
16. *Documento final*, p. 203.
17. Ibid., p. 7.

18. When interviewed by Enrique López Oliva in early 1989, he summarized the Cuban church as "a Church that is alive, and would like to contribute more, with all its members serving the common good, to the social fabric of the nation . . . a Church that loves this country and wants to collaborate in its progress." *La religión en Cuba*, año 2, no. 3 (March 1989), pp. 7–8.

19. It is significant that the Cuban media have treated these developments so favorably. See, for instance, the articles in *Granma Weekly Review* by Carlos Cabrera, "In Praise of Work," July 17, 1988, p. 3; and by Milagros Oliva, "Catholic Seminary Students Help Build Polyclinic," August 6, 1989, p. 7.

20. For a further analysis of this development, see Kirk, *Between God and the Party*, pp. 135–137, 155–157.

21. The text of that address contained the following:

> In order to promote these objectives, the Party has to be a consistent, enlightened ally in the struggle to weed out the remains of inequality and discrimination for reasons of sex, gender, or any other kind. This means, among other matters, the need for sincere communication with social sectors possessing specific interests—among them those believers with religious credos who share our life and assume our project in favor of social justice and meaningful development—even though in some matters their ideology may be different from ours.

See the Convocatoria, "El futuro de nuestra patria será un eterno baraguá!" *Granma*, March 16, 1990, p. 5.

22. French religious journalist Stanislas Maillard has also noted recently that in each province, offices directly responsible to provincial party leaders will be set

up with the specific obligation to evaluate claims concerning religious discrimination by practicing Christians. See Stanislas Maillard, "La fin de l'exil intérieure," in Maurice Lemoine, ed., *Cuba: 30 Año de Révolution* (Paris: Autrement Revue, 1990), p. 124.

23. The following is an example:

> From a strictly political viewpoint . . . I think that one can be both a Marxist and a Christian, and work together with the Marxist Communist to change the world. The important facet of both sets of beliefs is that we all seek to suppress the exploitation of workers by their fellow human beings, and that we all struggle for a just distribution of social wealth, as well as the provision of equality, fraternity, and dignity for all people.

Frei Betto, *Fidel y la religión* (Havana: Consejo de Estado, 1985), p. 333.

24. José Félix Pérez Riera, "Un signe d'espérance: La relève sacerdotale et religieuse," *Missions Etrangères*, vol. 21, no. 7 (February 1984), pp. 19–20. It has proved difficult to obtain more updated figures, although it is generally admitted that the level of religious vocations in Cuba has slowly decreased in the last five years.

25. Interview with Archbishop Jaime Ortega Alamino, Havana, January 1985.

26. Stanislas Maillard notes similar figures: from 7,000 for all of Cuba in 1976 to 20,000 in Havana alone in 1986, most of whom—he claims—were between twenty and thirty years of age. See Maillard, "La fin de l'exil," p. 129.

27. Jorge I. Domínguez, "International and National Aspects of the Experience of the Roman Catholic Church in Cuba," mimeo, May 1987, p. 16.

28. See Gabriel Molina, "The Popes Have Never Encouraged Confrontation with Cuba," *Granma Weekly Review*, July 9, 1989, p. 4.

CHAPTER 9

Evangelicals and Competition in Guatemala

EDWARD L. CLEARY

The election of Jorge Serrano Elías, an evangelical Protestant, as president of Guatemala and the active involvement of evangelicals in Peru in presidential politics shocked many observers. Are evangelical Protestants numerous enough in Latin America to feel that they could affect national politics? And why are they in politics, anyway? Latin American evangelicals had been assumed to be nothing but otherworldly and to care only about their own members.

Characterization of Protestants in Latin America are numerous and often misleading.[1] Stereotypes of Protestantism derived from North America or from Latin American prejudices about Protestants obstruct the view of what has been occurring. Evangelical Protestant religion, often with an independent nationalistic character, has surged mightily in Latin America, and the consequences for Latin Americans and those who deal with Latin America are worth considering.

In this chapter I attempt to show that what is taking place in Guatemala is neither simply the expansion of Protestant religion nor losses by the Catholic church but a reorganization of religion that cuts across organizational lines in response to structural changes. Religion grows or declines or reshapes itself in a context of changing socioeconomic conditions and political arrangements. As I describe this context at the outset, my primary focus remains that of the growth of Protestantism in Guatemala, and of how it poses the possibility of conflict and competition for the Catholic church. But I emphasize that one cannot explain Protestantism without a parallel understanding of competing religious organizations—Catholicism and native religions.[2]

Guatemala is a vivid example illustrating an extreme case of the situation of Protestants in Latin America. Chile, Brazil, and Guatemala are the main sites for the growth of evangelical religion in Latin America. There Pentecostal Christians have grown in numbers to a much greater degree, but growth has been experienced in most Latin American countries. David Martin has described this expansion in *Tongues of Fire*, and David Stoll has written *Is Latin America Turning Protestant?*[3] They and a number of others have attempted to offer general explanations for the rise of Protestantism. We shall see to what extent and how this has occurred in Guatemala.

Theoretical Framework

Theorists of sociology and anthropology built a general theory of modernization in which societies such as Guatemala would be transformed into increasingly complex entities. In this view, such processes as bureaucratization, urbanization, industrialization, and secularization are active in producing a complex, modern society. Secularization would affect religion, bringing about religion's demise (most Western intellectuals have anticipated the death of religion)[4] or at least its being pushed to the margins of society.[5] Some European theologians, in response to such thinking, began to sacralize the secular, one of them even calling for worship through work on Sunday.

Modernity and religion as mutually exclusive thus became the simplest way of formulating a major paradigm in the sociology of religious phenomena in Western societies. Nowhere was the paradigm thought to have greater relevance for formerly Catholic countries than France.[6] Empirical studies of French Catholics confirmed the decline of religion as inevitable in a society in which modernization is an ongoing process, and this type of research "formed the backbone of research in the sociology of religions until the late 1960s."[7]

Such a view has been called into question by analysts[8] and by careful historical and field research along various lines, including popular religion, invisible religion, and new religious movements.[9] The theoretical shift in France—and the perspective I adopt here—leads to a view of secularization not as a decline of religion in the modern world but as a process of reorganization of the work of religion in a society, a process whereby religion restructures itself to meet the challenges brought on by socioeconomic changes.

David Martin in expanding his theoretical conceptions of secularization allows for the possibility that Catholics and Protestants may be at play in the field of religion in developing countries, finding their own way and reorganizing themselves to fit changing circumstances.[10] Other theorists, such as Daniel Levine, also have been delving into popular movements in developing countries in attempts to explain *comunidades de base* and other revitalization movements (or, greater lay participation) especially at the grassroots in contemporary Catholicism.[11]

Levine and others point to the larger social processes taking place in Latin American (and presumably in other modernizing) countries and note specific factors—agrarian concentration, large-scale migration, improved transport, expanded literacy, and access to media—as combining to undermine long-standing ties between elites and masses. "Popular sectors were then made available for new kinds of organization and experimentation."[12] Massive social movements affect especially (but not only) lower classes among which both evangelical religion and basic Christian communities flourish.

The approach taken here is a historical-structural one.[13] It points to class formation and reformation and economic conditions that allow individuals to transfer allegiances from one group to another (as from Catholic or historical Protestant churches to evangelical Christian and sect churches) and new sets of behaviors within groups (such as empowerment of individuals previously largely passive). Such an approach does not allow one to specify why any particular person joins a particular church or assumes for the first time in his or her life a leadership position in a church. But as Eckstein says, the approach accounts "for the conditions that prompt groups of people, in the aggregate, to act as they do."[14]

A historical-structural approach furnishes a more ample view of Guatemalan religion and society than do most publications on Protestantism in Guatemala (or Latin America, for that matter), which emphasize descriptions and analyses of religion as denominations or sects with little more than their own organizational histories. By contrast, a structural approach provides illumination of the larger religious picture and the class dynamics that are reshaping social and religious relationships.

Several theories for the expansion of Protestantism in Latin America have been advanced.[15] Publications began giving prominent attention to the massive flow of resources—missionaries, money and goods, and television programming (Jimmy Swaggart, especially)—to Guatemala. These publications pointed to a purported conspiracy between the "religious right" in the United States and conservative elements, including the military, in Guatemala to promote a particular kind of law-and-order Protestantism and to stem the influence of progressive Catholicism.[16] In contrast, the explanation offered here emphasizes endogenous factors—socioeconomic and religious changes within the country—as more appropriate for assessing influences on religious conversion, but acknowledges exogenous influences as well. (Many Catholics are believed to have identified themselves as *evangelicos* to escape torture or death.)

Thus, I attempt to highlight the changing social and economic conditions of Guatemalan society in this century that facilitated religious change. These changes, which are extensively documented especially by many superior anthropologists,[17] are easier to highlight for rural areas, but find an intensified counterpart in life in cities.

Socioeconomic Changes

Rural Society

A major factor in (and part of the traditional explanation for) the expansion of evangelicals in Guatemala was, as Hubert Miller remarks, "the Catholic church's failure to develop a native clergy and an adequate number of clergy to minister to its flock. This situation provided a favorable environment in which evangelicals could work and gain converts. This was particularly true in rural areas where the clerical dearth was most obvious."[18]

The Catholic church in Guatemala suffered more than any other national church in Latin America prolonged debilitation at the hands of anticlerical liberals. John Lloyd Mecham noted that Guatemala presented a unique case in that anticlerical laws persisted so long without change.[19]

As far as can be gathered from oral and written histories and apart from an occasional evangelical pastor or Catholic priest, very little outside religious influence penetrated traditional Indian communities in Guatemala for a rather lengthy period, from at least the 1910s to middle 1940s. These communities were mostly free of direct Catholic control and could devote themselves to life within a Christo-pagan religious organization.[20] Maryknoll missionaries who went to Guatemala in the early 1940s reported no priests resident in rural areas of Huehuetenango or San Marcos.[21] During the Guatemalan revolutionary period (1945–1954), only three priests were ordained, and the ratio of Catholics to priests stood at 16,039 to 1.[22]

Changes in Guatemalan rural society have been noteworthy: First, modern capitalist relations of production expanded, dislocating traditional peasants and freeing peasants from ties that bound them to established ways and institutions. Second, increases in population greatly aggravated the problems of subsistence from agriculture for many farmers and pushed and pulled them into migration and into different economic arrangements. Third, a social awakening began in the Indian population.

The timing (but not the occurrence) of these changes is open to speculation. David McCreery, an economic historian, places the structural changes (the effects of which may not have shown up fully until later) as early as the 1870s. The system before that time largely depended on traditional Indian communities for training a work force and for taking care of workers during the off-seasons or when they became sick or ill.[23] After 1920, growers of coffee for an export market relied increasingly on "free labor." For a long time, economists and anthropologists have described the increases in seasonal labor migration from highland communities to work on the coffee plantations on the Pacific coast.[24] The work was disagreeable, especially in terms of disruption of community life and customs, and not well remunerated. Given the marginal appeal of the work, Guatemalan governments supported efforts to force Indians to work periodically in coffee and sugar harvests on the coastal plantations.

Demand for seasonal work remained strong, except for a hiatus during the 1930s and 1940s, as Guatemala's large growers diversified crop production, emphasizing cotton through the 1950s and 1960s. This ensured continued demand for a seasonal work force, largely supplied by Indian community members. By the early 1970s, Guatemala's export sector was booming and outperformed that of most other Latin American countries. Thus, for decades economic market forces and government pressures brought external and effective forces for changes in life patterns and loyalties, including to native religion, within Indian communities.

Guatemala's population increased from 3 million to 5.6 million from 1950 to 1973. This growth brought greater divisions in land, as the average size of farms in Guatemala from 1950 to 1970 dropped from 8.1 to 5.6 hectares. In the western and central highlands, the situation grew even more acute: By 1975, the average size of a farm unit decreased to 0.85 hectare per person.[25] More farmers became landless, and about a fourth of the rural work force at this time were counted as not owning land.

Large landowners, with profits increasingly assured, sought more land. Latifundia owners proceeded at a greater pace to incorporate Indian village land, often cheaply and frequently fraudulently. This increased local underemployment and forced families into less productive lands or left them without access to self-sustaining land resources.[26] Growers also applied increasing amounts of land to export production. Guatemala found itself importing staples, such as corn and beans. Both forces, population and export economies, squeezed peasant families: more persons to feed in the community, more persons to work the communal land, less land available.[27]

The internal problems brought on by economic and social changes increased through the years in the Indian communities of highland Guatemala. Among these stresses were private ownership of land where communal use was the norm, increasing class formation within villages, alienation of resources to outsiders, declining productivity, and overcropping. These problems strongly affected the personal lives of community members, raising questions of personal identity and emotional security previously assured by community life and religion practiced therein.

The connections between economic and religious change become clearer at the grassroots level. Sheldon Annis, in attempting to explain the change to Protestantism in Guatemala, emphasizes the "bombardment of twentieth-century forces" fracturing the cultural equilibrium of communities in the Guatemalan highlands.[28] These forces affect the

> community's very idea of self—who people think they are, what they think their community is and means. It is this change that has opened a new receptivity to Protestantism. . . . Such receptivity, I believe, begins with the stresses and strains that are pulling apart the *milpa*-based economy. . . . Most *milpa* farmers now find themselves under pressure. Individually they have less land and more dependents than ever, so making a living is harder and harder. On the other hand, for a significant minority, things are getting better.
>
> Taken together, these two trends mean that wealth and class differentiation are rising. This undercuts the traditional cultural equilibrium, which was based on social egalitarianism (or at least the assumption of shared poverty). Protestantism finds fertile ground for converts among those who are alienated from the traditional economy. To those who are economically marginalized by abject poverty or socially marginalized by increased entrepreneurial activity, Protestantism says: "Come to me."[29]

Annis further suggests that at the heart of motivation for conversion lies "the desire to tame what is feared to be out of control."

By at least the late 1950s, anthropologists noted that the imputed closed character of many indigenous communities had changed drastically, affected by the factors just mentioned. Most drastically changed was the civil-religious *cargo* system.[30] Men and their families in highland communities participated in an indigenous politico-religious system of offices and associated burdens, or *cargos*. As persons advanced in the system, they contributed more of their resources, notably wealth, to religious celebrations, receiving prestige in return. This system had the effect of redistributing wealth in the communities and of often siphoning small surpluses from Indians to wealthier Ladinos.[31]

Within these changing life patterns, early on, in the 1930s and 1940s, Pentecostal Protestant leaders began work in Indian communities.[32] Contemporary Catholic influence in the central and western highlands largely came after the penetration by Pentecostals. Catholic priests typically began working in different communities from where Pentecostals had made inroads, but were affected by much the same economic and social forces impinging on other native communities. Resistance to Catholic priests by the mostly Indian population in the rural areas was strong at least in the 1940s and 1950s. Kelly, for example, notes the "abundance of indifference" on the part of Ladinos and "great deal of superstition" among the Indian population.[33] As late as 1959, the bishop of Quezaltenango had to have recourse to military authorities to avoid mass rioting by Indians who would not cede the local church to a priest in Olintepeque. Five years later, the priest, Father James Flaherty, was able to take up residence peacefully in the community.[34]

Gradual openness to missionaries, both Catholic and evangelical, must be understood "in terms of strains that had developed within the traditional order as a result of population growth and economic changes."[35] Religious entrepreneurs thus find the door open to meet displaced religious demands with a religion more adequate to changing life conditions.

Economic conditions and religion in rural areas intermingled in the case of Catholicism, as they had for Pentecostals. As the disintegration of Guatemalan traditional social ties and economic organization occurred, new marketing arrangements became possible. Cooperatives and credit unions began appearing in Guatemalan small farming areas, introduced by Catholic missionaries (at this time principally Maryknoll and Sacred Heart missioners) in the late 1950s and 1960s. Within a ten-year period, 145 agricultural, consumer, and credit cooperatives carried on business in the country, with 27,000 members. Ten years later, 510 cooperatives operated in the country, with membership up to 132,000. Davis reports that cooperatives were having a major impact on Indian political attitudes, marketing strategies, and agricultural techniques.[36] One should note that here religious influence was both proactive and reactive. These changes in marketing strategies and other economic arrangements that tended to cut out or reduce the influence of Ladino brokers and overseers were looked on poorly by non-Indians. Adams notes the "conquest-ridden psychology that still persists," pointing out that "efforts by Indians to negotiate the economic and political rules of the game are seen as seditious."[37]

Also occurring within reformed Catholicism,[38] especially in the areas of Quiché and Huehuetenango, was the formation of catechists and Catholic Action members. In the Huehuetenango region and throughout Latin America, Maryknoll and other missionaries emphasized catechists as bridges (one reason being that missionaries often lacked fluency in native languages) to native cultures and as a way to extend the influence of the church where priests were scarce and native priests virtually unknown. In the Quiché area, Spanish missionaries also sought to make as many of the adult laity as possible active in contemporary Catholicism through Catholic Action. Thousands of Indians in the region became members, thereby further disrupting patterns within traditional communities, especially with respect to conflicts about traditional religious observances and the economic consequences of diminished participation.

By the middle and late 1970s, a political awakening was occurring among the Indians. Ricardo Falla described one area in his study of a movement of religion conversion by Catholics rebellious against traditional religious beliefs; Kay Warren carried on a masterful study of the change in religious symbolism from traditional Indian religion to contemporary Catholicism and the resulting conflicts.[39] Indians who acted as leaders, teachers, and organizers in modern economic and religious organizations had self-perceptions different from those of leaders in traditional institutions: They held active views of what Indians might accomplish in Guatemalan society, developed more direct ties with other Indian leaders, and began speaking about greater political participation in Guatemalan society than Indians were accustomed to express. Brintnall wrote about Aguacatán, Huehuetenango, in 1976: "Previously repressed hostilities against the Ladinos are now receiving open and politically concrete expression."[40]

The extensive changes affecting rural life accelerated in the late 1970s and into the 1980s. In these times of great flux, an act of God occurred. A massive earthquake shook Guatemala in 1976 and left devastation that touched many Guatemalan lives. The homeless, the unemployed, and the widowed and orphaned often suffered loss or loosening of customary economic and social arrangements and meaning by which they lived.

A great wave of repression followed in the wake of these changes. A full explanation of this reaction is too lengthy to detail here, but key to this discussion are the societal disruptions and the religious movements that were a part of the 1980s. Up to a million Guatemalans (in a population of eight million) found themselves displaced; 100,000, mostly adult workers, died; and more than 250,000 fled the country.[41] Forced settlement of many Indians into strategic hamlets and into obligatory service in civil patrols exacerbated the disruptions of community and religious life. No other Latin American country has undergone similar changes on the same scale and in such a relatively brief period. The dislocations of many persons from ties to local communities and the reforging of personal relations, including religious ones, opened the way to renegotiation of allegiances to traditional institutions.

Urban Society

Guatemala's character as a rural country has been changing; more than 40 percent of the population is now urbanized.[42] Although Protestants are well represented in both urban and rural areas, as attested by the large number of Protestant church buildings that have sprung up seemingly everywhere in Guatemala, historically in major Latin American growth areas, such as Brazil and Chile, Protestantism has had a disproportionate growth in urbanizing areas. Emilio Willems attributes this urban growth of Protestantism to both protest against social inequalities and a reaction to disorganizing aspects of urban life.[43]

Guatemala City as the dominant metropolis has grown from 600,000 to 2 million inhabitants in thirty years. In large part this growth occurred through large-scale migration from rural areas. Some of the migrants brought Protestant convictions with them, but almost all migrants faced the same challenges. This influx from the *campo* was not accompanied by proportionate growth of stable urban employment or of urban services. New immigrants found themselves scrambling for regular employment, affordable housing, and networks of friends and associates with whom to interact. The numbers of persons within Guatemala City and its environs seeking new social and economic ties over the last three decades taxed the urban planning capacity of Guatemalan civic leaders. At the same time, many evangelical pastors saw opportunities for conversions at these critical life points of the migrants.

In Guatemala City the high rates of mobility, lack of stable employment, and few emergency resources made the social or economic bases for enduring associations among migrating families difficult to sustain. Although what Bryan Roberts calls the "more formal" Protestant groups (such as Lutherans and Methodists) did not typically maintain branches in neighborhoods, the less formal Pentecostal groups expanded everywhere in Guatemala City, kept their doors open, and maintained a high degree of accessibility to the networks of relations within which new members became encapsulated. These churches involve members actively in the life of the group and helped to form these very networks; ministries of many kinds are delegated, and participation in work of various kinds is expected of members, almost from the very beginning. Tasks and offices are thus divided up, teamwork is developed, and lively interaction is stimulated. Lonely persons without clear meaning or direction in their lives find new purpose. They also find status, occupying a position within the group, even though less status is often afforded them in secular life.

Bryan Roberts' study of Guatemala City in the 1960s helps explain the attraction and mechanics of Protestant groups.[44] In contrast to the neighborhood Catholic churches that then did not offer stability in social relations, Protestant groups provided such stability, which aided individuals in the day-to-day problems of coping with life in a large city without kin or friendship that marked their lives in villages and towns. Belonging to a moral community attracts members and offers relations members can count on in a fragile and sometimes hostile environment. What Roberts noted in the 1960s became ever more common among the expanding evangelical groups in Guatemala City.

The teaching of the groups and the demands they make fit well the current situation in Guatemala. Many of the groups emphasize the otherworldly aspects of Christianity. Suffering in this life matters little because considerations for the life to come dominate. The Bible read in a certain way prepares one for a series of disasters in this life. Dislocations from family and friends, earthquakes, political upheaval, and financial setbacks all have ready interpretations for people. Moreover, as Roberts notes, "sect doctrine also provides them practical means to alleviate dangers of economic insecurity."[45] Cutting out smoking and drinking and petty crime brings considerable savings or separates one from persons likely to lead to deviant behavior and facilitates positive self-presentation, noted by employers or customers. Such practices, changes in behavior for many former Catholics, would be short-lived without the doctrine of a community of believers, a remnant in a bad world, because key to changing behavioral patterns has been a community of supportive relationships and a sustained expectation of personal responsibility. The example of conversion to a sober or otherwise "successful" life has been a powerful magnet to others in the neighborhood to join evangelical groups.

To summarize, changes in rural and urban society acted as social influences, outside the individual. First, persons who became converts had reached a crisis in their lives; some serious change in their environment had occurred. This, Lofland describes as a turning point; whatever they had done was disrupted, failed, or completed.[46] Indigenous *cargo* religions or folk Catholicism lost their hold over their participants. Second, established group members forged strong affective bonds with new members. Third, the new members' previous ties and allegiances to groups were weakening; these ties became less and less attractive in the case of *cargo* religious obligations or weakened to virtual nonexistence for migrants to cities. Fourth, a period of intensive interaction with the new groups took place. Attention given to potential members in Pentecostal churches often enthralled them and forged long-standing friendship ties; entering Catholic Action, becoming a catechist, or joining a *comunidad eclesial de base* also offered new members intensive interaction with friends or colleagues.

Protestant Presence and Growth

"The truth is, that before World War II, the Protestant presence was barely noticeable in Guatemalan society."[47] Such a statement by a prominent Guatemalan writer shows the difficulty of knowing what was going on in Guatemala during the first half of this century. Travel was difficult, telephones were almost nonexistent, and many groups, Catholics and Protestants, had little desire to communicate their findings with one another. In a word, information about Guatemala's social situation was fragmentary, and descriptions of religion tended to be one-dimensional and institutional. Twenty years after World War II, Richard Adams and his team of researchers made a first attempt at a study of Guatemalan society viewed on a grand scale.[48]

A few desultory attempts were made by Protestant missionaries to enter Guatemala before the Presbyterians arrived in 1882, which marked the recognized beginning of Protestantism in Guatemala.[49] These attempts are not worth recounting except that the roving salesmen (*colpor-*

teurs) who brought Protestant Bibles with them gave some Guatemalans contact with a world larger than their own and paved the way for others at least to satisfy curiosity about Christianity that was neither Catholic nor Christopagan.

But if the Protestant presence was, on the surface, barely noticeable in terms of chapels, schools, and clinics, Protestantism nonetheless had gained a strong grounding in the country. By 1937 Kenneth Grubb reported that the evangelical community numbered 40,657 members (committed adults) in a population of 2.2 million.[50] Neither Mexico nor any other Central American country could match the achievement in Guatemala.

Why growth in Guatemala thus became a question that a handful of churchpeople were discussing as early as the 1930s. There is nothing especially mysterious or miraculously sudden about evangelical growth in the country, although miraculous occurrences were recorded in the early days of the Guatemalan Pentecostals. Protestants had the door opened wide to them and only reluctantly responded to the invitation to come to Guatemala. One of the strongest leaders in Central American history, sometimes referred to as "El Patrón," Justo Rufino Barrios, like many of his contemporaries, was determined to keep the Catholic church out of the political space he and his Liberal Party wished to control.[51] Not only did he and other Liberal leaders of Guatemala manage to pass extremely limiting legislation against the Catholic church, making the restrictions stick much more effectively than most other Latin American liberals, well into the 1930s, but Barrios went personally to New York to solicit Presbyterian ministers to proselytize in Guatemala.[52]

Barrios never left the Catholic church, but he helped obtain buildings at favorable terms for a Protestant school, sent his children to the school, and urged his ministers to do the same. Pablo Burgess, a chronicler who knew Barrios, wrote: "The fact, generally accepted by friends and enemies, is that it was General Barrios himself who brought Protestant missions to Guatemalans and has given them privileged position and a certain prestige that has greatly contributed to their success."[53]

For a long time in its history, Protestantism was not missionary; it was reactionary to the Catholic church and conservative of its own resources. Protestant ministers in Latin America tended their own congregations, largely European in origin and English or German in language. As a missionary spirit began to burn in the hearts of Protestants in the latter part of the nineteenth and early twentieth centuries, a majority of worldwide mission leaders were able in 1908 to state that mission goals meant especially the Christianization of Asia and Africa. Latin America was considered by the majority at Edinburgh to be minimally Christian.

Thus, the goal of evangelizing Latin Americans in Spanish and seeking converts among them is relatively new. And although Barrios and

Liberal leaders removed many of the restrictions against Protestants and muzzled to some extent the Catholic church, they could do little to restrain discrimination against Protestants by persons who were culturally Catholic and were offended by the new preaching and foreign ways.

Assertiveness marked the Protestant way to do things in Guatemala for two notable pioneers. Albert Edward Bishop entered Guatemala in 1899 as part of the Central American Mission. Bishop, then 38, had been a merchant in Abilene, Kansas, and he modified merchandising techniques for his long ministry in Guatemala. Within six years, Guatemalans would be hearing the message of Bishop and other Protestants in ways that were exceptional to most of Latin America. J. G. Cassel wrote in 1905 that in practically every town or village on the 140-mile trek from Guatemala City to San Marcos, one would find a Protestant adherent or someone friendly to Protestantism.[54]

The aggressiveness of the Strachans was also exceptional. When Henry and Susanna Strachan came to Guatemala after sixteen years of work in Argentina, they were appalled at what they found in Central American Protestantism: a slow pace of conversions and a kind of inferiority complex. The remedy for this, they felt, had to be a more aggressive form of evangelism. Their work, which eventually became the Latin American Mission, foreshadowed the strong appeal of Billy Graham, Luis Palau, and Jimmy Swaggart in live and televised mass meetings in Latin America.

Henry Strachan, of Scottish descent, and Susanna, of Irish, understood the values of a culture that fundamentally is oral, not literary, in orientation. As Allan Figueroa Deck and others have remarked, the Spaniards never succeeded in making Latin America a predominantly literate region.[55] This facet has been a great cultural obstacle for missionaries from the United States and a tradition of literacy. The Strachans, as few others, seemed to grasp intuitively the orality of Latin American culture. (Pentecostalism, especially evident in the televised preaching of Jimmy Swaggart, has exploited more fully than most other Christian religions this aspect of Guatemalan culture.)

Between 1921 and 1934, the Strachans organized massive evangelization campaigns in most of Spanish-speaking Latin America, including Guatemala.[56] The Strachans employed eloquent Spanish-speaking preachers of differing denominations, drawing wider support than previous sectarian efforts. Preachers appeared in theaters, tents, and the open air. The Strachans and their collaborators used music, fireworks, and posters to attract audiences. Latin Americans had seen nothing like this kind of public religious display. Hundreds of persons began professing evangelical religion, and many thousands heard for the first time the Protestant message. They were handfuls of people compared to the masses of persons in Latin America. But historians such as Wilton M. Nelson believe that these campaigns moved Protestantism in Central America through its inertia and started it on an era of modern growth that began in 1935.[57]

The Presbyterians and Central American Mission built strong urban bases, but they emphasized rural work among Guatemalan Indians. Here the Catholic presence was weakest, and the challenge of reaching out to groups largely untouched by Christian evangelization was great. Central to missionaries from a literate missionary tradition was translation of the New Testament and eventually the whole Bible into Cakchiquel and other Meso-American languages. Cameron Townsend, working then with the Central American Mission, went on to help establish the Summer Institute of Linguistics/Wycliffe Bible Translation Society eventually found in many Latin American countries.[58]

Pentecostal Ascendancy

In rural areas Pentecostal Christians, who have developed the greatest following among evangelicals in Guatemala and throughout most of Latin America, were quietly and effectively working. Within the changing life patterns of Indian communities, early on, in the 1930s and 1940s, Pentecostal Protestant leaders began work in Indian communities (an early influence many institutionally oriented histories of Protestantism ignore). Church of God leaders encouraged community members to reorganize their lives into evangelical congregations. As Everett Wilson notes, "Guided by assertive missionaries and aggressive local leaders, evangelical converts who represented *the social elements most subject to dislocation* arrogated effective control of their communities to themselves." So well did this early work progress that Pentecostalism *became a vehicle of ethnic expression*.[59] This was no sudden change, or "explosion," as some writers on Protestant phenomenon would have us believe.

Pentecostals, once a very minor variant of world Protestantism, account for well over half of evangelicals in Guatemala. The largest of the church groups, the Assembly of God, reported 100,000 fully enrolled members. If one uses the multiplier of 2.5 currently favored by researcher Clifton Holland, then Assembly of God attendees are in excess of 250,000.[60] Their numbers are nearly matched by the Church of God (Cleveland, Tennessee) and by two prominent Guatemalan churches that broke away from parent churches: Principe de Paz from the Assemblies of God and Elim from the Central American Mission.

Churches began splintering notably in the 1960s and 1970s. Guatemalan pastors broke off and formed their own national churches, virtually all of them in the Pentecostal vein. It was an era of a neo-Pentecostal/charismatic spirit worldwide in which Catholic charismatics were forming a large contingent. The common denominators in these church divisions were Pentecostalism/neo-Pentecostalism and a desire to pull away from foreign leadership and to form something more Guatemalan.

In Virginia Burnett's judgment, Protestantism failed to spread before the 1960s because "American missionaries presented the faith as a foreign belief system which offered little more than alienation to most Guatemalans."[61] She particularly faults the paternalistic leadership of the groups from the United States and their strong reliance on external works, such as schools. The older Pentecostal groups, in my view, did not share the same degree of foreign handicaps that Burnett mentions, nor does Wilson share Burnett's view of the early Pentecostals as becoming paternalistic and having thereby a negligible effect.[62] In the accounts of the early Pentecostal missionaries, indigenous leadership assumed central importance. Key to understanding the appeal of such groups, historian Wilson believes, is control over their own lives that Pentecostals felt religion bestowed on them.[63]

Character of Pentecostal Religion

A major authority among Pentecostal scholars, Robert Mapes Anderson, describes Pentecostal and charismatic Christianity as centering "on the emotional, nonrational, mystical, and supernatural: miracles, signs, wonders, and the 'gifts of the Holy Spirit.' Supreme importance is attached to subjective religious experience of being filled with or possessed by the Holy Spirit."[64]

The character of the main thrust of Protestant churches changed dramatically at this time. The newer Pentecostal movements (after 1960) in Guatemala, as the older ones, may be viewed as protesting against the formalistic, rationalistic, and increasingly secularizing trends of the mother non-Pentecostal churches. Pentecostal leaders, clergy and lay, came from the poor and lower-middle class groups, typically had little advanced education, and were, at the beginning, from the outermost fringes of Guatemalan society.

The social background of Pentecostalism as it arose as a movement in the United States thus persisted in Guatemala. The groups involved in the beginnings of the Pentecostal movement in the United States included the poorest of the poor, black and white: tenant farmers, "hired help," and residents of the Appalachian "hollers." Further, many of the early preachers were black in predominantly white congregations. Virtually all the first pastors and evangelists lacked a higher education; they came from the same sources as their adherents.

With this kind of social background, Pentecostals in Guatemala, as in the United States, were able to separate themselves at the beginning of the movement from the influences of the dominant social structure. A "cultural reconstruction" achieved by the churches (described by Nida in 1952) began to take place. Here class background as it emerged in the Pentecostal movement assumes a special importance. As Wilson points out, "Latin American indigenous churches have been largely the creation of the upper-lower and lower-middle classes, the 'creative minority,' in Toynbee's phrase, whose aspirations give leadership to the socially inert masses." Wilson sees this tendency "reflected in the occupations and social standing of the emergent pentecostal leaders."[65] The appeal to come apart from the world also implied the ability of preachers to control interpretation of events in the world outside. This allowed pastors and preachers to explain social and economic strains in terms of good and evil and to concentrate the attention of members on self-discipline, helping one another, and aggressively reaching out to make new converts.[66]

The ideas at the core of Pentecostalism are critical to an understanding of its spread[67] (and possible imitative effects in Catholicism). Its prescientific and nonrational vision of life, especially as expressed in its worship, serves many functions in a rapidly changing society. Members are allowed emotional outbursts, pleadings, protestations of hope despite deplorable circumstances, and warm and complete acceptance within a group of persons who share in this expressive subculture and who promise their support and lead newcomers in worship services through allusions and direct testimonies to the successful lives these old-timers live in emotional havens within a fast-moving, turbulent society. Older Pentecostal practitioners, through the effect that Pentecostalism had on their lives, can point to discipline (and sobriety), hard work and subsequent promotion, greater wages and greater desire to save, and obedience to authorities at work and in civil society. These are qualities thought to be needed in the socioeconomic development process, an analysis made at the beginning of this chapter.

This kind of subjective religion gives emotional expression to many of the feelings experienced by persons caught up in the shifts to a more modern society in the country. Healing, Holy Spirit baptism, and wonder-filled happenings satisfy many of the longings of adherents. Many expressions of feelings customarily expressed diminished when fiestas, celebrations, and pilgrimages were deemphasized in an adult Catholicism growing increasingly rational and in a native religion increasingly losing its hold over and taking its economic toll on Guatemalans (native religion greatly depleted the economic surpluses of its sponsors). Feeling hurt and bewilderment and isolation from family and acquaintances, and lacking many expressions of changing popular culture, Guatemalans turned in increasing numbers to another expressive subculture.

Indians who were accustomed to believing in a life of the spirits and in shamans found a life of the spirit much alive in frequent services and healing ceremonies readily available without dependence on the specialized office of a native shaman. Many of the same needs were evidently felt by Ladinos on the fringe of a society in which changing economic productive arrangements were taking place and in which old allegiances had been challenged.

Major shifts occurred in class structures and social movements in Latin America in the 1970s and 1980s, especially in cities. Alejandro Portes, among others, notes the decline of traditional organized movements, such as labor unions, and the emergence of new social movements receiving increasing attention, such as squatter organizations, women's groups, and church-sponsored grassroots communities.[68] These movements organize members in neighborhoods, not typically by occupation, as Drogus shows in Chapter 4 in her discussion of basic Christian communities (CEBs). Pentecostal Christians constitute movements similar in many regards to these communities.

Persons cut loose from old ties thus formed new movements, especially Pentecostalism. Embracing both traditional (nonscientific, subjective) and modern (rational, objective) ideas and behavior, Pentecostalism served as a bridge attracting hundreds of thousands in Guatemala. In concrete terms, for persons in a transition to a more modern mode of life (and often to greater poverty), Pentecostalism offered emotional release and effective control over one's life. Many other religious organizations did not have the same capacity to pull in participants. Moreover, Pentecostals often denigrated the cold and rational approaches of traditional Catholicism and old-style Protestantism.

From where did the converts come to the new style of religion expression? As already noted, non-Pentecostal Protestants became Pentecostals in large numbers through conversion of their organized churches to Pentecostal bodies, a move that may be only slowly perceived by the members. But Luis Corral Prieto (a Catholic priest studying at the Protestant university in Guatemala City) in his study of Protestantism found that most of the individual converts were from Catholicism. Clifton Holland, head of the research teams surveying Protestants in Guatamala in 1980–1981 and 1990–1991, believes that many of these Catholic converts were charismatic/Pentecostal Catholics.[69] One presumes that some were disenchanted with the slow progress of their church toward something more expressive or were reacting to the social stances of some Catholic leaders.

A ground-breaking study—and one that fits well here—was conducted by Timothy E. Evans in the late 1980s.[70] Evans, a sociologist, conducted the most extensive study known of religious conversion in Guatemala. He searched the country for a region that would make his study representative of the larger Guatemalan population (city and rural, Indian and Ladino, and the like). He chose the diocese of Quezaltenango and through Mayan interviewers sought reasons why large numbers (about 30 percent) were choosing especially Pentecostal Protestantism.

Evans concludes that the majority rejected Catholicism and chose Pentecostalism because they wanted to keep the sacred separate from the profane. Reform Catholicism, for them, had mixed the sacred with the secular in ways that were unacceptable. Pentecostalism offered them an acceptable expression of the sense of the sacred. For many, Evans believes Pentecostalism is a contemporary expression of beliefs similar to those previously expressed through traditional religions, such as Mayan religion or mystical Catholicism.

Increasingly converts, especially from traditional Protestant groups, came from the middle and upper-middle classes to independent neo-Pentecostal churches. A religion once practiced on the fringes of society now could be seen under the Guatemalan blue-and-white tents previously reserved to society parties or in hotel auditoriums of the more prosperous zones of Guatemala City and other urban centers of power and privilege. To the very early Sunday morning worship service for servants was added a late-morning service for the *patrones*. Many stories are heard about the first conversions from the middle class occurring through conversations between the *senora de la casa* and the maid and through curiosity about the change in lifestyle evidenced by the servants.

Many tales are told as well about the "push" factors—the negative features that were presumed to drive some Catholics from their older allegiance. High on the list of reasons given by observers in Guatemala is the expressed dissatisfaction of many middle- and upper-class Catholics with the social and political stands of Catholic leaders.[71] This complex subject has not been fully explored by social scientists and has been greatly complicated by abortive revolutionary ties of a few Catholic leaders in Guatemala and by a culture of rumor in a society where the free press is not a long-standing privilege.

Pentecostals and Catholics: A Closer Look

Through decades of change, Guatemalans have become ready for new forms of social organization and of social meaning. Pentecostal Protestants and reform Catholics offer both—and often attempt to do so aggressively. Billboards, newspapers, radio, and television all carry their messages. If one word could characterize the situation, it would be *assertiveness*.

To observe more closely what has been happening on the contemporary religious scene, I chose one of the newer sections of Guatemala City at random for on-site study. To the north and west of the much older downtown area lie La Florida and the other subdivisions that make up Zone 19, one of the municipalities of the city; the area began to be settled in the 1960s. In 1980 and 1981 a group of Protestants cooperated in

enumerating all the Protestant churches of this area as part of a larger
study of Central America by Proyecto Centroamericano de Estudios
Socio-Religiosos (PROCADES), a research and publication center head-
quartered in Costa Rica.[72] Walking or riding a bus the length and breadth
of this section of Guatemala City, almost ten years after the PROCADES
survey, one finds much the same church groups as recorded in the La
Florida study of 1981. The number of persons attending services on a
Sunday (or Saturday, for Adventists) appears to be stable or declining,
ranging from a handful at one church to several hundred at another for
the main Sunday service.

Worshipers jam into Catholic churches in La Florida and neighboring
colonias, sometimes five hundred or a thousand at a time, for the
numerous Sunday masses. James Scanlon, a longtime Maryknoll mis-
sioner in Guatemala, began establishing a parish in the new *colonia* of
Carolingia. To Scanlon, the multiplication of evangelical churches seemed
endless, but at least in a smaller *colonia*, as Carolingia, the scale of
competition was a good deal less than in La Florida.

In 1989 Scanlon and his parish welcomed back 1,800 persons who had
been attending Protestant churches.[73] When Scanlon transferred from the
western highlands in the early 1980s to work in Guatemala City, he drew
on two strengths: (1) his experience of working closely with lay Catholic
leaders in Huehuetenango and (2) the pool of reformed Catholics available among the new migrants or in nearby areas of the city. Together he
and his lay leaders fanned out through the neighborhood, knocking on
doors, inviting, challenging. The laypersons formed a core of some two
hundred leaders, mostly fifteen to forty years old, for forming and breathing life into the new parish. Scanlon also increased efforts at bringing back
Catholics who had identified themselves, at least for a time, as *evangelicos*.

Clifton Holland, considered a major figure among Protestants attempting to put numbers on evangelical growth in Latin America, directed
the 1980–1981 PROCADES study of Guatemala and directed a similar
study in 1990–1991. Holland believes Catholics are stemming the tide of
evangelical growth. Protestants will continue to grow, but the high rates
of growth in Guatemala peaked, he believes, in 1980.[74] Another researcher, Timothy Evans, believes the Protestant growth rate in the
Quezaltenango region began to decline in the period 1986–1990.[75]

For the future, Bruce Calder, a longtime historian of religion in
Guatemala, has this view:

> The Protestants are not likely to decline in numbers in coming years.
> Rather they will continue to expand in numbers and influence, though
> at ever slower rate until some kind of equilibrium is established between
> active believers. . . . This point will be reached when the Evangelicals
> have exhausted the supply of nominal Catholics and of others who are
> open to but as yet uncommitted to organized churches and religions.[76]

What is apparent in the section of Guatemala City surveyed and throughout much of Guatemala is that a general religious awakening is taking place, for Catholics and Protestants alike. General agreement among Catholics and Protestants interviewed supports special reports like *La Hora*'s "Guatemala, Christian Awakening." The paper cited the great expansion of churches and missions among evangelicals and greater Sunday attendance and lay leadership among Catholics.[77] "The Catholic lay movements are so numerous, we cannot keep track of them all," remarked Bishop Juan Gerardi Condera.[78] Interviews conducted over ten years with veteran missionaries confirm these impressions. In two of the movements I studied, 50,000 lay Catholics were reported to have gone through the often intensive conversion experience of the Cursillos de Cristiandad and some 3,000 young persons and adults participated in El Camino Mejor retreat movement, two of the many active lay movements in Guatemala.

Kay B. Warren, whose important work on the changes in religious symbolism and political involvement helped establish a better understanding of the religious changes taking place in Guatemala fifteen and more years ago, remarks that Catholicism as she observed it in San Andres "came on the scene like Protestantism."[79] She points to the emergence of what she calls a "folk Catholic" belief system whose adherents hold values calling for universalism and the end to ethnic subordination.[80] These are values similar to those described as operative in the lives of many Pentecostals.

Both Protestantism of a particular kind and a Catholicism fostered by Vatican II and interpreted by clerical and lay leaders in Guatemala offered forms of religion suitable to changing social and economic conditions in which traditional Indian religion (with its strong economic implications) was breaking up. In effect, Pentecostalism and reform Catholicism offer bridges for the socioeconomic and political changes taking place in the country. Both offer symbolic systems by which a person can live a life adapted to changed conditions and the attitudes and values useful in a chaotic, modernizing society: competence in expressiveness, control over one's life, and altruism in attempting to influence family and neighbors. What Levine described as "popular sectors . . . then available for new kinds of organization and experimentation"[81] describes well the situation of many evangelicals and lay Catholics in Guatemala.

A key statistic for assessing the strength of the Guatemalan Catholic church, given its reliance on leadership from its ordained clergy, is the number of seminarians (Table 9.1). However, even if large numbers of students persevere to ordination, the number of new priests will hardly be enough to meet the needs of a growing population. But the increased numbers show the notably increased vitality of the Catholic church in Guatemala. And the increases of national priests would mean greater freedom from reliance on foreign clergy and a further Guatemalization of

Table 9.1   Catholic Seminarians in Guatemala in Philosophy
and Theology

1972	1987	% Change
69	483	637

Sources: Statistical Yearbook of the Church 1987; Catholic Almanac 1975.

the Catholic church (as is occurring among evangelicals). Further, the increased presence of students from Indian and poor backgrounds in seminaries and the greater adaptation of seminaries to these students also foretells a church with a more national face.[82]

Especially at the grassroots, leadership has been provided by religious sisters. They conduct established schools and educational outreach programs, run hospitals and clinics, and work in remote communities. Their numbers in Guatemala increased 30 percent from 1972 to 1987.

When judged by statistics, impressionistic reports, and personal observation and interviews over a decade, evangelical Protestants and reform Catholics all have been successful. A religious awakening is taking place in Guatemala on a grand scale, and the revival has many witnesses.

Political Consequences

The Catholic church in Guatemala has found itself increasingly constrained by religious competition with Protestant, especially Pentecostal, churches. The main thrust of this chapter has been to point to the social and economic conditions that have led to the great expansion of Protestantism. The same forces also fostered a greater religious intensity among a notable segment of Catholics. A word remains to be said about religious organizations and politics.

Given the underdeveloped state of scholarship about contemporary religion and politics in Guatemala, it is too early to develop a systematic explanation. But an attempt should be made to indicate how Catholics and Protestants have responded in their political behavior, as well as in their "religious" attitudes, to the present-day economic and political influences.

Most evangelical churches in Guatemala have been extremely conservative, and many have professed to be "apolitical." The kind of Protestantism that El Patrón fostered avoided political conflict and supported the status quo. It was silent in public about partisan politics and offered no public judgments about repression of persons (except on an ad hoc basis about its own members), suppression of human rights, or ethical issues of work or democracy. Through most of their histories, the dominant Protestant churches assumed that kind of apolitical stance. Jean Pierre Bastian, Protestant historian and editor of *Cristianismo y Sociedad*, describes this as a covert and effective political stance in support of the status quo—that of a client to patron.[83] Except for Roberts's classical study of neighborhood politics,[84] researchers on evangelical groups have noted little overt political activity until the catastrophic events of 1976.

There were several compelling reasons for the apolitical stance, especially because most Protestants were from the lower strata of society until the late 1970s. Wilson observes that for the "overwhelming majority of new evangelicals, the rewards of conversion, apart from transcendent or subjective satisfactions, were solely those derived from *association with community*."[85] The small in-group community became all-important. Further, the group frequently was or believed itself misunderstood or held in contempt. Roberts concluded that "Protestants' lack of political participation is due to their enclosed social organization." They thus become "a self-contained society within the larger society." This view did not imply, even in the 1960s, that Protestant groups did not enter into politics. They acted as active pressure groups, blocking efforts of neighbors to organize the communities to improve living conditions. They fought to keep themselves independent of Catholics and acted as divisive forces in Guatemala City.[86]

Pentecostal groups duplicate in important ways depictions of similar groups in the United States, which are criticized for emphasizing individual salvation as a response to difficult social and political conditions. J. W. Sheppard responds that this behavior is appropriate for outsiders who are not likely to define their situation as amenable to a political solution.[87] Early participants in the Pentecostal movement saw political solutions as impractical and unwise because they were outsiders to most political processes and could see no way to effect political solutions; further, lacking power or prestige, they had no way to change the system.

As a value-oriented (not a norm-oriented) movement, Pentecostals have reconstructed values and norms and redefined their world. The Pentecostal movement has been successful in part because of its ability to isolate itself from the influences of the dominant social structure. Appeals have been made over and over by preachers to come apart from the world and be separate. As Sheppard mentions, this "allowed the ministers to control the interpretation of world events."[88]

A notable change occurred after the February 1976 earthquake. Protestants, especially neo-Pentecostals, shouldered their way into the public arena, gaining conspicuous attention. With help from their counterparts in the United States, they rushed to the forefront of assistance efforts, pushed aside cooperation with Catholics and some Protestants, and "affirmed their respect for constituted authorities" (military dictators) and their desire to collaborate with the military in the future.[89]

There followed a highly confusing (to religious participants and to outside observers) period.[90] The assistance approach developed during the time of a natural catastrophe allowed some Protestant groups to control vast quantities of money and material resources, to reinforce their power to co-opt rural Protestant sectors (neo-Pentecostals especially recruit among other Protestants), and to mobilize Protestant popular religion for the ruling interests of the military and the groups benefiting from control and stability.

In the warlike situation from 1978 to 1983 some evangelicals, such as Presbyterians and primitive Methodists, suffered death and persecution. But unlike them or many Catholics, most Protestants were not subject to persecution or held under suspicion. Controversy among church groups abounded during this period and was compounded when a neo-Pentecostal, General Efraín Ríos Montt, assumed the presidency (by coup, not by ballot) in 1982.

The religious right in the United States, including Pat Robertson, greatly increased the tensions and confusions of the period by pledging vast amounts of support for Ríos Montt and, at least implicitly, for his ambitious relocation and pacification efforts. A million (in a population of eight million) persons were relocated; thousands died; many were terrorized.

Key issues for evangelicals were anticommunism and anti-Catholicism. The military found these themes especially congenial. As Clifford Kraus, correspondent for the *Wall Street Journal* writing in *Inside Central America* mentions: "Evangelical Christianity became a principal element of counterinsurgency—with the army helping to build churches for survivors."[91]

Ríos Montt's removal as president in 1983 was a setback to those evangelicals who favored a wedding of a certain kind of Pentecostalism and the presidency. Some evangelicals began regrouping (one is always acutely aware of fragmentation among evangelicals in Guatemala), and in 1987 an ad hoc group circulated a position paper, "The Political Task of Evangelicals: Ideas for a New Guatemala." The paper acknowledged the political inexperience of the Protestant community and serious political errors of the Ríos Montt presidency.[92]

The larger world has changed drastically in the period from when Jorge Serrano Elías left the presidential palace as adviser to Ríos Montt in 1983 and returned as president in 1991. Communism has receded as a world force and now may or may not motivate guerrillas in Guatemala. Attempts at national reconciliation, including the involvement of guerrilla representatives as major actors, have achieved major importance, and the

Catholic church has been prominent in this effort. Bishop Rodolfo Quezada became president of the National Reconciliation Commission; Serrano Elías was positioned by his side as a member.

Individual Catholics and Protestants

How then to explain politics in Guatemala and the support of many Catholics for Ríos Montt or Serrano? To presume politics like those of the United States helps not at all. Guatemala is developing economically in a pattern different from that of North America or Europe. If economically based stratification systems are the basis for politics in North Atlantic countries, then Guatemala represents the case of a country where the processes of migration, urbanization, and other socioeconomic changes continue to outpace industrialization and fail to produce a working class conscious of its political interests. This creates competition and instability among all the sectors of the population.

The system of stratification emerging in Guatemala thus provides a basis for political control imposed from above. An apparent identity of interests, especially stability, exists between those of differing economic positions. As Roberts points out, "The poor [of Guatemala City] are quite prepared to cooperate with professionals and middle-class politicians in an attempt to improve their position."[93] Indeed, Ríos Montt might have been elected to the presidency. Serrano, to a great extent his surrogate, won the presidential election in 1990 on the basis of a platform stressing control, security, and a common pulling together to save Guatemala from chaos and a downward economic spiral. Catholics and Protestants from very different social positions brought Serrano to power with much the same economic interests in mind. It is no wonder, then, that committed Catholics worked diligently in the Serrano campaign.[94] He represents a safeguarding of perceived interests, rich and poor.

Protestantism now has a long history in Guatemala, and many Protestants have found acceptance as first-class Guatemalans. Jorge Serrano Elías qualifies as one of them. His election, the first of a Protestant as president, represents the coming of age of Protestants in public life. But his performance may be severely circumscribed. In Guatemalan politics the military has the controlling interest.[95] Independent action on the part of the president may not be easily accomplished.

Corporate Voices

From Barrios's point of view, the Catholic church, at least its hierarchy, the agency Barrios most feared, has become among the most outspoken and most admired by progressives in Central America.[96] In an atmosphere of limited democracy and lessened repression, the Catholic church in

Guatemala is finding a role in politics by attempting to define major political issues. It does this by framing issues in moral, ethical terms, emphasizing notions of distributive justice and participation of citizens in the common good.

But the place of the Catholic church in the public arena is now more limited because it is not the only public religious voice in Guatemala. Other religious traditions within contemporary Guatemalan Christianity have spokespersons and clear, simple messages with (increasingly, they believe) a political mandate. The Catholic church now competes with other voices speaking from the religious platform, an unaccustomed and perplexing position.

Walled up by legal restrictions and beaten down by liberal governments for a long period and later by a repressive army, the Catholic church has found a modest and active voice in contemporary politics and a renewed place in society. Sometimes favored and protected in a hostile environment, evangelical Christians, if not churches, have also found a voice in national politics. These are the prominent—but not only—faces of religion reorganizing to meet the challenges brought on by modernity. Neither the original builders of modernization theory nor El Patrón can rest easily.

Notes

Helpful comments used in the revision of this chapter were made especially by Hannah Stewart-Gambino, Bruce Calder, Lesley Gill, Hubert J. Miller, Philip Williams, Everett A. Wilson, Eugene TeSelle, and Edward T. Brett and are gratefully acknowledged.

1. For a general history of Protestantism in Latin America, see Hans-Jurgen Prien, *La historia del cristianismo en América Latina* (Salamanca: Sígueme, 1985); for individual countries, see Comisión de Estudios de Historia de la Iglesia en América Latina (CEHILA), *Historia general de la iglesia en América Latina*, 9 vols. (Mexico City: Paulinas, 1984). See also Jean-Pierre Bastian, *Historia del protestantismo en América Latina* (Mexico City: Centro de Comunicación Cultural CUPSA, 1990). Extensive bibliographies appear in David Martin, *Tongues of Fire: The Explosion of Protestantism in Latin America* (Oxford: Blackwell, 1990); David Stoll, *Is Latin America Turning Protestant?* (Berkeley: University of California Press, 1990); and *Bibliografía teológica comentada del area latinoamericana* (Buenos Aires: Instituto Superior Evangélico de Estudios Teológicos, 1973/74), vol. 1/2.

2. See also Rodney Stark, "Introduction," in Stark, ed., *Religious Movements: Genesis, Exodus, and Numbers* (New York: Paragon, 1985), pp. 7–8.

3. Martin, *Tongues of Fire*; Stoll, *Is Latin America Turning Protestant?*

4. For a discussion of the meaning of secularization and its variations in national contexts, see, for example, David Martin, "Secularization and Its Discontents," in Brian R. Wilson, ed., *Religion in Sociological Perspective* (New York: Oxford, 1982), ch. 6, pp. 148–179; and Martin, *A General Theory of Secularization*

(Oxford: Blackwell, 1978).

5. Martin, *General Theory of Secularization*; Richard K. Fenn, *Toward a Theory of Secularization* (Ellington, Conn.: Society for the Scientific Study of Religion); Bryan Wilson, "The Secularization Debate," *Encounter* 45, pp. 77–83; Wilson, "The Return of the Sacred," *Journal for the Scientific Study of Religion* 18, pp. 268–280; Rodney Stark and William S. Bainbridge, *The Future of Religion* (Berkeley: University of California Press, 1985), p. 1.

6. Daniele Hervieu Leger, "Religion and Modernity in the French Context: For a New Approach to Secularization," *Sociological Analysis* 51, SS (1990), p. S15.

7. Ibid.

8. The literature on secularization is vast. See, for example, Jeffrey K. Hadden and Anson Sharpe, eds., *Secularization and Fundamentalism Reconsidered: Religion and Political Order*, vol. 3 (New York: Paragon, 1989), and other volumes in the series.

9. See especially Hervieu Leger, "Religion and Modernity."

10. Martin, *Tongues of Fire*, pp. 3–4.

11. Daniel Levine, "Popular Groups, Popular Culture, and Popular Religion," *Comparative Studies in Society and History* 32, 4 (1990), p. 722.

12. Ibid.; Alejandro Portes, "Latin American Class Structures: Their Composition and Change During the Last Decades," *Latin American Research Review* (hereafter *LARR*) 20, 3 (1985), pp. 7–40; Portes, "Latin American Urbanization in the Years of Crisis," *LARR* 24, 3 (1989), pp. 7–44.

13. See, for example, Susan Eckstein, "Power and Popular Protest in Latin America," in Eckstein, ed., *Power and Popular Protest: Latin American Social Movements* (Berkeley: University of California Press, 1989), pp. 1–60.

14. Ibid., p. 56.

15. Edward L. Cleary and Eugene TeSelle, "Evangelical Surge in Latin America: An Analysis," *Latin American and Caribbean Contemporary Record* 9 (New York: Holmes and Meier, forthcoming).

16. Stoll, *Is Latin America Turning Protestant?*

17. Among many examples are Carol A. Smith, ed., *Guatemalan Indians and the State: 1540–1988* (Austin: University of Texas Press, 1990); Smith, "Survival Strategies Among Petty Commodity Producers in Guatemala," *International Labour Review* 128, 6 (1989), pp. 791–813; Smith "Local History in Global Context: Social and Economic Transitions in Western Guatemala," *Comparative Studies in Society and History* 26, 2 (1984), pp. 193–228; Anthony Winson, "The Formation of Capitalist Agriculture in Latin America and Its Relationship to Political Power and the State," *Comparative Studies in Society and History* 25, 1 (1983), pp. 83–104; David J. McCreery, "Debt Servitude in Rural Guatemala, 1876–1936," *Hispanic American Historical Review* 63, 4 (1983), pp. 735–759; McCreery, "An Odious Feudalism: Mandamiento Labor and Commercial Agriculture in Guatemala, 1858–1920," *Latin American Perspectives* 13, 1 (1986), pp. 99–117; Richard N. Adams, "The Conquest Tradition of Mesoamerica," *The Americas* 46, 2 (1989), pp. 119–136; W. George Lovell, "Surviving Conquest: The Maya of Guatemala in Historical Perspective," *LARR* 28, 2 (1988), pp. 25–57; Robert M. Carmack, ed., *Harvest of Violence: The Maya Indians and the Guatemalan Crisis* (Norman: University of Oklahoma Press, 1988); Lynn Stephens and James Dow, eds., *Class, Politics, and Popular Religion in Mexico and Central America* (Washington, D.C.: Society for Latin American Anthropology, 1990). For an overview of anthropological and historical literature, see Carol A. Smith and Jeff Boyer, "Central America since 1979: Part 1," *Annual Review of Anthropology* 16 (1987), pp. 197–221.

18. Hubert J. Miller, private communication, May 1, 1991.

19. John Lloyd Mecham, *Church and State in Latin America* (Chapel Hill: University of North Carolina, 1934), p. 370. See also Hubert J. Miller, *La iglesia católica y el estado en Guatemala, 1871–1885* (Guatemala City: Universidad de San Carlos, 1976); and Mary P. Holleran, *Church and State in Guatemala* (New York: Octagon, 1974).

20. As Lesley Gill cautions: "Priests may not have celebrated mass in Indian communities, but Catholic influences penetrated the countryside in many and powerful ways, e.g., through landlords, in market centers, and during fiestas." Private communication, May 20, 1991.

21. Interviews, 1981–1991, David Kelly, James Curtin, Bishop Richard Ham, Daniel Jensen, Carroll Quinn, Maurice Healy, Ronald Michaels, and other Maryknoll missioners.

22. Miller, private communication, May 1, 1991.

23. McCreery, "An Odious Feudalism," p. 104.

24. See, for example, Shelton H. Davis, "Introduction: Sowing the Seeds of Violence," in Carmack, *Harvest of Violence*, p. 15.

25. Ibid.

26. David McCreery, "Coffee and Class: The Structure of Development in Liberal Guatemala," *HAHR* 56, 3 (August 1976), p. 457.

27. Smith depicts well the alternative, nonagricultural sources of income among peasants. Smith, "Survival Strategies."

28. Sheldon Annis, *God and Production in a Guatemalan Town* (Austin: University of Texas Press, 1987), p. 140.

29. Ibid., pp. 140–141.

30. Smith, "Local History," pp. 211–212; Kay B. Warren, *The Symbolism of Subordination: Indian Identity in a Guatemalan Town* (Austin: University of Texas Press, 1978), p. 16.

31. See, for example, P. A. Kluck, "The Society and Its Environment" in Richard F. Nyrop, ed., *Guatemala: A Country Study* (Washington, D.C.: U.S. Government Printing Office, 1984), pp. 68–70.

32. Everett A. Wilson, "Identity, Community, and Status: The Legacy of the Central American Pentecostal Pioneers," in Joel A. Carpenter and Wilbert R. Shenk, eds., *Earthen Vessels: American Evangelicals and Foreign Missions, 1880–1980* (Grand Rapids, Mich.: Eerdmans, 1990), pp. 133–151; Charles W. Conn, *Where the Saints Have Trod: A History of the Church of God Missions* (Cleveland, Tenn.: Pathway, 1959), pp. 131–138. Stanley Howard Frodsham, *With Signs Following: The Story of the Pentecostal Revival in the Twentieth Century* (Springfield, Mo.: Gospel Publishing House, 1946), p. 216, mentions graduates of the bible school in El Salvador working in Guatemala.

33. David Kelly, "Maryknoll History, Guatemala–El Salvador Region: 1943–1969," mimeo, Guatemala City: Maryknoll Missioners, 1969, pp. 5–6.

34. Ibid., p. 16

35. Douglas E. Brintnall, *Revolt of the Dead: Modernization of a Mayan Community in the Highlands of Guatemala* (New York: Gordon and Breach), p. 73.

36. Davis, "Sowing the Seeds," p. 21.

37. Adams, "Conquest Tradition," pp. 126, 129.

38. Reformed Catholicism refers to changes in Catholicism perceived by Indians as opposition to traditional practices, including abusive drinking and costly sponsorship of saints' day celebrations. See Hans C. Buechler, *The Masked Media: Aymara Fiestas and Social Interaction in the Bolivian Highlands* (The Hague: Mouton, 1980), pp. 282–283. See also Thomas E. Lengyel, "Religious Factionalism and Social Diversity in a Mayan Community," *Wisconsin Sociologist* 16 (Spring–Summer 1979), pp. 83–84.

39. Ricardo Falla, *Quiché rebelde: Estudio de un movimiento de conversión religiosa, rebelde a las creencias tradicionales, en San Antonio Ilotenango, Quiché (1848–1970)* (Guatemala City: Editorial Universitaria, 1980); Warren, *Symbolism.* See also Brintnall, *Revolt*; and Annis, *God and Production.*

40. Brintnall, *Revolt*, p. 76.

41. Carmack, *Harvest of Violence*, p. 295.

42. Patrick Johnstone, *Operation World*, 4th ed. (Waynesboro, Ga: STL Books, 1986), p. 200.

43. Emilio Willems, "Protestantism and Culture Change in Brazil and Chile," in William D'Antonio and Frederick B. Pike, eds., *Religion, Revolution, and Reform* (New York: Praeger, 1964).

44. Bryan Roberts, "Protestant Groups and Coping with Urban Life in Guatemala City," *American Journal of Sociology* 73 (1968), pp. 753–767; Roberts, *Organizing Strangers* (Austin: University of Texas Press, 1973).

45. Roberts, "Protestant Groups," p. 761.

46. John Lofland, *Doomsday Cult* (Englewoods Cliff, N.J.: Prentice-Hall, 1960), pp. 31–62.

47. Emilio Antonio Nuñez, "The Influence of Protestantism in the Historical Development of Guatemala," *Theological Fraternity Bulletin* 1 (1979), pp. 6–7.

48. Richard N. Adams, *Crucifixion by Power: Essays on Guatemalan National Social Structure* (Austin: University of Texas Press, 1970).

49. For a small Latin American country, Guatemala has more than the usual number of histories of Protestantism; many of the histories have limited utility, being written along institutional lines. See especially Virginia Garrard Burnett, "A History of Protestantism in Guatemala," Ph.D. diss., Tulane University, 1984; Burnett, "Protestantism in Rural Guatemala, 1872–1954," *Latin American Research Review* 24, 2 (1989), pp. 127–142; Burnett, "God and Revolution: Protestant Missions in Revolutionary Guatemala," *The Americas* 46, 2 (1989), pp. 205–233; Gennet Maxon Emery, *Protestantism in Guatemala: Its Influence on the Bicultural Situation, with Reference to the Roman Catholic Background* (Cuernavaca: Centro Intercultural de Formación, 1970); Virgilio Zapata Arceyuz, *Historia de la iglesia evangélica en Guatemala* (Guatemala City: Genesis, 1982); Luis Corral Prieto, "La iglesias evangélicas," *Estudios Teológicos* 13 (January–June 1980), pp. 1–199; Wilton M. Nelson, *Protestantism in Central America* (Grand Rapids, Mich.: Eerdmans, 1984); and Kenneth B. Grubb, *Religion in Central America* (New York: World Dominion, 1938).

50. Grubb, *Religion*, p. 67.

51. See, for example, Miller, *La iglesia.*

52. Iglesia Evangélica Nacional Presbiteriana de Guatemala, *Apuntes para la historia* (Guatemala City: Iglesia Nacional Presbiteriana de Guatemala, 1980), p. 40.

53. Pablo Burgess, *Justo Rufino Barrios* (Guatemala City: Editorial Universitaria de Guatemala, 1972), pp. 329–330.

54. J. G. Cassel, quoted by Mildred Spain, *And in Samaria* (Dallas, Tex.: Central American Mission, 1954), p. 163.

55. Allan Figueroa Deck, *The Second Wave: Hispanic Ministry and the Evangelization of Cultures* (New York: Paulist, 1983), p. 43ff.

56. Zapata, *Historia*, p. 174.

57. Nelson, *Protestantism*, p. 46.

58. One of the Protestant inventions emanating from Central America has a controversial history. Several points of view about the Summer Institute of Linguistics are expressed in the following: David Stoll, *Fishers of Men or Founders of Empire?* (Cambridge, Mass.: Cultural Survival, 1982); Robert B. Taylor, "The

Summer Institute of Linguistics/Wycliffe Bible Translators," in Frank A. Salmone, ed., "Missionaries and Anthropologists," pt. 3, *Studies in Third World Societies* 26 (1985), pp. 93–116; and Soren Hvolkof and Peter Aaly, eds., *Is God an American?: An Anthropological Perspective on the Missionary Work of the Summer Institute of Linguistics* (London: Survival International, 1981).

59. Wilson, "Identity," p. 140. (emphasis mine).

60. Holland, interview, October 30, 1990.

61. Burnett, "History," p. 2.

62. Ibid., p. 5.

63. Interview with Everett Wilson, August 1, 1990.

64. "Pentecostal and Charismatic Christianity," in Mircea Eliade, ed., *The Encyclopedia of Religion*, vol. 11 (New York: Macmillan, 1987), p. 229.

65. Wilson, "Identity," p. 148; Eugene A. Nida, "The Relationship of Social Structure to the Problems of Evangelism in Latin America," *Practical Anthropology* 5 (1958), pp. 101–123.

66. See J. W. Sheppard, "Sociology of Pentecostalism," in Stanley M. Burgess and Gary B. McGee, eds., *Dictionary of Pentecostal and Charismatic Movements* (Grand Rapids, Mich.: Regency, 1989), pp. 794–799.

67. Two of the many surveys and analyses of Pentecostalism are Donald W. Dayton, *Theological Roots of Pentecostalism* (Metuchen, N.J.: Scarecrow, 1987); and Killian McDonnell, *Charismatic Renewal and the Churches* (New York: Seabury, 1976).

68. Portes, "Urbanization," p. 36; Elizabeth Jelin, *Los nuevos movimientos sociales*, 2 vols. (Buenos Aires: Centro Editor de América Latina, 1985).

69. Corral Prieto, "La iglesias," p. 65; Holland, interview, October 30, 1990. See also Guillermo Cook, "The Evangelical Groundswell in Latin America," *Christian Century,* December 12, 1990, pp. 1175–1176.

70. Timothy E. Evans, "Religious Conversion in Guatemala," Ph.D. diss., University of Pittsburgh, 1990.

71. Interviews, February 1981 and July 1990.

72. *Directorio de las iglesias, organizaciones y ministerios del movimiento protestante: Guatemala* (San Jose, Costa Rica: PROCADES, 1981).

73. Interviews with Carroll Quinn, July 19, 1990, and October 3, 1990.

74. Holland, interview, October 30, 1990.

75. Evans, interview, February 9, 1991.

76. "The Response of the Catholic Church to the Growth of Protestantism in Guatemala," *Historia general de Guatemala*, vol. 5 (Guatemala: Fundación para la Cultura y el Desarrollo, forthcoming).

77. *La Hora*, July 18, 1990.

78. Interview, July 16, 1990.

79. Interview, December 1, 1990.

80. Warren, interview, December 1, 1990; and Warren, *Symbolism*.

81. Levine, "Popular Groups," p. 722.

82. Interviews with Pablo Vizcaino, rector, and faculty, Seminario Mayor de la Asunción, Guatemala, July 19, 1990.

83. Bastian, "Religíon popular Protestante y comportamiento político en América Central: Clientela religiosa y estado patrón en Guatemala y Nicaragua," *Cristianismo y Sociedad* 88 (1986), pp. 41–56.

84. Roberts, "Protestant Groups."

85. Everett A. Wilson, "The Central American Evangelicals: From Protest to Pragmatism," *International Review of Missions* 77, 305 (January 1988), p. 97.

86. Roberts, "Protestant Groups," p. 766.

87. Sheppard, "Sociology," pp. 796–797.

88. Ibid., p. 797.

89. "La nueva junta directiva de la alianza evangélica de Guatemala," *La Nación*, July 17, 1976, cited by Jean-Pierre Bastian, "Religión popular protestante y comportamiento político en América Central," *Crisiantismo y Sociedad* 86 (1986), p. 49.

90. An orientation to this period is ably provided by Bruce Calder in "The Response of the Catholic Church to the Growth of Protestantism in Guatemala," *Historia general de Guatemala*, vol. 5 (Guatemala: Fundación para la Cultura y el Desarrollo, forthcoming).

91. Clifford Kraus, *Inside Central America: Its People, Politics, and History* (New York: Summit Books, 1991), p. 41. See also Jorge Pixley, "Algunas lecciones de la experiencia Ríos Montt," *Cristianismo y Sociedad* 76 (1983), p. 9.

92. See commentary on the document in *Private Organizations with U.S. Connections: Guatemala* (Albuquerque: Inter-Hemispheric Education Resource Center, 1990), p. 9.

93. Roberts, *Organizing Strangers*, p. 348.

94. Interview with Eduardo Rottman, July 16, 1990.

95. Research on the Guatemalan military is well established. See, for example, Jim Handy, "Resurgent Democracy and the Guatemalan Military," *Journal of Latin American Studies* 18, 2 (November 1986), pp. 383–408; Carol A. Smith, "The Militarization of Civil Society in Guatemala: Economic Reorganization as a Continuation of War," *Latin American Perspectives* 17, 4 (1990), pp. 8–41; Jennifer Schirmer, "The Guatemalan Military Project: An Interview with General Héctor Gramajo," *Harvard International Review* 13, 3 (1991), pp. 10–13. Michael Richards, "Cosmopolitan World View and Counterinsurgency in Guatemala," *Anthropological Quarterly* 3 (1985), pp. 90–107; Gabriel Aguilera Peralta, "Terror and Violence as Weapons of Counterinsurgency in Guatemala," *Latin American Perspectives* 25 (1980), pp. 91–113; and on the origins of military as an institution, see Richard N. Adams, "The Development of the Military," in his *Crucifixion by Power: Essays in Guatemalan Social Structure, 1944–1966* (Austin: University of Texas Press, 1970), pp. 239–277.

96. See, for example, *Envío* 9 (May 1990), pp. 105–106; and Tom Barry, *Guatemala: A Country Guide* (Albuquerque, N.M.: Inter-Hemispheric Education Resource Center, 1990), p. 100.

CHAPTER 10

Conclusion:
Politics and Religion — Crisis,
Constraints, and Restructuring

EDWARD L. CLEARY

The studies contained in this volume call attention to what is occurring at a critical juncture of religion and politics in Latin America. The preceding chapters depict the broader ways in which religion has been shaped by the social, economic, and political environment. Authors also have shown religion entering actively into the lives of individuals and organizations, thereby shaping society and culture. The interaction of social forces, culture, and religion is crucial to the understanding of the changing position of religion in Latin America, religion which has found the ground shift beneath its feet.

None of the contributors argue forcibly for a special point of view in the theoretical framing of their studies. They have looked carefully, described what they and other researchers found, and have interpreted the relations of religion and politics in a national context. But all the authors carry into their research ideas about how to organize and interpret and, at least implicitly, have been affected by theoretical considerations. So it is important to point out prevailing theoretical influences.

Theoretical Considerations

Three theoretical paradigms have dominated the field of study of religion and politics in the countries of Asia, Africa, and Latin America.[1] These are: modernization/secularization theory, world-system theory, and critical theory. I presume that modernization theory has most affected the writers and is the best known to readers. In outline, modernization theory postulates that, as societies progress, a division of labor takes place whereby institutions become more complex in organization and specialized in function. Instead of the tribal chief acting as family, political, and religious ruler, those three functions have been separated and taken over by individuals and groups within family systems, political parties, and religious organizations. Politics, education, medicine, and other institutions become more detached from religion, and religion becomes less diffused throughout society and more limited to practice in churches or families. Religion thus becomes increasingly separated from politics and enters its own sphere.

Closely allied with modernization theory in the minds of many social science practitioners is secularization theory. In some formulations secularization would mean the demise of religion (see Chapter 9). Secularization of this type has not occurred in Latin America. Instead the preceding chapters describe the lively practice of religion in countries from Nicaragua and Guatemala to Chile. The enthusiastic reception given David Stoll's *Is Latin America Turning Protestant?* and David Martin's *Tongues of Fire* acknowledges for the first time the grand scale of the "explosion" of Protestantism in Latin America. But, contrary to many expectations, Catholicism also flourishes. Its innovations are imitated in a broad sense by national churches in many parts of the world, lay Catholics by the millions have been actively engaged in the church with a sense of responsibility and ownership, and seminaries are filled or nearing capacity.[2]

Religion in Latin America has been remolded by the changes in larger society. Catholicism, the dominant religious institution in Latin America, has received the most attention. But significant changes are taking place as well in Protestantism and spiritist and native religion.[3] The fundamental basis for societal changes affecting religion is that religion is an institution deeply embedded in society and exposed to the broader social environment. Key to understanding societal changes as they affect religion is not to focus on the ups and downs of style or fad. Rather, at issue are long-term changes in Latin American society and culture effected by great forces.

The magnitude of social forces that have impacted on Latin America since World War II is decisive for understanding religious change. These forces include: concentration of agrarian land holdings and food production, vast migrations from rural to urban settings, shifts from agriculture to commercial and industrial production and marketing, increased literacy, frequent reception of radio by almost every person and of television by probably half the population, and unprecedented settlement by migrants in marginal urban areas.

In their work on grassroots movements Levine, Mainwaring, and a number of others have pointed to these societal changes and the effects they have wrought.[4] Levine recalls Max Weber's use of *crisis*, modifying the drift of Weber's argument to fit what is taking place in Latin America. Thus a great many Latin Americans have gone through experiences of displacement, cutting of family and friendship ties, loss of family status, suffering of various kinds, and have witnessed violence and untimely death. These experiences have had several effects, two of special consequence for religion: loss or reduction of previous allegiances (allowing for new ties) and pressure for innovation (since old ideas and ways frequently do not work well in the new context).

Levine explains:

> Crisis (in the Weberian sense of expanded trade, broadened scale of action, and emerging challenges to legitimacy) made religion a particularly likely focal point for change. Religious themes and metaphors (as Bible stories) are culturally familiar, and thus provide a convenient place from which to begin any effort at cultural reconstruction. Religious innovations . . . make sense in the setting of "crisis," . . . as a consciously chosen and highly prized avenue for change and self fulfillment.[5]

Adaptations to changing societal conditions for the Catholic church meant innovations in religious messages, drawing new meaning from old founts. Liberation theology is one such innovation, marking a distinct change of method, viewpoint, and emphasis from traditional theology. Liberation theology, in contrast to traditional formulations is: existentialist, christocentric, communitarian, participatory, and egalitarian. The founts searched for innovation in religious message were above all the Bible and secondarily the fathers of Vatican Council II (Karl Rahner, Yves Congar, and others), whose strength lay especially in the Fathers of the Church and *reinterpretation of tradition*.

Key for understanding the change in religious discourse in the Latin American church is to see how the systematic statements of liberation theologians have been accepted and formulated by the institutional church. A vivid example of this reformulation of viewpoint and language is the case of the Brazilian bishops, who, in a 1986 publication of CELAM (Latin American Bishops Council), described the Brazilian church as having these goals and messages:[6]

General Objective of Pastoral Action

To Evangelize:
the Brazilian people in the process of socioeconomic and cultural
    transformation
from the truth about Jesus Christ, the Church, and human beings
in the light of preferential action for the poor
aimed at the integral liberation of men and women
in increased participation and communion
oriented to a just and fraternal society
announcing the fulfillment of the Kingdom

The above offers a stark change of message from the traditional, otherworldly views of Brazilian and other Latin American bishops that were typically communicated in the first two-thirds of this century. Who is the audience that is presumed to be receptive to the innovations in religious messages? According to Levine, the new Catholics or Pentecostals who are responding to the messages are similar to the "masterless persons" of Puritan revolutionary times, "individuals free of old constraints but not yet bound to definitive new arrangements. . . . A prime source of new leadership and an avid clientele for innovations in religious discourse that underscore equality, identity, and an independent capacity to reason, judge, and act together."[7] As a result, Levine believes that a great transformative moment in cultural and political history has arrived in Latin America.[8]

Hannah Stewart-Gambino, in her introduction to this volume, lays the groundwork for understanding the three major challenges to the Catholic church in Latin America that also act as constraints on its activities in the public arena: neoconservative influences within the transnational church, limits of political activity within a democratic society, and the mounting competition of Pentecostal churches.

Influence of Transnational Church

The transnational character of the Latin American churches remains as important today as it was earlier in this century when many Latin American national churches needed missionary assistance and outside agencies for its survival. The Peruvian church remains largely a missionary church, as do many other Latin American churches, which still depend strongly on foreigners for their clergy needs.

The direction of transnational influence has changed in important ways. In the late 1950s and early 1960s the Vatican was a major player in influencing the progressive direction of the Latin American church.[9] Rome had a direct and positive influence on the genesis of the progressive church in Latin America, especially evident in Brazil, the largest of the progressive churches. The Vatican modernized structures of the Latin American church by creating many diocesan-sized units (dioceses, vicariates, and other geographic units with a bishop as head) and by encouraging decentralization from Rome through national bishops conferences. Without the national bishops conferences, the Brazilian and other churches would have floundered. The Brazilian church's considerable identification with justice issues reflected the impulse of the larger church, especially as expressed by John XXIII and Paul VI, who captured attention with their emphasis on Third World issues.

Now, in contrast to progressive support, some countries have shown the effects of strongly conservative Vatican actions. The churches of Brazil, Peru, Nicaragua, and Chile have exercised the most independence with respect to Vatican leadership.[10] They have felt the Vatican influence fall like hammer blows. While journalists reported encounters between the Vatican and prominent liberation theologians Leonardo Boff and Gustavo Gutierrez, a much more profound influence has been taking place in the naming of bishops. This is the most effective way to change the orientation of a church. The appointment of bishops means evolutionary and far more lasting change than episodic events.

While appointments of conservative bishops to replace progressive or moderate ones were highlighted in Brazil and Peru, not all new appointees were conservative. It is enough that a new bishop not express active support for grassroots communities or that he emphasize legal concerns in his leadership rather than focus on major pastoral innovations of the Latin American church, such as lay leadership, grassroots communities, and strategies for the poor. These innovations, dependent on voluntary participation, tend to wither without support from above. As Jeffrey Klaiber points out in Chapter 5, the majority of Peruvian bishops are neither conservative nor progressive. But the "powerful weight of Rome," as Klaiber describes it, is the determining factor that inclines centrist bishops to support the conservatives.

In places where economic and other changes have made the lives of grassroots participants and pastoral leaders especially difficult, the greatest hardship in the retrenchment of some bishops is: "The tendency to kill enthusiasm in pastoral agents who need encouragement in the face of astronomical inflation, immense debt, a cholera epidemic, traffic in drugs, and an increasingly cruel guerrilla element, experienced in the Peruvian church."[11]

Moreover, progressives in the Latin American church have always been a minority, but were able to ally themselves with a large group of moderates in the leading progressive churches. Conservative forces have not received the same degree of attention by social scientists as progressives or moderates, but conservatives have long been a major force and their influence understated.[12] The drama of the Latin American church has involved conservatives in prolonged battles over new theological or organizational paradigms and over aspects of reform viewed from conflicting understandings of Vatican II and its interpretation for Latin America. Progressive theologians and pastoral leaders created innovations of liberation theology, options for the poor, and base Christian communities. In response, conservatives counterpoised their paradigms and programs: spiritual liberation from personal sin, poverty of spirit, apolitical stances from the rank and file, acquiescence in educational programs designed by elites unsympathetic to social reform, and strengthening of parishes without small grassroots groups.

Conservatives from outside countries and agencies have strongly attempted to influence the direction of the Latin American church.[13] Ralph Della Cava characterizes this as "Euro-Latin Alliance," supported especially by the conservative wing of the West German Catholic bishops who set out "to 'conquer' Rome."[14] The conservative impetus is much more extensive than this coalition, and its measure has yet to be taken by historians. Many groups, including Opus Dei and the Institute for Religion and Democracy, worked hard in Latin America, as well as in Washington and Rome, to reestablish conservative priorities. And they succeeded in many ways. The contributors to this volume and many others have described the impact of their efforts in Nicaragua, Peru, and Brazil.

In Della Cava's view, conservatives in Brazil are not about to assume dominant leadership of the church. But conservatives in Brazil have several significant sources of influence: espousal of the democracy of elected parties (understood in an elitist fashion); support for popular religious expressions; access to European conservative groups and resources; and a base within the Brazilian hierarchy,[15] no longer only in Rio and Porto Alegre but also in the Northeast, the region that acted as the greatest driving force of the Brazilian church.

Since the early 1980s various accounts have described a Vatican offensive in Latin America.[16] However—and this is seldom acknowledged—neither the direction of Vatican influence nor the instructions of the pope have been uniform. Rome has encouraged progressive leadership of national churches in various countries, such as Bolivia and Guatemala where the nomination of key archbishops and the pope's visits were seen as victories for the progressives. Replacement of conservative Cardinal Mario Casariego with Próspero Penados del Barrio as archbishop of Guatemala City rejuvenated the Guatemalan church and placed it clearly on the path of Vatican II reforms. The Cuban church's opening in Cuba has been carefully nurtured by papal nuncios. In Venezuela, John Paul II was believed to have given Venezuelan bishops instructions to begin speaking up about social issues.[17] Following the pope's visit to Venezuela, bishops issued statements about major issues of unemployment and housing,[18] drawing the attention of other churches for the first time.

Has the impact of the neoconservative movement been overestimated? In Brazil and Peru, despite the conservative proclivity of the Brazilian and Peruvian bishops, conservatism imposed from outside or above has problematical force when lacking popular support. Drogus cites the large number of effective and well-motivated priests, sisters, and pastoral agents in Brazil who have internalized the main tenets of liberation theology.[19] Then, too, the progressive agenda usually has the backing of church pronouncements, as in the Medellín documents or encyclicals dealing with peace and justice themes. Further, the Brazilian church especially does not have enough priests and must continue to rely on whatever pastoral agents are working, progressive or not.[20] Froehle makes the same argument for Venezuela. Another observer points to a new awareness of the social and religious problems causing changes in previously conservative priests who became bishops. (Oscar Romero comes prominently to mind.)[21]

Andrew Greeley argues that the Catholic "restoration" has had a significant effect on the ecclesiastical institution, especially through appointments of bishops, but very little effect on the life of the typical Catholic in the United States. He shows the conservative element of the church as small and believes that the restorationist strategy can be counterproductive.[22]

Klaiber is one of the first writers to describe the progressive counterweight to the neoconservative movement in Latin America. He cites these reasons: (1) the missionary character of the Peruvian church, which allows progressive enclaves to exist and to flourish; (2) the strength of the progressive church since 1968 (and the Medellín conference); and (3) pressure from a society racked by numerous woes that may force conservatives and moderates to choose positions associated with the progressive church.

Church, Democracy, and National Contexts

The foremost achievement of the church in politics in Latin America has been its substantial contribution to the establishment of democracy. Samuel Huntington assesses the church's influence as second only to socioeconomic development as the strongest factor in the turn to democracy in the 1980s.[23]

This contribution has been especially evident in Chile and Brazil. For Chile, Stewart-Gambino describes the effective role of the bishops and John Paul II as mediators and moderators in the exceedingly difficult compromises necessary for coalitions to defeat Pinochet and to establish a unitary oppositional force to dictatorship in the country. For Brazil, Della Cava judges: "There is absolutely no doubt that in their moment of unity in the early and mid-1970s the Vatican, the Brazilian episcopacy, the network of CNBB intermediate organizations as Pastoral Commission for Land (CPT), and the priests, nuns, laity, and poor of the 'People's Church' played a crucial role in augmenting democratic pressures in Brazil."[24]

One can point to neutrality, weakness, and inertia at various points in the defense of human rights by the institutional church and these should not be understated. But in the process of learning how to deal with repressive military governments the institutional church carried on courageous denunciations of episodic and structural injustices. The church helped to delegitimize the arbitrarily assumed and prolonged military governments and helped to force a transition to democracy. The church also fostered and protected democratic structures growing at the grassroots in society, such as basic Christian communities, new social movements, and nongovernmental organizations.

The Chilean church deserves special merit for the role that its bishops played in the drama of the return to democratic party rule long before the wishes of General Pinochet. In the years of the Allende government, the church (despite the reservations of many prelates and lay people about the socialist plans of the government) attempted to maintain the continuance of the system of democratic rule. Some observers have argued that this was the church's finest moment.

After Allende's downfall, the church offered the only safe space in society to groups, such as sports clubs and neighborhood associations, which also allowed political parties to maintain influence and leadership cadres and to communicate policy. After 1983, despite reluctance to enter the political arena, the archbishop of Santiago fostered the tortuous process of dialogue necessary to lead to an alliance of political parties. Pope John Paul II in word and symbol threw his weight toward the restoration of the party system of democracy in Chile. On numerous occasions the church acted as mediator and at a few crucial times moderator, as well.

The period from the 1970s on marks a clear turn in the history of the Catholic church from its previous ambiguous or clouded record in dealing with authoritarian governments in Latin America and elsewhere.[25] Nonetheless, acknowledgment of this key role by the church in Latin America has been slow, especially among observers of the Protestant expansion in Latin America. Some of these observers point to the democratizing influence of Protestantism or Pentecostalism in Latin America in contrast to their presumptions of the ineffectiveness of Catholicism in dealing with democracy.

Some observers expect the church to recede from the public arena as political parties and other civic organizations take their rightful place there. If that occurs the church's most important role in future politics may be a continuance of its status as mediator, moderator, or mentor of democracy.

When military rule controlled most Latin American countries, a similarity of church and politics in varying national contexts was presumed to exist. Since then great differences between countries in degrees or stages of democracy have become increasingly clear. These cultural differences affect the church and the various roles it is called upon to play. First, the ability to discuss without penalty basic issues of society, such as who shall benefit from services governments provide and the proper role of the military in civil affairs, forms the basis of democracy and is shown not to exist in some countries with the facade of elected presidents and congresses. Civic culture, which affirms or denies support for democratic institutions (as basic trust in the legal system), also varies from country to country. Intermediate structures (parties, unions, national commercial associations) have to be functioning as instruments to articulate the demands of elite members and people at the grassroots. Finally, popular organizations and movements of citizens greatly enhance the experience and benefits of democratic life. Leftist sociopolitical options and the current role of the military are secondary considerations.

Debating Major Issues

Fundamental to democracy is the capacity in a given society for citizens to debate major issues of the society in a public forum. In Central America (Guatemala, Nicaragua, and El Salvador) the absence of the capacity to carry on this debate has been a major issue. In Central America one hears: "La democracia es un engaño." (Democracy is a deceit.) To rely for analysis on the technical aspects of democracy (such as free elections to the presidency and to congress), as many analysts do, is far too narrow a criterion of democracy. Perspectives of the broadest possible scope, including the ability to debate underlying societal issues, such as land tenure, the function and performance of military forces in internal security, distributive justice and which social groups should benefit most from the political system, and administration of justice with equality before the law, are needed to judge the condition of democracy in a country.

One may argue that in Nicaragua political life and relations among political actors have definitively been altered.[26] In Guatemala and El Salvador major issues are excluded from public debate and to discuss them invites death. These issues include: unfavorably representing presidential policy or conduct; reports about specific military or police personnel responsible for human rights violations; reports on large land holdings; investigations into governmental corruption; military involvement in drug traffic; and the benefits and economic structures controlled by the military. Instead of criticism and analysis, there are daily reports of terror. The president and the congress, the press and university and labor representatives may denounce events; they may not point to underlying causes or perpetrators. Thus Guatemalans and El Salvadorans do not have as yet a democratic method of government, that is, an opposition free to discuss the major issues of society. Against the backdrop of the struggles between capitalist/landholders and the marginalized groups, the electoral process and largely sham presidential-congressional interactions are weak measures unlikely to produce definitive results.[27]

The Guatemalan bishops, as their pastoral letters demonstrate, understand that the fundamental obstacle to change in Central America is the entrenched power of oligarchies and their domination of the mechanisms of legitimization. The dominant bishops in Nicaragua, by contrast, never seemed to understand the need to challenge the oligarchical system that supported the Somozas and to establish a more representative political environment.

The leading contemporary, progressive episcopal conferences (Guatemala, Bolivia, and Brazil) are marked by an ability to understand the underlying issues of the democracies in their countries, including the participation by networks of citizens in building up the grassroots structures of civic society, provision of basic public services (as sanitation, health, and schooling), the representation of class interests in public debate, and the acceptance of political conflict in the public arena within tolerable limits. By contrast, the Peruvian episcopacy spent much political currency in a fight over peripheral religious controversies associated with candidates for a presidency. The bishops would have promoted more fundamental change through measures for the establishment of a working democracy, one including grassroots movements.

Civic Culture

A further consideration for functioning democracy in a country is the rooting of a strong civic culture. The contrast between Chile and Peru says much about the variations in national political cultures and the responses that might be called forth by church bodies. The accounts of Hannah Stewart-Gambino and Jeffrey Klaiber in this volume have to be read against differing histories in Chile and Peru and differing views in those countries of what a person in society is, how one responds to civil law, and how power is manipulated in the political system. Peruvians often find themselves oppressed by police and military applying arbitrary measures to control corruption or guerrilla activity. Chileans debate with profound conviction the necessity to punish military officials for offenses committed during military rule as a means of reestablishing the rule of law, not primarily as retribution. For Chileans one of the primary tasks after the election of a civilian president was restoring the credibility of the court system of law.

Tina Rosenberg offers one way to describe differences in viewpoint of persons in differing civic cultures: those of citizens (Chile) versus inhabitants (Peru). *Citizens*, she says, believe the political system offers them a voice and a way to satisfy basic needs. Citizens attempt to solve everyday problems through civic institutions; they settle disputes through the judicial system, not through private violence. They trust in a *rule of law* and abide by the rules of the political game. For them, power is less important than law. *Inhabitants* by and large do not trust in civic institutions and do not resort to the justice system. They use bribes to influence officials and habitually seek brokers to manipulate bureaucratic regulations.[28]

The church in Chile has the luxury of debating whether to back away from politics because of the strength of its civic culture. The churches in many other Latin American countries where persons are more inhabitants than citizens have a number of potential political functions to play, such as tutoring for democratic roles, helping to foster respect for rules by which justice can be achieved, framing debates about civil society in terms of rights and obligations, and acting as voice of persons notably excluded from the benefits of society.

Intermediate Structures

The presence of intermediate structures that function effectively in society, such as unions, professional groups, the press, and universities, helps to articulate demands and to express the interests of various groups in society. Stewart-Gambino shows Chile as a society with an effervescence of political parties, unions, and other associations representing the spectrum of interests in the country and with universities and press free to express themselves. Church groups there, contrary to Brazil, are not reported as considering sponsorship of their own parties or unions. The Chilean church helped to ensure the institutionalization of parties, unions, and associations that have their own autonomy.

Bruneau, Hewitt, and Drogus generally portray Brazil in an intermediate position. Brazil has parties and unions that represent large groups of middle-class and stable working populations but lacks adequately organized representation for many other groups. The Brazilian church attempts political advocacy for major groups, such as the millions of landless persons through, for example, *Pastoral da Terra.*

At the other end of the spectrum is Guatemala, lacking in intermediate structures sufficient to support a democracy. Guatemala suffers not only a lack, but an intolerance, of parties and unions that have attempted to represent other than the controlling interests. Hundreds of centrist party and union officials have been murdered, and the press and the universities have been muzzled. In such a society in need of structures of democracy and a culture to support them, the church has a far more difficult task than in Chile, and one that has left a long list of threats, murders, and exiles.[29]

Are all classes represented well in society? Fundamental to understanding the church's interest in this issue is the major debate that has raged over the mission of the church, the image of the church that best expresses its self-understanding and that controls to some extent how it will act in society.[30] As stated at Medellín and repeated by many national episcopal conferences, the church has a preferential option for the poor. This would appear to be a clear mandate, but the neoconservative movement has attempted to cast doubt on this option by emphasizing the church's "universal call" to all classes.

Here the actions and contemporary thrust of the Brazilian church may count for a great deal. This church has been one of the bellwethers for the Latin American church, first in justice issues and second in specific concern for groups and persons marginalized in society.[31]

Bruneau, Hewitt, and Drogus assure us that the Brazilian church will not abandon "its justice orientation" nor its special attention to the poor. At the same time they point to a "spiritualizing" tendency in Brazilian Catholicism. Bruneau and Hewitt call this a "devotional" tendency; Drogus describes the trend as one emphasizing the "sacramental and liturgical." Pressed for further explanation, Bruneau and Hewitt point to a trend toward a widening of the gap between religion and politics in Brazil. Bruneau and Hewitt reject the secularization theory in the sense of the diminishing, even disappearing, of religion. Religion flourishes in Brazil, they believe. But as Brazil becomes a more industrialized society (with the world's tenth largest economy), religion and politics will occupy increasingly separated spaces. Hewitt explains that religion in Brazil is becoming more like that of Europe and Canada, increasingly observant of a wall between the two institutions. The thrust of the Brazilian church will be proselytization and evangelization with less political overtones than in the past. Bruneau changes the metaphor: "The religious window will be wide and evident in Brazilian culture and less overlapping with the political window. What the Brazilian church is doing is rearranging itself within the religious picture."[32]

Regarding the other church most closely associated with liberation theology, that of Peru, Klaiber shows that for priests working in the slums distinctions such as Bruneau and Hewitt describe are impossible to make. These priests are described as carrying on a variety of activities *with* the poor, doing whatever comes along that is necessary to promote life in difficult circumstances.

Further, in many countries of Latin America the church may have to reprise its role of "voice of the voiceless," not as spokesperson against repressive military governments but as the voice of millions who are falling through the cracks of the economic and political systems.

Grassroots Movements

Often hidden from the view of travellers and ignored by social scientists who focused on elite group leaders, grassroots movements have helped to change the face of Latin American politics and religion through the years. These groups, their ideologies, and their links to larger units of society and to the church have been emphasized in recent research as "new social movements" in Latin America.[33] As made clear in the previous chapters in this book, these groups in Latin America are key to understanding the disparities of political response in a complex organization.

The social movements (which are much wider than church-sponsored ones) and the Catholic church itself have been depicted as helping to transform Latin America. The transformation began in Brazil and Chile at mid-century (before Vatican II) and in many other countries through the 1960s and 1970s.[34] Ordinary men and women, typically with the encouragement of priests and other church workers, began organizing a large part of their religious and civic activities through small grassroots communities, often with political consequences.

Along with social movements and base Christian communities, non-governmental organizations (NGOs) form part of the ferment of the social and economic organization taking place at the grassroots. These groups number from two hundred to over a thousand in most Latin American countries.[35] Often established in response to military repression or natural disaster, these organizations continue to be important in helping to organize the lives of lower-class persons. They often have ties to churches and have created programs with extraordinary range, from lending $US 50–100 to help start a micro-enterprise to teaching environmentally safe small gardening techniques for slum dwellers. These groups have achieved political significance and, as Stewart-Gambino says: (they) "represent a partial transformation of the historical political arena in Chile."

The political implications of these communities and the larger movements of which they are a part gained prominence as direct military rule gripped most Latin American countries. These communities might have remained unnoticed had it not been for the repressive climate and the struggle for human rights in which many communities became embroiled. They became carriers of the symbols of popular resistance and survival.

The churches, local and national, had to make hard decisions about these groups (often accompanied by threats of death or exile). By defining the space that the base Christian communities occupied as church space and by making public statements on behalf of the rights the groups espoused, the national churches acknowledged the political implications. The Vatican, the CIA, military governments, and many activists in Latin America and North Atlantic countries took notice and began choosing sides. For some base community members the choice was lethal.

These communities occupied a prominent place in the churches studied, with the exception of Cuba. Basic Christian communities among the new social movements became icons, targets, or instruments, depending on one's point of view. The Medellín and Puebla conferences said that basic Christian communities are the preferred strategy of the Latin American church and elevated the communities to "being church," and not just parish, organizations. Esteem for the basic Christian communities, however, was not bestowed by many conservative and moderate bishops. Colombian bishops, for example, directed their church through a five-year process of reaffirming the parish as preferred pastoral strategy, deliberately excluding *comunidades de base* from preferential treatment.

Thousands of community members died at the hands of repressive military governments. But the community movement succeeded in helping to displace repressive governments and to establish elective governments in their countries. Political actors and analysts focused on these communities for their political potential, for example, as surrogate political parties.

Beyond unresearched speculations about the putative political potential of the communities, major figures in the field of religion and politics, such as Levine and Mainwaring, have spent years of carefully attuned research listening to grassroots community members and their motivations.[36] What they discovered and the questions they raised to a large extent corresponds with what Carol Drogus vividly portrays. She finds that members of base Christian communities are primarily driven by religious motivations. The communities are essentially neutral in political orientation and only take on a political character as specific issues arise. These communities do not make good surrogate political parties at the state or national level but have been effective at the local level in addressing a variety of neighborhood, and occasionally citywide, issues. What Drogus has shown highlights the importance of messages and reinterpretations: participants in the active grassroots groups filter the messages communicated. Believers at the grassroots are constantly reinterpreting religious messages to suit their circumstances and needs. Out of such reinterpretations are born changes in popular culture and popular religion and account as well for the disparities in messages held by elites and grassroots members.

The Chilean, Peruvian, and Venezuelan churches whose grassroots activities have been described above will continue, I believe, to be with the poor, focusing on smaller scale politics and working in ways that fit none of the typical political categories.

Great internal changes have occurred in community members in attempting to understand that their religion has social implications. This occurs as a crisis for many. Drogus describes this for base Christian community members as a "revelatory experience, giving them practical skills and opening up a realm of unimagined possibilities for participation in the public arena." True crises demand clear decisions to step in one direction or another, and Drogus notes parish members who turn away from participation in the communities, thinking them communist or Protestant options. A similar empowerment is available for new members of Pentecostal churches who are able to make choices, gain social competence, and find opportunities for treasured expression of deeply felt needs.

Community members are effectively remaking popular culture. These men and women are working hard to reshape religion and culture to meet their needs. Levine describes this as a "search for new coherence driven by men and women making themselves into different individuals and communities; . . . What changes is their own sense of self and their capacity to act and to judge."[37] Since society gains long-term effects from changes in popular culture, these changes in individual citizens may be more influential for the course of democracy in Latin America than the explicit activities of electoral government for which popular culture is a kind of subsoil.

However, the crucial question becomes the point of articulation between popular culture increasingly stressing independence and active participation and "viable institutions, such as political parties, that people trust and that serve their needs."[38] Drogus believes it is difficult to show how people becoming organized and empowered in popular circles can reach further into politics and society to have a larger effect.[39] In Brazil, for example, basic Christian communities have not reduced skepticism about electoral politics and national political parties without which representative democracy will not function. Further, the state needs to respond to grassroots demands so that the state becomes "theirs," a part of their lives and expectations. Resolving the debt crisis is crucial; otherwise the achievement of grassroots groups in creating a citizenry will be diminished.[40]

Grassroots membership holds implications not only for civil society but for the church, as well. Several issues, consequences, and general trends are still playing themselves out in Latin America and are subject to speculation. Bruneau, Hewitt, and Drogus have suggested a spiritualizing trend and a growing de-emphasis on these communities in the Brazilian church. Hewitt goes so far as to forecast the demise of these communities.[41] By contrast, Madeleine Adriance and Kevin Neuhouser see these communities as having a momentum of their own.[42]

Given the dynamic nature of popular culture and religion in contrast to the presumptive overwhelming support for traditional ways, one may expect new forms of organizing religious and cultural lives to emerge. Creative pastoral agents in the Brazilian church have been experimenting with *a igreja da rua* (church in the streets) to reach the multitude of homeless found on the streets of São Paulo. Catholic charismatics may act as bridges to the megachurch model, meeting a variety of needs, from clinics to singles clubs, especially for middle-class Catholics. But above all, competition can serve to breathe new life into the small grassroots church.

Leftist Options and Role of Military

Missing from the case studies in this volume is a discussion of notable pressures from the left. The dismantling of the Soviet political system, the anomaly of Cuban communism, and the partial demise of the Nicaraguan revolution have had a profound effect, yet to be measured, on Latin Americans. Christian intellectuals who sought a "third way"—not capitalism, not Soviet-style communism—have been hard pressed to articulate political and economic alternatives. The Christian left is muted in many countries. University students, a major audience for the left, are described as profoundly apathetic to politics and inclined to "individualism."[43] Little is known about the effect of events in Eastern Europe on basic Christian community members who had only vague notions of *socialismo*.

Cuba stands as an ever more glaring anomaly among Latin American countries. Restrictions are placed upon the church due to Marxist-Leninist directives, reinforced by the efforts of clerics and active Catholics to unseat Castro in the early days of his regime in ways that the government considered seditious. Equally important an issue has been legal and informal restrictions placed upon actively practicing members of the church. Restrictions frequently have been understated in depictions of religion in Cuba. Church-going Catholics have been excluded from mainstream schools and other channels that lead to upward mobility in occupation and income. Exclusion of practicing Catholics from Communist party membership, a condition for advancement to many positions in Cuban society, was absolute until the Party Congress of 1991.

Nonetheless, to stress restrictions overlooks the subtle and highly delicate history of negotiation, accommodation, and adjustment that both the church and state have been making in Cuba. Through those subtle changes, the church has found a place in Cuban society. This place, as John Kirk tells us, has become increasingly visible as younger Cubans, often for the first time, make their way to Catholic and Protestant churches and many more Cubans than ever before choose Christian ceremonies for key moments of their lives.

The changes in the Cuban church involved more than hostages accommodating captors. From the grassroots up, the Cuban church went through a process of years of introspection about its mission, previous behavior, and stance toward a revolution with many flaws. Cuban Catholics through ENEC (National Church Congress) chose to try to work with the state, albeit painfully, toward social justice objectives.[44]

Radical Christians point to the Nicaraguan revolution as the only revolution in history, at least in modern times, in which Christians actively participated in a revolution on the basis of their religion. Catholics and Protestants at the grassroots and in elite positions took part in the Nicaraguan revolution to a degree that characterized the revolution as: (1) nationalist, (2) Marxist, and (3) Christian in inspiration. The Nicaraguan revolution did not employ these three elements in equal measure, and many supporters of the Nicaraguan revolutionary process increasingly felt reservations about the Sandinista's authoritarian manner of governing in Nicaragua. Nonetheless Christians in the revolution were supported by thousands more outside the country who were struck by the impact that social Christianity apparently was having.

Partial defeat of the Sandinistas in the elections of 1990 (loss of presidency but not of control over important municipalities and organizations) brought a sense of failure to many participants and a reluctance to discuss further religion and revolutionary options. For other participants, though, their goal was improving the situation for the majority who are poor and their work continues.[45] Overall, participants in the revolution could point to these gains: altered relations of power within the country, extension of education and of medical care to new groups, and more extensive land ownership. Radicals and military leaders, looking on from Guatemala or El Salvador, increasingly found reconciliation and formation of political parties within the system better options than violence.

In the classic conceptualization, the military was an arm of the state. During the 1960s the military in many Latin American countries achieved a degree of autonomy from the state and made itself into a much stronger institutional voice in society, an evolution from the usual fostering of personalistic *caudillo* leadership. This changing military appeared in many Latin American countries, using its role as *árbitro* (arbiter of the constitution) and creating various doctrines to fit the military's national leadership roles, such as the doctrine of national security.[46] While the military continues to attempt to control the political environment of the state in Guatemala, El Salvador, and to a lesser extent, Honduras, in other countries the military is less evident. But it is never far behind the scenes. In Venezuela, the paragon of Latin American democracy, a military coup attempt in early 1992 showed not only a segment of the military ready to take over government but large segments of the population applauding the effort. In Peru, more than half of the political support of President Fujimori is estimated to come from the military.[47]

The *carapintadas* (the camouflaged faces) of leaders of military revolts against a civilian president in Argentina was only an outward sign of military discontent with those leaders who sought justice for crimes committed under military governments in Brazil, Argentina, Uruguay, and Chile. That the Chilean church has been drawn into that controversy bespeaks a civic culture in which the church has been embedded to a considerable extent. The Chilean church is expected to speak and is given public weight, while Bruneau and Hewitt report that many practicing Catholics in Brazil no longer support the taking of public political positions by the church hierarchy.

The one lesson the Latin American church may have carried away from its long, increasingly acute, and unwanted conflict with the military from the late 1960s to the early 1980s is that the military are constantly learning and attempting to adapt to changing circumstances in society so that institutional size, weight, and strength can be maintained through new rationales and new strategies. The military remains a forceful actor in Latin American politics, maintaining a large share of national expenditures, despite economic hard times.

Pentecostals and Competition

In their analyses of religion and politics in Latin America, social scientists seldom included Protestants, except as participants in episodic events. But, as this survey recounts, the flooding of Protestants through Latin America has reached a point where the strong presence of Protestants cannot be ignored.

For every practicing Catholic in Brazil, Chile, and Guatemala there is, most likely, an equal or greater number attending Protestant or native religious services. As early as 1982 Bruneau pointed out that the Brazilian bishops were coming to realize the "religion practiced by the majority of the population is not that promoted by the institution, a point dramatized by the rapid growth of other religious movements—particularly Protestant sects and spirit-possession cults."[48]

How large is the growth of Protestants? Exaggerated estimates, favored by partisan missionary spokespersons, describe Guatemala as 50 percent Protestant by 1990 and other countries following closely behind this exponential growth. For a single index of Protestant growth, David Barrett, editor of *World Christian Encyclopedia*, recommends the estimates of Protestant representation in Latin America and the Caribbean made by Patrick Johnstone in various editions of *Operation World*.[49] Among the countries studied, the estimates of Protestants are: Chile, 22 percent; Guatemala, 20; Brazil, 17; Nicaragua, 9; Peru, 4; Venezuela 3; and Cuba, 2. If the practicing Catholic population is about 10 to 15 percent, as is commonly believed, then it is clear why "church-growth" enthusiasts (a school of thought centered in Fuller Seminary, Pasadena, California) speak of *campos blancos*—wide fields of opportunity for conversion of the majority of Latin Americans—a religiously inert group who are Catholic by culture but not by active participation as well as formerly active Catholics disillusioned by the changes in their church.

Bruneau and Hewitt view the Brazilian Catholic church as still possessing a religious hegemony over 80 percent of the population but as having its religious monopoly seriously threatened by evangelical growth. Even though large numbers of Brazilians identify themselves as Catholics, the growth rate among Protestants is nearly double that of Catholics. In

Peru, Klaiber notes the newly prominent place of evangelicals in public life, and in Venezuela, Froehle recalls a recent period of evangelical growth from 47,000 to half a million members in 14 years.

In some cases this Protestant growth has been fostered by governments displeased with the performance of the Catholic church in human rights. Chile's military government, under President Pinochet, opened the military to Pentecostal evangelization efforts, extended social benefits to Protestant ministers, and held a major ceremonial occasion, *Acción de Gracias*, in the largest Pentecostal church in Chile. Guatemala's military gave Pentecostal and other Protestants favored places in resettlement and other government projects while excluding Catholics.

For the most part the segment of Protestantism attracting the largest number of converts is Pentecostalism. In the past, sociologists constructed theories to explain this growth in Latin America as churches offering "havens for the masses." Froehle's evidence contradicts this point of view, as does evidence from Guatemala. Rather, as Levine remarks, it is also the long-time urban residents with property that Pentecostalism attracts.[50]

Further, one can no longer speak of Pentecostalism as a unitary phenomenon. Neopentecostalism is a rapidly growing segment of the Pentecostal wing proven to be especially attractive to the middle and upper levels of society. Many Neopentecostals are said to expect health and wealth from the hand of God. Neopentecostalism has a different history and differing emphases from classic Pentecostalism.

The key assumption made by many theologians and church growth advocates, that Catholicism declines as Protestantism advances, is not verified by the research. The Catholic church is enjoying an awakening to a degree unknown in contemporary history. The seminaries in most countries are filled or are nearing capacity. Millions of lay persons perform active roles in the institutional church. Hundreds of lay movements within the Catholic church mimic the hundreds of non-Catholic churches. To a considerable extent Catholic lay movements compete directly with non-Catholic churches for the loyalties of Latin Americans. Aggressive lay Catholics may be found knocking on the same doors as non-Catholics.

For many middle- and upper-class Latin Americans whose preference is for a religion practiced without the scrutiny of neighbors, it has come as an unwelcome intrusion to receive ten or fifteen invitations, often with social pressure, from persons in the neighborhood to attend their churches, including the Catholic parish. An effect of Pentecostal competition and Catholic response has been the movement of religious convictions into much greater public view in recent years.[51]

For persons whose interest is the Christian enterprise rather than denominational gain, this enlivening of religion in Latin America is a win-win situation. But this would downplay a strong sense of competition.

"We [Protestants and Catholics] steal from one another's nominal members" remarks Clifton Holland after reflecting for many months on statistics reported to him from Central America.[52] Intense and unfriendly competition has reduced gains in ecumenism noted in the 1970s.

Many former Protestants, a category only faintly understood, can be found in Latin America. Pentecostals, as well as Catholics, recruit these former members of Protestant churches. Virginia Burnett noted a marked change in Guatemala as Pentecostals took many of their converts from former members of other Protestant churches instead of from former Catholics.[53] Of special concern are former church members who have gone through an emotional maelstrom of the religious experiences available in many churches and have emerged disoriented or burned out.

When considering why so many Catholics, nominal or active, converted to Protestantism, one cannot assume that converts sought in their new religion a change while Catholicism had remained static. In fact, changes in Catholicism pushed Catholics seeking a religion emphasizing mysticism toward Pentecostal churches. In sum, a marketplace of lively religion exists in Latin America, and Latin Americans, having few restraints, choose more freely than ever the religion with the emphases closest to their own preferences.

The freer competition points out theological or cultural constraints that bind Catholicism in its competition with Pentecostalism. Three restraints are noteworthy. The first restraint is scarce resources, especially in the number of priests. The recent increases in the number of seminary students is not nearly enough to satisfy the enormous needs of the large and ever-growing Latin American population. Not only have priests been in short supply but the scarcity is likely to continue due to lack of flexibility in recruitment and training. Six years of advanced education and a separate culture are required for candidates to the priesthood in societies where literacy is far from universal or where unmarried life is not well understood. Pentecostal ministers require a much shorter education, received in short courses while one exercises ministry in apprenticeship stages and family life continues. The Pentecostal pattern of becoming and being a minister is much closer to that of the numerous semi-educated preachers who formed the backbone of the growth of religion in the North American frontier.

The resulting multiplication of non-Catholic ministers means that in some urban settlements or rural parishes a single priest has to counter the efforts of 25 to 40 competing ministers. In a section of Guatemala City where 55 percent of the population is non-Catholic, Father James Scanlon reported feelings of belonging to a minority religion, "of being suffocated by storefront churches on all sides." In assessing the magnitude of priests to non-Catholic ministers in Guatemala, I estimate about one priest for every eight non-Catholic ministers; I presume that imbalance is becoming commonplace in other countries.

Another restraint on the performance of the Catholic church is the "foreign factor" in countries where the majority of clergy are foreign-born, such as Venezuela, Peru, Nicaragua, and Guatemala, leaving them to suffer the weaknesses of "missionary" churches, as Klaiber describes them.

Further, the Catholic church is often hampered by another important inflexibility, that of its organizational structure. The Christian church took almost a thousand years to refine the idea of the parish as the basic local unit and point of contact for its members. Catholics (and historical Protestant churches) are unlikely to create an innovation to take its place. Thus the Catholic church marks its maps with parish boundaries while the evangelical world sees no similar limits and multiplies congregations along the lines of the black church in the United States, with loyalty to pastor and preference for ritual style but with hardly any regard for territorial exclusivity. This gives evangelical and Pentecostal pastors the capability of locating with flexibility and of concentrating buildings and personnel in places where newcomers find themselves rebuilding their lives through new associational ties.

Nonetheless, the lack of flexibility in clergy and organizational structures in the Catholic church can be overemphasized. Priests, such as Scanlon in Guatemala City, have shown themselves capable of mobilizing hundreds of lay persons to extend the outreach of the Catholic church and to return significant numbers (1,800 in one year in Scanlon's parish) to the practice of Catholic religion. Clifton Holland believes this lay outreach and revitalization efforts among lay Catholics working with priests have "stemmed the tide of Protestant growth in Central America." Hence, studies of the Protestant explosion will need a parallel understanding of the reactions and reshaping of Catholicism.

Contemporary Catholics active in the awakening of Catholicism are not typically traditional laypersons passively responding to mobilization efforts of their pastors, but persons who have internalized their religion often through a sustained small group experience as part of a larger grassroots movement. Through study they have formed their convictions on shared scriptural reflections and, through interaction with evangelical neighbors, have learned to express reasons for their beliefs. Intense competition has added urgency to the pastoral mandates of the Medellín and Puebla conferences for *pastoral de conjunto*—joint ministry of priests and laypersons—as the preferred strategy of the Latin American church.

A slower rate of growth but one of considerable magnitude signals the strong Protestant presence in Central America, and no guarantee exists that the rate of growth will not again accelerate. But, as Levine argues, observers would be better off if they forgot numbers and concentrated on the larger dynamics of the religious situation in Latin America.[54]

Conclusion

Religion as part of Latin American culture is changing and adapting; it forms part of the dynamics of society and politics. Religion has not disappeared but flourishes with changing faces—many more Pentecostals are now evident and the Catholic presence is more vivid.

Latin Americans, often motivated by new Catholic and Pentecostal messages, are forging new associational ties and gaining new political skills at the grassroots. They also have a new firmness of purpose. They have capitalized on their new ties to build a myriad of lower-level movements, limited to localities or single purposes. They suffer the agony of being dependent on political parties for articulation of their interests. Many grassroots needs are not well met by contemporary governments.

Other Latin Americans, working at elite levels as politicians, planners, and economic elites, struggle to find an economic basis for government in increasingly technological societies. They may succeed in creating new forms of governments besides democracy—as yet without a name—forms better-suited to the situation of Latin America in the sociopolitical environment of the 1990s. It is a creative agony, and the church, too, searches for its place.

Notes

Comments that were especially useful in the shaping of this chapter were made by Daniel Levine, Hannah Stewart-Gambino, Thomas Bruneau, James Malloy, Eduardo Gamarra, and Carol Drogus. Special gratitude is expressed to Gaddis Smith, director, and Nancy Ruther, associate director, of the Yale Council for International and Areas Studies, and to the community of St. Mary Priory, New Haven, for offering a congenial environment.

1. The three prevailing theoretical approaches are well described by Robert Wuthnow, "Understanding Religion and Politics," *Daedalus* (Summer 1991), pp. 1–20. See also, Wuthnow, *The Restructuring of American Religion* (Princeton, N.J.: Princeton University Press, 1988).

2. Edward Cleary, "The Vitality of Religion in a Changing Context," *Latin American and Caribbean Contemporary Record*, vol 8. (New York: Holmes and Meier, in press).

3. See, for example, *Boletín Teológico*, 23, 4 (December 1991), entire issue dedicated to evangelicals and politics in Latin America; and Diana D.G. Brown, *Umbanda: Religion and Politics in Brazil* (Ann Arbor, Mich.: UMI Research Press, 1986).

4. See especially, Daniel H. Levine, *Popular Voices in Latin American Catholicism* (Princeton, N.J.: Princeton University Press, 1992); and Levine and Scott Mainwaring, "Religion and Popular Protest in Latin America: Contrasting Experiences," in Susan Eckstein, ed., *Power and Popular Protest: Latin American Social Movements* (Berkeley: University of California Press, 1989), pp. 203–240.

5. Levine, "Protestants and Catholics in Latin America: A Family Portrait," paper prepared for Conference on Fundamentalisms Compared, The Fundamentalism Project, University of Chicago, November 1991, pp. 21–22.

6. Consejo Episcopal Latinoamericano, *Hacia un mapa pastoral de América Latina* (Bogotá: CELAM, 1987) p. 437.

7. Levine, "Protestants," pp. 29–30.

8. Levine develops argumentation and presents research findings in his *Popular Voices*, which complements perspectives portrayed in this volume.

9. On the progressive church see especially, Mainwaring and Alexander Wilde,"The Progressive Church," in Mainwaring and Wilde, eds., *The Progressive Church in Latin America* (Notre Dame, Ind.: University of Notre Dame Press, 1989), pp. 1–37.

10. Mainwaring, "Democratization, Socioeconmic Disintegration, and the Latin American Churches after Puebla," in Cleary, ed., *Born of the Poor: The Latin American Church since Medellin* (Notre Dame, Ind.: University of Notre Dame, Press, 1990), p. 144.

11. Interview, April 19, 1991.

12. See, for example, Ralph Della Cava, "The 'People's Church,' the Vatican, and *Abertura*," in Alfred Stepan, *Democratizing Brazil: Problems of Transition and Consolidation* (New York: Oxford University Press, 1989), pp. 143–167.

13. For a view of the neoconservative challenge, see Mainwaring and Wilde, pp. 29–32.

14. Della Cava, " The 'People's Church,'" pp. 153–154.

15. Della Cava, "The 'People's Church,'" pp. 159–160.

16. See, for example, *Pope John Paul II and the Catholic Restoration* (New York: St. Martin's Press, 1981).

17. Interviews, Raul Davila, Sept. 14, 1988 and Luis Ugalde, March 12, 1989.

18. Venezuelan Bishops Conference, "The Church Speaks for the Unemployed," (1986) and "They Will Build Their Houses and Live in Them," (1987) in Cleary, ed., *Path from Puebla: Significant Documents of the Latin American Bishops since 1979* (Washington, D.C.: National Conference of Catholic Bishops, 1988), pp. 313–320 and 321–329.

19. Interview, Sept. 25, 1991.

20. Thomas Quigley, Office of International Justice and Peace, U. S. Catholic Conference, interview, Sept. 23, 1991.

21. Philip Berryman, interview, Oct. 14, 1991.

22. Andrew Greeley, "Who Are the Catholic Conservatives?" *America* (Sept. 21, 1991), pp. 158–162.

23. Huntington, "Religion and the Third Wave," *The National Interest* (Summer 1991), p. 35.

24. Della Cava in "The 'People's Church,'" p. 162.

25. For a summary and references on the church's past record, see Brian H. Smith, *The Church and Politics in Chile: Challenges to Modern Catholicism* (Princeton, N.J.: Princeton University Press, 1982), p. 283.

26. Edelberto Torres-Rivas, *Repression and Resistance: The Struggle for Democracy in Central America* (Boulder, Colo.: Westview Press, 1989), p. 150.

27. Jeffrey Stark, "Going for Baroque: Ways of Thinking about Democracy in Latin America," *Journal of Interamerican Studies* 31, 1 (Spring 1991), p. 175.

28. Tina Rosenberg, "Beyond Elections," *Foreign Policy* 84 (Fall 1991), pp. 77–78.

29. See especially, Robert Carmack, ed., *Harvest of Violence: The Mayan Indians and the Guatemalan Crisis* (Norman: University of Oklahoma, 1988); and

Donna Whitson Brett and Edward T. Brett, *Murdered in Central America: The Stories of Eleven U.S. Missionaries* (Maryknoll, N.Y.: Orbis, 1988).

30. For an important discussion on this aspect of the analysis of the church, see Mainwaring, *The Catholic Church and Politics in Brazil, 1916-1985* (Stanford: Stanford University Press, 1986), pp. 3–7.

31. Brazilian Catholics through several movements called attention to educating "non-persons" to facilitate taking their place in modern society. See, for example, works of Paulo Freire, especially, *Pedagogy of the Oppressed* (New York: Continuum, 1981).

32. Interviews, Sept. 16 and 17, 1991.

33. See especially Susan Eckstein, ed., *Power and Popular Protest: Latin American Social Movements* (Berkeley: University of California Press, 1989); David Slater, ed., *New Social Movements and the State in Latin America* (Amsterdam: CEDLA, 1985); and Diane Davis, review of Eckstein, *Journal of Interamerican Studies* 31, 4 (Winter 1989), pp. 225–234.

34. See, for example, Huntington, "Religion."

35. Interview, Brian Smith, January 29, 1992.

36. Daniel H. Levine, "Popular Groups," pp. 718–764; Levine and Mainwaring, "Religion and Popular Protest," pp. 203–240; and Mainwaring, "Grassroots Popular Groups and Politics in Brazil," in Mainwaring and Wilde, *The Progressive Church*, pp. 151–192.

37. Levine, "Popular Groups," p. 759.

38. Carol Drogus, private communication, Nov. 2, 1991.

39. Interview, Dec. 5, 1991.

40. David Lehmann argues that without institutionalization of mechanisms of access to the state by grassroots groups, democracy will be weakened, not strengthened. See his *Democracy and Development in Latin America: Economics, Politics, and Religion in the Post-War Period* (Philadelphia: Temple University Press, 1990), p. 206.

41. Hewitt, *Base Christian Communities and Social Change in Brazil* (Lincoln: University of Nebraska Press, 1991), p. 108.

42. Adriance, *Opting for the Poor: Brazilian Catholicism in Transition* (Kansas City, Mo.: Sheed and Ward, 1986); and Neuhouser, "The Radicalization of the Brazilian Catholic Church in Comparative Perspective," *American Sociological Review* 54 (April 1989), pp. 233–244.

43. David Miller, "Latin American Students Giving Up Political Activism, Turning Inward," *Pulse* 26, 19 (Oct. 11, 1991), pp. 2–3.

44. See "National Encounter of the Cuban Church," in Cleary, *Path from Puebla: Significant Documents of the Latin American Bishops since 1979* (Washington, D.C.: National Conference of Catholic Bishops, 1988), pp. 91–99.

45. Rafael Aragón and Eberhard Loschcke, *La iglesia de los pobres en Nicaragua: Historia y perspectivas* (Managua: n.p., 1991).

46. See the helpful discussion of military doctrine and discourse in Alfred Stepan, *Rethinking Miltary Politics: Brazil and Southern Cone* (Princeton, N.J.: Princeton University Press, 1988). See also the church's reaction to military doctrine in the 1970s and early 1980s in Cleary, *Crisis and Change: The Church in Latin America Today* (Maryknoll, N.Y.: Orbis, 1985), pp. 157–159.

47. Interview with James Malloy, co-director of a large-scale study of political elites in Peru, Bolivia, and Ecuador; February 15, 1992.

48. Bruneau, *The Church in Brazil: The Politics of Religion* (Austin: University of Texas Press, 1982), p. 151.

49. See David Stoll, *Is Latin America Turning Protestant?: The Politics of Evangelical Growth* (Berkeley: University of California Press, 1990), pp. 333–334.

50. Daniel H. Levine, "Protestants," p. 18. Philip Williams reported similar findings in a study in El Salvador in 1991-1992. (Williams, interview, Jan. 20, 1992.)

51. In many rural areas residents know the religion of everyone else within a community, and this knowledge became the basis of persecution as informers for repressive military or paramilitary forces pointed to *catequistas* (Catholic activists) as dangerous; most *evangélicos* (Protestants) as safe; and *los de la costumbre* (followers of the Indian religious customs) as probably alright.

52. Interviews, Oct. 30, 1990 and Jan. 17, 1991.

53. Virginia Gerrard Burnett, "A History of Protestantism in Guatemala," Ph.D. dissertation, Tulane University, 1986, pp. 190–191.

54. Levine, "Protestants," p. 32.

About the Contributors

Thomas C. Bruneau is chairman and professor in the Department of National Security Affairs at the Naval Postgraduate School, Monterey, California. His work on the church in Brazil helped to define the field of study of religion in Latin America. He is author of *The Church in Brazil: The Politics of Religion* and *The Political Transformation of the Brazilian Catholic Church.*

Edward L. Cleary is visiting professor at Yale University and director and professor of Hispanic studies at the Pontifical College Josephinum, Columbus, Ohio. He is author of *Crisis and Change: The Church in Latin America* and editor of *Born of the Poor: The Latin American Church since Medellin* and *Shaping a New World: An Orientation to Latin America,* among others.

Carol Ann Drogus is assistant professor in the Department of Government at Hamilton College. She has written on women in grassroots communities in Brazil.

Brian Froehle has worked for two years in CISOR, a research center in Caracas, Venezuela. He is completing his dissertation in sociology at the University of Michigan on the church in Venezuela.

W. E. Hewitt is a member of the Department of Sociology at the University of Western Ontario. He is author of *Base Christian Communities and Social Change in Brazil* as well as a number of articles on Brazil.

John M. Kirk is professor in the Department of Spanish at Dalhousie University. He has written extensively on Cuba and other Latin American topics. He is author of *Between God and the Party: Religion and Politics in Revolutionary Cuba* and editor of *Cuban Foreign Policy Confronts a New International Order* (with H. Michael Erisman).

Jeffrey Klaiber teaches at the Catholic University in Lima and has been a resident of Peru for more than 25 years. He recently completed the second edition of his history of the church in Peru, *La Iglesia en el Peru,* and has published numerous other works on Peru.

Hannah Stewart-Gambino is a member of the Department of Government at Lehigh University. She is author of *The Catholic Church and Politics in the Chilean Countryside* and numerous other publications on the church in Latin America.

Philip Williams is a member of the Department of Political Science at the University of Florida and has taught at the Universidad Simon Canas, San Salvador. He is author of *The Catholic Church and Politics in Nicaragua and Costa Rica.*

Index

223

About the Book

Changes in Latin America have created a new political game with new rules, argue the authors, and the Catholic church, the "voice of the voiceless" in the 1980s, will find itself increasingly constrained in its political activity in the 1990s. The church will have to respond to limits placed on it by the Vatican and by strained human and financial resources. It also faces competition from a massive surge of evangelical Protestantism. The authors address these new situations, looking in depth at Brazil, Chile, Cuba, Guatemala, Nicaragua, Peru, and Venezuela.